INTELLIGENT
TUTORING
SYSTEMS
Evolutions in Design

INTELLIGENT
TUTORING
SYSTEMS
Evolutions in Design

Edited by

Hugh Burns
University of Texas

James W. Parlett
Air Force Human Resources Laboratory

Carol Luckhardt Redfield
Southwest Research Institute

 Psychology Press
Taylor & Francis Group

NEW YORK AND LONDON

First Published 1991 by
Lawrence Erlbaum Associates, Inc.

Published 2014 by Psychology Press
711 Third Avenue, New York, NY 10017

and by Psychology Press
27 Church Road, Hove, East Sussex, BN3 2FA

*Psychology Press is an imprint of the Taylor & Francis Group,
an informa business*

Library of Congress Cataloging-in-Publication Data

Intelligent tutoring systems: evolutions in design / edited by Hugh
Burns, James W. Parlett, Carol Luckhardt Redfield.
p. cm.
Includes index.
1. Intelligent tutoring systems. I. Burns, Hugh II. Parlett,
James W. III. Redfield, Carol Luckhardt.
LB1028.5.I5534 1990
371.3'34 — dc20   90-38257
                                                         CIP

ISBN 13: 978-0-805-80682-3 (hbk)
ISBN 13: 978-0-805-80683-0 (pbk)

Publisher's Note
The publisher has gone to great lengths to ensure the quality of this
reprint but points out that some imperfections in the original may be apparent.

Contents

6

Representing, Acquiring, and Reasoning
About Tutoring Knowledge   127
Beverly Woolf

Building a Tutoring System, *127*
Tools for Representing Tutoring Primitives, *129*
Tools for Representing Discourse Knowledge, *136*
Summary and Future Opportunities, *144*

7

Generating Coherent Explanations to
Answer Students' Questions   151
Liane Acker, James Lester, Art Souther, Bruce Porter

Representing Fundamental Knowledge, *152*
Related Work on Question Answering, *155*
Question Types, *158*
Determining the Content of a Question Response, *160*
Discussion, *169*
Conclusions, *173*

8

From Training to Teaching:
Techniques for Case-Based ITS   177
Christopher K. Riesbeck and Roger C. Schank

Case-Based Teaching, *178*
Case-Based Reasoning, *180*
Indexing Cases, *182*
Connecting Language to Knowledge, *184*
Tutorial Plans, *185*
A Case Study, *187*
Long-Term Goals and Vision, *190*
Summary, *192*

9

The Role of Domain Knowledge in the Design of an Intelligent Tutoring System
Pamela K. Fink

10

Representing and Teaching High Performance Tasks Within Intelligent Tutoring Systems
J. Wesley Regian

11

Technology Assessment: Policy and Methodological Issues for Training
Eva L. Baker

12

The Future of Intelligent Tutoring Systems   265
Carol Luckhardt Redfield and Kurt Steuck

Author Index   285

Subject Index   291

Preface

When advanced computer tools and techniques are used to build instructional systems, such systems earn, perhaps too easily, the right to be modified by the word *intelligent,* just as — again too easily perhaps — we create terms and disciplines like *artificial intelligence.* So in the 1990s our educational and training establishments are witnessing evolutionary advances in intelligent computer-assisted instruction (ICAI) and the emergence in the research laboratories of intelligent tutoring systems (ITSs).

This volume is a collection of 12 chapters on issues related to the evolutionary design and the practical future of ITS. The collection follows in the tradition of *Foundations of Intelligent Tutoring Systems* (1988), edited by Martha C. Polson and J. Jeffrey Richardson, and *Intelligent Tutoring Systems: Lessons Learned* (1988), edited by Joseph Psotka, L. Dan Massey, and Sharon A. Mutter. The two earlier volumes were also published by Lawrence Erlbaum Associates. The 9 chapters in the Polson and Richardson volume present a general foundational text that defines the major theoretical components of an ITS, among them expert knowledge bases, robust instructional environments, and modules for student diagnosis and remediation. The Psotka et al. volume is oriented more toward applications of that theoretical base, with 18 chapters on technical training domains, electronic troubleshooting, instructional planning, and more. Likewise, the first volume resulted from papers delivered at the Air Force Human Resources Laboratory's Research Planning Forum on Intelligent Tutoring Systems held in San Antonio, Texas, in September 1986; the second volume resulted from sessions sponsored in October 1986 by the Army Research Institute in the small village of Smugglers Notch, Vermont. Obviously, 1986 was a banner year for artificial intelligence and for the application of artificial intelligence (AI) to education and training. In the 3 years since, some of the visions and short-term issues have been explored and better defined. For example, vigorous projects in qualitative simulation have been established at the major academic research centers and intelligent computer-assisted instruction testbeds are now important baseline programs in the Air Force and National Aeronautics and Space Administration (NASA). Another example includes the creation of AI tools for instructional development, especially tools for rapidly prototyping lessons and instructional environments. Indeed, the intelligent tutoring design paradigm is evolving, and that is what this book is about — that dynamic evolution. ITS design challenges are being confronted as knowledge engineering representations become more intuitive, as tutors for teaching specific knowledges and skills in sophisticated domains are demonstrated — orbital mechanics, F-16 avionics maintenance, economics, Pascal programming, helicopter bladefolding operations, radar maintenance, to name but a few. These ITSs show promise and some even provide actual instructional effectiveness data.

This enthusiastic climate existed in April 1989 when the Air Force Human Resources Laboratory sponsored its second Research Forum on Intelligent Tutoring Systems in San Antonio. In many ways an encore, the forum established as its theme the dimensions of ITS design as that design was evolving in those ITSs that seemed the most promising under various research conditions. The forum also was envisioned as a place where a lot more about the potential of ITSs to meet users' needs had to be said.

The chapters here synthesize each speaker's formal presentations, many of the audience's responses and comments, and even many of the most intriguing conversational challenges uttered during breaks and luncheons, even on strolls down San Antonio's Riverwalk: "The theory is too static; loosen up." "Get the interface right and you don't need AI." "We want more flexibility upfront; in fact, we want flexibility designed in everywhere." "We need more tools for the just plain folks." "What is simulation doing on a picture of an ITS?" "How much does one of these things really cost?" "Will ITSs be useful for teaching high performance skills?" Besides facing the questions asked at the forum, each of these authors had the summer to rethink and revise their chapters. During the summer, each of these authors was challenged to ask the questions we should be answering in the 1990s: "How can knowledge bases generate explanations?" "Will case-based reasoning techniques be worth pursuing in the ITS framework?" "Will high performance skills be successfully taught in an ITS design?" "Are there dimensions of ITS design which the research laboratories are ignoring, and ignoring at the customer's peril?" So our authors, like Yeats in 1927 in his poem "Among Schoolchildren," found themselves exploring "the long schoolroom questioning."

ACKNOWLEDGMENTS

Many people need to be acknowledged for their contributions to the organization, planning, and overall execution of this project. We derived a good deal of momentum from everyone associated with the first ITS Forum and were encouraged to think about the second almost from the rap of the closing gavel: Martha C. Polson and J. Jeffrey Richardson kept us working toward that goal. Colonel Harold G. Jensen, commander of Air Force Human Resources Laboratory, enthusiastically supported with the necessary funding as well as endorsed the ambitious program of research. Martin Goland, president of Southwest Research Institute, was a strong supporter and ally, an ally especially concerned with nurturing connections among the academic, the government, and the industrial sectors of the education and training community. Without the generous support of Robert MacDonald, Robert Brown, and Robert Savely of NASA's Johnson Space Center, this project would not have had a vehicle for its implementation. The leadership of the University of Houston at Clear Lake's Research Institute for Computing and Information Sciences (RICIS), in particular Glenn Houston and Glenn Freedman, made the willingness of NASA and the Air Force to cooperate a financial and political reality. The often hectic administrative workload was managed skillfully by Rose Reyes, Elia Martinez, Beatrice Moreno, Debra Aguirre, and Veronica Perez—many, many thanks. Needless to say, we are grateful to these colleagues; we understand how such efforts take immense bureaucratic patience and deserve heartfelt thanks.

The four moderators for the forum's major sessions also stimulated all of us to explore, evaluate, and envision these new evolutionary frontiers in education and training systems. Susan Chipman has been a long-time sponsor from the Office of Naval Research (ONR) and—perhaps better than anyone else in the field—is able to relay the historical evolution of knowledge-based computers and education; indeed, ONR has historically been the most consistent funding source from research and scholarship in the AI and training world. Joseph Psotka of the Army Research Institute insured that issues of literacy, hypertext environments, and basic cognitive skills were discussed fully cogently. Frank Hughes of NASA's Johnson Space Center conjured up images of the space station and imagined astronaut-students "floating" to their schoolrooms; he brought his sense of wonder and his sense of reality to his panel. Kurt Steuck of AFHRL's Intelligent Systems Branch orchestrated the instructional sessions and themes, reminding us of the value and complexity of one-on-one tutoring with or without machines.

Of course, we owe a special thanks to all of the contributors. They began their work in January 1988 as conference advisors, helping us bring the right issues to the floor. In April, they delivered their papers and defended them before the invited audience. Through the summer, they extended, revised, rewrote, and edited them to make them "just so." These are the people who deserve the kudos for this volume; we greatly appreciate their willingness to do the real cognitive work. Over the past few months, we appreciated Glynda Hull's special encouragement to confront the issues of basic literacy in our various ITS projects. Obviously, we are also grateful to Hollis Heimbouch of Lawrence Erlbaum Associates for leading this new editorial team through the maze. Whenever we felt guilty for our delays, she somehow made us feel we were ahead of schedule.

Finally, as you read and perhaps study these chapters, we sincerely hope that this book helps you in your own research and development efforts with ITSs. We also hope these wonderfully powerful machines will soon be used effectively and efficiently in your classrooms. Like the ITSs we are striving to develop, we will have to become even more multidimensional — experts, students, instructors, communicators — to succeed in tomorrow's integrated, high technology schoolhouses. Indeed, we are all deeply engaged in and challenged by these important evolutions in ITS design.

Hugh Burns
James W. Parlett
Carol Luckhardt Redfield

The Evolution of Intelligent Tutoring Systems:
Dimensions of Design

Hugh Burns
University of Texas at Austin
James W. Parlett
Air Force Human Resources Laboratory

Acts of instruction—training, tutoring, teaching—must be integral acts, indivisible, whole. Yet to a designer, they are composed of many interactions—personal, highly collaborative interactions, filled with moments of increasing expertise, of understanding what was not understood, of being challenged to know important things in personally useful and publicly usable ways.

In the 21st century, professional credibility will depend in part on how well educators have kept up with technology in general and the development and use of intelligent tutoring systems (ITS) in particular. Plainly stated, modern educators cannot afford artificial intelligence illiteracy in tomorrow's electronic schoolhouses. They cannot afford it for their professional lives; they certainly cannot afford it for their students' futures. An "intelligent" computer is clearly on the practical horizon. Educators and trainers need to be able to exploit it, and—better yet—need to influence the design and evaluation of ITSs. In fact, the credibility of educators as master teachers or tutors depends on moving their future classrooms to singularly, scholarly, social conversations with one human at a time. This, in itself, should not be surprising.

What should be surprising to us today is how far some of the research and developments have come. The literature and scholarship of ITSs is maturing on an international level. To complicate the matter, instructors trained before the widespread use of the microcomputer are often particularly wary of computer-based instruction of any sort. They perceive computer-based instruction, first, as a technology whose time peaked in the 1960s and 1970s and, second, as a symbol of all that mechanizes individual human performance. This bias is unfortunate, but real in all too many instances. This apprehension about technology stands in opposition to another roadblock facing ITS designers, researchers, and implementers. All too often, educators, administrators, and managers of technical training respond to the push of technology overzealously and none too wisely. Although it is disheartening to encounter a schoolhouse of any sort where technology is shunned, feared, or ignored, it is almost equally disheartening to enter a schoolhouse where administrators have responded to the demands of technology by hurling fistfuls of money at the problem with no real conceptual understanding of it. The result, predictably, is a schoolhouse full of fancy hardware platforms, but no design/development staff (or funding for such a beast) in sight.

Designing, developing, and evaluating ITSs are not so much strategic matters—what things to do—as they are an integrated technical enterprise—how to do it. Figure 1.1 portrays the overall evolving architecture of a practical intelligent tutoring system.

It is difficult to separate the dancer from the dance; nevertheless, in *Foundations of Intelligent Tutoring Systems* (Polson & Richardson, 1988), the foundational anatomy was used to discuss research issues within each of the separate components. These components were an expert module, a student diagnostic module, an instructional module, an intelligent interface, and a user. This classification has allowed the research community to focus attention on issues; for example, representing expert knowledge, designing student bug libraries, developing rules for teacher intervention, presenting intuitive computer work spaces and, for some, preliminary evaluation of ITSs since 1987. Because designing intelligent tutors is such an interdisciplinary activity, attending to the anatomy piece by piece often ignored the synergy that a wholly integrated system could achieve. Now we are wiser and more ambitious. This companion piece to *Foundations of*

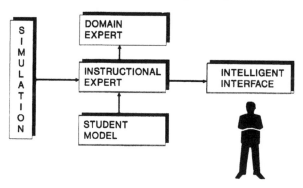

FIGURE 1.1   Intelligent tutoring system architecture.

Intelligent Tutoring Systems broadens the issues to emphasize the interactivity of the major components in the design and further explores the dimensions of communication, instruction, and expertise.

THE HUMAN-MACHINE COMMUNICATION DIMENSION

Interactivity is undoubtedly the real strength and centerpiece of individualized instruction necessary to ITSs. The set of instructional activities in an ITS provides miniforums for investigating, exploring, and stimulating the learning processes (see Figure 1.2).

An ITS capable of helping students learn complex problem-solving tasks requires extremely flexible human-machine interfaces. To achieve the goal of designing and implementing flexible tutoring environments, we must begin by defining student-computer interactions; the evolution of system design is moving toward student-centered, reactive learning environments. The microworld design possibilities instantiated are now in "play" or "exploratory" environments capable of being realized in practical interactions in "real" domains. Advances in interface design have allowed us to explore more complex reasoning tasks, so researchers should now focus on the question of developing more formal specification tools that can be used to describe user behavior, independent of software implementation. This methodology resolves the problem of defining functionally equivalent but stylistically different interfaces.

Ideas about how people learn to read and write should also inform the construction and evaluation of ITSs. More than being able to represent the perspective of student users, more than seeing through student eyes— rather than through the eyes of developers, computer scientists, or domain

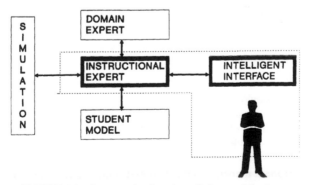

FIGURE 1.2 Communication knowledge architecture.

experts — ITSs will have to be developed so that students who are under-prepared in literacy skills have opportunities for success. The literacy demands in the future promise to be even more complex, especially in the area of group or team problem solving. Almost every college and university has already designated a portion of its students as deficient in the reading and writing skills necessary for competent academic work, and the numbers are approximately comparable for the literacy demands in the military. Current research contributing to a new plurality of cognitive and social understanding of literacy emphasizes these basic literacies. What we count as reading and writing or as good reading and writing is going to vary to some extent from context to context. We also know that when people sit down to read or write, they will bring strategies that range from functional to dysfunctional; however, even those reading and writing performances that seem bizarre or quite aberrant have a history and a logic. The notion of a "functional" learning strategy is not new; Van Lehn (1988) and others found such situations to occur often in domains like addition, subtraction, and programming itself. Shaughnessy (1977) theorized that similar "bugginess" was frequently present in the learning behaviors of basic readers and writers — a theory that Hull and Glaser (1989) validated in their research in syntactic remediation. Such ideas applied to the design, development, and evaluation of ITSs suggest simply that we cannot take for granted that our students, particularly those who are underprepared, possess requisite reading and writing skills for special tasks, like operating and learning from ITSs. Thus, we must plan to include bug libraries and strategies for remediation in reading and writing as a natural part of learning literacy practices. Solutions may include students working collaboratively, thus being able to negotiate the meaning and the construction of educational exercises. Other solutions, already in implementation in universities and technical training centers, include early diagnosis and remediation by humans. Computers — ITSs, really — must participate actively in the solution process.

THE INSTRUCTIONAL DIMENSION

One of the most obvious advantages of an ITS is simply achieving a more favorable teacher–student ratio. Any teacher or coach who is trying to improve performance of a skill can attest that the more one-on-one time spent, the greater the likelihood that a student's performance will improve (see Figure 1.3). Figure 1.3 depicts the interaction among the instructional module, the student model, and the learner-friendly intelligent interface — the territory where the evolution of the instructional power of a system will

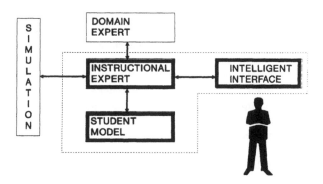

FIGURE 1.3 Teaching knowledge architecture.

take place. So ITSs potentially allow, even require, more one-on-one instructional efficiency and, thereby, leverage more instructional effectiveness.

But there are complications, the first complication is an overly simplistic view of instructors as knowledge brokers. Instructors have knowledge of domains, certainly, but instructional effectiveness is more often achieved because of the relationships good teachers have with individual students. Good teachers or tutors are able to take in the instructional context such that they know what the student does not know in terms of knowledge, and perceive what the student can and cannot do in terms of skill. Even trickier is representing the expert knowledge so that the student can comprehend the knowledge while exercising and mastering the skill. All of these instructional practices are often invisible to instructors themselves. The best tutors automatically adjust their relationships with their domain, a specific student, and their instructional repertoire. Make no mistake, ITSs are trying to achieve one-on-one instruction, and therein lies the complexity and the necessary flexibility of any potentially honest ITS design. Burton (1988) discussed at length instructional environments that would have this flexibility; most serious instructional systems following the SOPHIE research legacy have been intended to achieve total instructional robustness (Sleeman & Brown, 1982). So, designing and exploring instructional dimensions of new technologies is perhaps one of the greatest challenges facing ITS implementation. It is certain that the tutor must tutor, and any system that purports to do this effectively will be able to demonstrate a complex set of decisions about what expertise to give, the size of the knowledge to package, and the best way to present such material in the dimensions of time and space. What specific architectures might be proposed for such an instructional integration?

Proposed architectures for representing teaching knowledge in ITSs can be described both in terms of how that knowledge is understood by experts and how it can be represented by programmers in sets of domain-independent tutoring strategies. Teaching knowledge can also be used to develop methods to generate answers and explanations from instructional knowledge bases in which a coherent viewpoint is tailored to the individual student's needs. From a researcher's viewpoint, generating explanations is an important goal in the ITS design; what will be curious to see is how explanations are driven by the student diagnostic modules. Let us pursue this idea of explanation generation within the instructional module.

Artificial intelligence (AI) and education have come to be thought of in potentially useful ways, thus ITS designers have set up their own holy grail. The grail is, as you might have guessed, the capability for a large-scale, multiuser knowledge base to generate coherent definitions and explanations. It goes without saying that if a student asks a reasonable question, then an ITS should have an answer. Knowledge engineers are able to predict and write "canned" answers catching students' questions by recognizing key word patterns and expected terms that need to be defined. But "caning" explanations defeats the intelligence potential for a system to be able to write a program and infer appropriate responses. Most tutors since Socrates have valued questioning and answering instructional strategies. It seems to many of us in AI and education that the true potential for ITS will be in areas where uncertainty is high and information is combinatorially explosive. For example, if there were a knowledge-based expert system on the subject of designing ITS, what questions might be anticipated? An ITS should be able to present fairly easily a definition of an interface. But it would be more difficult for an ITS to generate an explanation to open-ended questions such as "What is knowledge?" "What is the interaction here between student diagnostic modules and expert module?" Simply put, definitions should be easy to present, but often are only useful very early in an instructional interaction. Inferred questioning and explanation generation will take powerful inference engines. Will there be substantial differences in the patterns of acquiring instruction among the various subjects? Of course. Consequently, tools to encode an instructional expert to control knowledge in intelligent tutors will involve representing multiple knowledge concepts and proposing alternative teaching tactics.

Many educators feel that today's inflexible or brittle software does not significantly help them meet the specific needs of their students. Likewise, educators are not always comforted when computers actually reach their students with appropriate, individual help. It threatens, perhaps, the sense of their own position and authority in the classroom.

Much of this brittle software sits on the shelf—abandoned, ignored, unevaluated. If an institution is enthusiastically pursuing advanced computer applications, then such programs are viewed as evolutionary, as improvable, as buying into teacher-controlled modifications. Instructors want more control over supplementary materials; they want to have authority over software prescriptions. It is appropriate for them to have that authority. Because they want the capability to reinforce their students personally, instructors should be able to customize software. These ITSs should be electronic mirrors, reflecting what students want to do and allowing them to think more about their choices, but simultaneously reflecting the shifting and flexible notion of a teacher's goals. In whatever way an instructor perceives the art of skill development, an ITS must allow more individual opportunities for instructors to intervene precisely in the learning process.

Although some of the brittleness and inflexibility is the fault of designers working in the tight memory constraints, some fault also rests in the politics of ITS development, especially in the academic arena. Many tutoring systems are begun by graduate students or postdoctoral researchers whose financial support is, not surprisingly, grant or research-fund based. These systems, although potentially functional, exist (or are brought into existence) to answer specific research questions, and the system itself is relegated to the shelf when either the research questions are answered or the funding runs out. Designers and research developers are often not motivated or perhaps financially able to excise the brittleness from their systems. Besides, new grants or research questions await them. Technology transition is what is missing.

Technology transition must begin with vigorous evaluation and assessment of the systems. All too often we ignore, gloss, or otherwise sidestep the question: Do these things work? We are not sure whether evaluation and assessment is the work of ITS designers and researchers or the work of (as yet) nonexistent technology transition experts. But such work, as Baker (chap. 11, this volume) points out, needs to be done.

Some ITSs already provide recordings of a student's problem-solving processes so that students and instructors alike may observe and review the tutoring interactions as well as the expert performance in the system. Such recordings offer a time-compressed view of the tactics involved in solving a technical problem. The "compression of process" allows for past habits to become more visible and to more fully inform future decisions by students and designers alike. In the long term, as more and more "artificial intelligence" is designed into ITSs, applications then will be truly individualized. These trends are unmistakable. Yet until such hardware and software matures and until such computing power can be made widely available both in our culture and in our educational centers, researchers must keep investigating how humans learn and how intelligent computers may surprise us even more.

Intelligent tutoring systems must be designed to give students a strategic sense of purpose, to encourage them to work appropriately with an outcome in mind, to coach them to perform efficiently, and to have them recognize what they have learned.

Intelligent computer-assisted instruction (ICAI) is often controversial because it must take an explicit instructional point of view, and its value is determined by how robust the instructional environment is designed, how "smart" the subject matter expert is, and how capable and flexible the "instructional expert" is within the machine.

Because computer-based tutoring is still poorly codified and hotly debated in professional circles, reaching a consensus about a specific ICAI lesson's effectiveness would be difficult if not impossible. This situation, however, means that ITSs are generally more likely to be appreciated widely as "tools" rather than as "tutors."

THE KNOWLEDGE DIMENSION

Trends in knowledge design for ITSs today suggest a balanced implementation of declarative facts and procedural skills. Instructors are fairly articulate about the domain facts and the skills they wish to see demonstrated in tutoring systems. Many are also concerned about the learning processes students use to master various technical skills, such as the specific troubleshooting or operational procedures used to solve the problem.

The current design of an ITS is closely tied to how the ITS presents the domain to a student: knowledge from the simulation, knowledge packaged as rules, frames, or scripts, or intuitive interfaces faithful to the knowledge behaviors of the subject matter (see Figure 1.4). Figure 1.4 highlights the dimensions of device or operational simulation, the domain expert, and the intelligent interface.

Domain knowledge is most often represented operationally. Although most ITS design is centered on the user interface, the domain obviously has evolutionary implications for how a tutor is conceptualized and how a student views the instruction. Most importantly, we believe, the knowledge acquisition process for domain representation will become the major research issue in tutoring development. We have all had the experience of trying to teach someone how to do something, only to realize that—although we understood the problem—we were unable to articulate

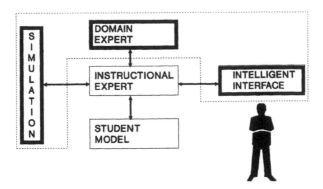

FIGURE 1.4 Domain knowledge architecture.

the steps in a comprehensible way so that the learner truly understood. Describing what we know so that a computer program can present that knowledge effectively is a complex task. The knowledge representation in our heads is not the knowledge representation in our computers.

So the design of domain knowledge structure will depict properties of the domain itself. Most domain knowledge design for an ITS will evolve from highly structured problems with a small set of expected, reasonable human behaviors in specific lesson sequences. In teaching maintenance skills or equipment operations, such explicit knowledges can be designed to present a particular viewpoint within the knowledge base based on meeting specific goals. Even in domains that have a less defined knowledge structure—such as programming, algebra, troubleshooting, or writing—relevant and often creative representations can be designed and presented. Nevertheless, representations are based on how experts understand and interpret the task domain.

How domain knowledge is represented and used in a computer program also depends on the task to be performed. The task—as it breaks down in the goals of a tutoring system—provides a viewpoint about the basic knowledge in the domain. For example, in the domain of jet engine mechanics, the task of diagnosing malfunctions generates various viewpoints of knowledge about aircraft, mechanics, and electronics. Such viewpoints might include a functional representation that fosters a simulation of how the engine works or an experimentally based representation that provides quick condition-action, pattern-matching capabilities. All high performance domains require both knowledge and physical skills.

What needs to be demonstrated? First, can an ITS train or teach efficiently? Can an ITS help students learn how to perform on the job more effectively? As we noted earlier we do not have enough empirical data to cite many significant differences.

As tools, ITS technology is used mostly for rapidly prototyping robust instructional environments. The "knowledge burden" of using a tool is obviously within the programmer. More and more, however, researchers are designing "knowledge-based tools" so that instructional specialists can work together with subject matter experts.

DESIGN DIMENSIONS: EVOLUTION – NOT REVOLUTION

The outlook for ITSs is bright. But understand one thing: Computers do what we ask and program them to do. As professional educators and trainers, we therefore must be wise about what we ask computers to do. Individual instructors should strive to be wise about achieving a balanced perspective when using computers. Technical trainers do not want to end up teaching artificial intelligence rather than their own technical specialty. We must all guard against letting machines and powerful computational features become more important than our students' performances. Intelligent training systems help instructors teach only if wise investments of time, money, and personnel are made. When educators witness the synergy of teacher–student–computer collaborations, then the odds are that real job-related operational processes will be better understood and success on the job will be more assured.

If we better understand the dynamic features of *communication,* then we can individualize instruction efficiently. If we better understand the nature of *teaching,* then we can design machines that can tutor effectively. If we have complex *domains* to simplify, then we can use expert representations and advanced integrated interfaces masterfully. All in all, an ITS can provide the right instruction for right people at the right time.

Intelligent tutoring systems are tools for the 21st century. With carefully considered decisions about how such intelligent systems will supplement education and training, our work in the enterprise of learning complex skills promises to be more efficient, more effective, and much more exciting. Can an ITS help a learner become a better technician, a better problem solver, a more independent thinker, a seasoned decision maker? Yes, and educators and educational technologies must lead novices to this journeyman's realization. This evolution represents quite a challenge for educators. But in the next few years, such challenges will seem more and more natural. As educators and administrators alike see the empirically validated proof of the new intelligent tutoring vision that innovative research scientists imagine, ITSs will one day be wisely and widely used.

REFERENCES

Burton, R. (1988). The environment module of intelligent tutoring systems. In M. C. Polson & J. J. Richardson (Eds.), *Foundations of intelligent tutoring systems* (pp. 109–142). Hillsdale, NJ: Lawrence Erlbaum Associates.

Hull, G., & Glaser, R. (1989). *Fruitful error*. Manuscript submitted for review.

Polson, M. C., & Richardson, J. J. (Eds.). (1988). *Foundations of intelligent tutoring systems*. Hillsdale, NJ: Lawrence Erlbaum Associates.

Shaughnessy, M. (1977). *Errors and expectations*. New York: Oxford.

Sleeman, D., & Brown, J. S. (Eds.). (1982). *Intelligent tutoring systems*. New York: Academic Press.

Turkle, S. (1984). *The second self: Computers and the human spirit*. New York: Simon & Schuster.

VanLehn, K. (1988). Student modeling. In M. C. Polson & J. J. Richardson (Eds.), *Foundations of intelligent tutoring systems* (pp. 55–78). Hillsdale, NJ: Lawrence Erlbaum Associates.

2

Managing Communication Knowledge

Kathleen M. Swigger
University of North Texas

This chapter describes communication knowledge and how it should be used in an intelligent tutoring system (ITS). After the previous discussion concerning user needs (see chap. 1), it seems appropriate to begin the book's technical portion with a description of communication knowledge, as this is the module that is most visible to the user. The communication module (or interface) is the only part of the tutoring system that students actually see and experience. As a result, all other modules in the tutoring system (expert, tutoring, and student module) must describe their functionality and representations in terms of what the student sees. In a very real sense, the communication module drives the student's understanding of the rest of the system.

In the past, communication knowledge has been defined as a specific module responsible for administering the interaction between the student and computer (Yazdani, 1987). As Woolf and McDonald (1985) argued, "The communication module is limited to generating grammatically correct and rhetorically effective output (1) to help the tutoring component do its job and (2) to interpret the student's responses in terms of the categorizations that the tutoring component is sensitive to" (p. 10). According to this narrow definition, the communication module is a single module that transmits appropriate messages from one logical unit of the tutoring system to another. More recently, the definition of communication knowledge has been expanded to include the entire tutoring system. Indeed, Wenger (1987) maintained that the primary purpose of an ITS is to provide the student with a set of operators that will cause or support the communication of knowledge. Thus, communication knowledge is both the interface and a series of sophisticated tools that actually drive the design of the entire system. The set of tools includes a vast array of interactive styles (menus, natural language, icons) and interactive devices (mouse, touch pads, speech recognition). The interface allows operations such as dragging, recognizing, throwing, relating, and so on. Under this broad definition, the designer of intelligent tutors is responsible for building a massive communication management system that controls and monitors a student's learning environment.

What follows is a discussion of how designers of ITSs confront the problem of creating systems that communicate rather than simply provide information; the distinction between communication management systems and information exchange systems is fundamental to this discussion. Furthermore, this chapter attempts to answer such questions as:

- What is communication knowledge in an ITS?
- How is it different from other types of communication?
- How does one represent and present communication knowledge?
- How does one evaluate an effective communication system?

This chapter tries to address the problem of how to provide an environment that facilitates learning. The reader should be warned that interface design or the construction of effective dialogues are not dealt with explicitly. This type of discussion can be found in other works (e.g., Dumas, 1988; Shneiderman, 1987). As a result, this is not a tutorial, nor a presentation of guidelines for creating effective interfaces; rather, it is a presentation of the theories and methodologies that should govern decisions about the role of communication in an ITS.

The first section of the chapter explains the relationship between communication, as defined in ITSs, and theories of communication, as developed by human communication researchers. The second section defines communication knowledge within the context of existing intelligent tutors. The third section discusses a methodology that may assist designers of communication knowledge. The fourth section discusses the question of evaluating the communication between student and tutor. Finally, this chapter concludes with a discussion of future research.

A DEFINITION OF COMMUNICATION

The broad field of human communication studies has a well-established body of knowledge about which intelligent tutor interface designers are largely unaware. The term *communication* has had a variety of meanings for different communication theorists. Its most restrictive definition refers to face-to-face communication and relates only to the function of referencing the transmission of information between two individuals (Bateson, 1951). This allows for only a few necessary functions to be fulfilled by the communication act, such as sending a message, receiving a message, and interpreting a message. Furthermore, the functions operating under this narrow definition tend to be flat and static, conveying very little of the context of the communication.

More recent definitions refer to communication acts that reference an external world of objects and events (Newcomb, 1953; Rogers & Kincaid, 1981). The simplest possible communication act involves one person (A) transmitting information to another person (B) about some object (X) (see Figure 2.1). The meaning of the conversation consists of *report* and *content* functions, and *command* and *relationship* functions. Thus, a successful communication act consists of managing or manipulating content and relationships in order to come to some agreement about object X. Under this definition, the communication act becomes a dynamic interchange of ideas and emotions. The functions or operators (i.e., command, report, relationship, etc.) are much broader and more expressive of a dynamic environment. Suddenly, there are operators that allow the user to express both the content and the context of the interaction.

Traditional person–computer interfaces have used the metaphor of communication in a restrictive manner, similar to the first definition of communication (see previous definition). The computer is seen as a passive partner engaged in information exchange with a user who gives orders or makes requests while the computer does the work (see Figure 2.2). Most computer users are not interested in communicating with computers, but rather want to use the computer to solve problems or accomplish a specific task. This model can be seen most readily in computer applications such as querying a database, using a word processor, or manipulating a spreadsheet. Here, the functions or operators are simple commands such as

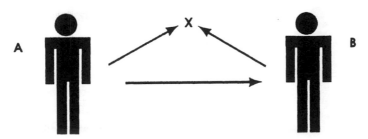

FIGURE 2.1. Person/person.

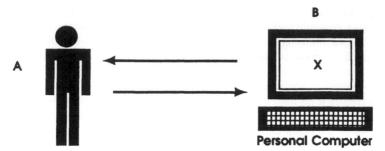

FIGURE 2.2. Person/computer.

"modify," "retrieve," "delete," and so forth. Even when users are allowed to use a direct interface device such as a mouse or touch panel, they are still engaged in an information-exchange activity. In an information-exchange activity, the person does not want to come to an agreement with the computer. The person merely wants to retrieve information about object X.

More traditional computer-assisted instructional (CAI) environments provide yet another metaphor of communication. Within a CAI environment the computer controls the communication act by soliciting information from the student in the form of questions and requests (Figure 2.3). Information exchange is again the purpose of the communication, but this time the computer is soliciting the information. Sometimes the computer even evaluates the student with respect to the quality of the information exchange. In this particular communication environment, the student is asked to retrieve information about object X.

Intelligent tutoring systems, more specifically student-centered intelligent tutors, try to model different levels of communication and adapt to the choices of the human user. Some of these systems (Fischer & Lemke, 1988) use the metaphor of iconic object manipulation to manage the interaction. This metaphor suggests that the student views items on the screen as objects that can be held in one's hand. Instead of referring to an

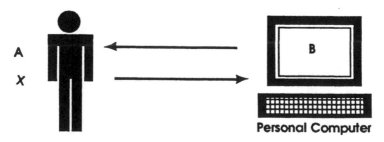

FIGURE 2.3. Person/computer.

object by its name, the student can use a mouse to point to an object or grab it and drag it across the screen. Some student-centered environments even allow the student to enter natural language expressions that communicate more naturally with the system (Brown & Burton, 1982). In a student-centered environment, the goal is to have the computer and the student gradually become partners and learn how to manipulate content and relationships in order to come to an agreement about the knowledge they share (Figure 2.4).

This type of communication management system (i.e., student-centered environments) seems most similar to the face-to-face communication represented in Figure 2.1, and is the type of communication required to make intelligent tutors more effective. Like face-to-face communication, student-centered tutors convey the meaning of the conversation through explicit operators that are supported by specific functions and relationships. Furthermore, both the functions and relationships are physically available to the student and can be manipulated much like real-world objects. Ultimately, these relationships and functions represent both the content and the context of the conversation. This is what gives student-centered tutors their power, and this is what makes the systems appear intelligent.

COMMUNICATION KNOWLEDGE IN INTELLIGENT SYSTEMS

There are two problems that must be solved by an ITS designer: (a) how to define the knowledge that the system is suppose to teach (e.g., knowledge about how to land an aircraft, knowledge about motion etc.), and (b) how to design a system that manages the interaction or relationship between student and computer so that the primary task can be achieved more quickly. Thus, communication knowledge in an ITS consists of the

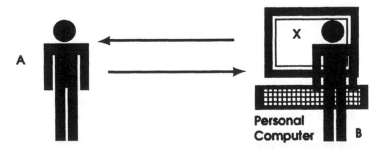

FIGURE 2.4. Person/microworld.

rules and facts that tell the system how to manage the student–computer interaction.

Generally, the design of the student–computer interactions consists of selecting appropriate interaction devices and interaction styles to fit a particular instructional style. Briefly, *interaction devices* are the physical objects (hardware) that allow the student to interact with the system and include such items as a mouse, touch pad, keyboard, light pen, and so on. *Interactive style* refers to the software that promotes the interaction, such as menus, command languages, and icons. Finally, the *instructional style* refers to a selected method of communicating or teaching the knowledge. One way to distinguish among these three elements is to think of instructional style as the observable two-way exchange of symbols and actions between student and computer, whereas interaction styles and interaction devices are the supporting software and hardware through which this exchange occurs (Hartson & Hix, 1989). However, the three items are so closely integrated that it is impossible to separate them when discussing the subject of communication knowledge. Thus, communication knowledge refers to the conversation between the student and the computer system and all the media necessary for that communication. Together these elements comprise what may be called *communication style*.

Traditionally, instructional designers and CAI authors have discussed communication style using terms such as *drill and practice, tutorial, problem solving, simulation,* and *games* (Bork, 1981). Similarly, intelligent tutors can also be labeled as games (WEST [Burton & Brown, 1982] and WUMPUS [Goldstein, 1982]), simulations (STEAMER [Stevens & Roberts, 1983] and SOPHIE [Brown & Burton, 1982]), tutors (WHY [Stevens & Collins, 1977]), drill-and-practice (BUGGY [Burton, 1982]), and problem solving (PROUST [Soloway & Johnson, 1984]). Although these categories convey very useful meanings for people interested in designing conventional software, they do not really describe the type of student-directed communication style that currently characterizes more creative tutoring systems. More recently, Fischer and Morch (1988) described three categories of communication styles that are more appropriate for student-centered interactions: *tutoring, consultation,* and *critiquing*.

Tutoring is important in the initial stages of training because students need to know something before they can ask questions. A tutoring system might be loosely defined as the arrangement of instructional sequences that eventually leads to the mastery of a specific goal. Thus, the designer of a tutoring system is responsible for arranging the sequences of instruction in a manner facilitating the mastery of a specific objective. This type of communication style is typically called *sequential dialogue* because it moves in a predictable manner from one part of the dialogue to the next (Hutchins, Hollan, & Norman, 1986). The communication management system, in turn, supports the instructional sequence and provides an interface guiding the student toward the goal. Thus, the major issue involved in constructing this type of interface is the question of moving the student toward the goal by limiting the user's choices to a finite number of selections. Although tutoring systems appear to be tolerant of students' responses, they impose a structure that can only react to anticipated responses. Examples of systems that use the tutoring approach include PROUST (Soloway & Johnson, 1984), the *LISP-Tutor* (Anderson & Reiser, 1985), and SOPHIE (Brown & Burton, 1982).

Consultation is used more frequently in expert systems than training systems. This particular model provides little support for learner-controlled functions. The computer controls the dialogue by asking the user to enter responses to specific questions (much like what happens when a student responds to a human consultant). Therefore, the system is responsible for managing an interface that facilitates information exchange. At the end of the consultation, students receive an answer to their question. Students can ask the system why it gave a particular answer, but they cannot volunteer additional information, nor can they pursue a particular line of reasoning. Examples of such systems include MYCIN (Buchanan & Shortliffe, 1984), and an early version of GUIDON (Clancey, 1987).

The critiquing model is used in a more student-centered environment and permits students to pursue their own goals. The computer interrupts only when the student fails to meet minimum criteria. Based on previous research (Carroll & McKendree, 1987), it is known that students learn only what is necessary to solve the current problem. Thus, the critic intervenes only when it is necessary and only with advice that is problem-specific. The critiquing approach provides information to the student only when it becomes relevant. The critiquing approach also allows the student to fail and make mistakes.

Often associated with the critiquing style of communication is the term *multithread dialogue,* a task-oriented concept referring to the multiplicity of task paths available to the student at any given instant during the lesson (Hill, 1987). The general term for this kind of communication is *nonsequential* or *asynchronous* dialogue. In contrast to sequential dialogue where the system presents the student with one task at a time, asynchronous dialogue makes all tasks available to the student at any time. Dialogue is asynchronous in the sense that sequencing of each task is independent of the others. At almost any point during the lesson, the student can select another task and, later, return to the first. Asynchronous, multithread dialogue is also called *event-based* dialogue because students actions initiate the actions or sequence of tasks (Ehrlich & Hartson, 1981). Interface management for this type of model is much more difficult because the system cannot anticipate every action the student takes. Instead, the designer must provide a flexible environment that allows the student to explore different paths of action.

For tutoring and consulting types of instructional systems, students interact mainly via the keyboard. They answer questions, select an answer, or react to specific prompts by pressing a key. For critiquing models of communication, students interact by directly manipulating the object itself through a direct manipulation device such as a mouse, touch pad, or voice (Shneiderman, 1983). The major portion of the interaction between student and computer is performed by movement of the object from one position to another, by dragging the object to a new location, or by changing the object's size or shape. Objects are also moved to indicate when an operation is to be performed on them (Tesler, 1981).

Two Examples of Student-Centered Tutors

To better understand student-centered tutors, we have developed two training systems that use different aspects of the critiquing approach. In order to help students better understand the relationships between *orbital elements* and *ground tracks,* we built an elaborate system that allows students to explore the "microworld" of orbital mechanics (Swigger, Burns, Loveland, & Jackson, 1987). The original training system was designed to teach students how to deduce orbital elements by looking at ground tracks. Ground tracks are two-dimensional displays that show the portion of the earth that a satellite covers as it circles the earth. The actual satellite path appears as a continuous line on a monitor. The ground track information is then used by Air Force crews to verify orbital paths of known satellites, to hypothesize about mission intent of unknown satellites, and to monitor space debris. The ground track, as well as the orbit itself, is a direct function of the orbital elements.

The orbital mechanics tutor, nicknamed OM, allows the student to explore the interactions between orbital elements and ground tracks. Students learn about ground tracks by changing orbital parameters, changing injection points, generating ground tracks, predicting ground tracks, and so forth. Additionally, there are several on-line tools that help students organize and systematize their information. These tools include a two-dimensional display that helps students conceptualize the effect of orbital parameters, definition and example windows that relate facts, a history tool that allows students to overlay previous work, and a prediction window that allows students to state relationships between variables (Figure 2.5). This system is designed so that students learn about orbital

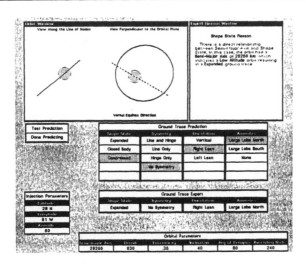

FIGURE 2.5. OM prediction window.

mechanics by gathering data, generating and testing hypotheses, as well as forming generalizations about the different orbital elements.

The communication management system for OM includes all the on-line tools and windows and a model of how students explore a microworld environment. The system monitors the students' actions and determines whether they are demonstrating effective inquiry skills. This is accomplished by associating all the on-line tools with specific categories of inquiry skills. When there is a sufficient amount of evidence to indicate that the student needs help, then the system suggests that the student select one of the appropriate tools.

This same approach was used to develop a tutoring system called Strategic Training Routes Architecture for an Intelligent Effective Reviewer (S-TRAINER), which is designed to assist in the debriefing of Air Force pilots who have completed a bombing mission (Swigger & Holman, 1989). The system has the ability to reason about tactical situations and provide plausible explanations about these activities. Prestored mission events serve as script templates that are matched against actual events and the time relation between events. After the air crews complete the training mission, the system diagnoses pilot and crew errors and generates a written evaluation of the mission along with a set of graphics that can be used to supplement the written report.

S-TRAINER contains an elaborate communication management system that determines significant mission events and uses this information to generate a training script. The training script consists of a list of significant events along with a list of graphic displays describing these events. All of the graphics are eventually shown on one of two screens. Each of the two screens, in turn, can be partitioned into a full, half, or quarter display. Thus the communication management system must decide on the content, type, and location of each display. In order to accomplish this task, S-TRAINER uses a series of rules that (a) suggest possible displays, (b) compute display times for each event, (c) determine whether to expand or reduce the number of displays, and (d) determine the correct flow of the script. Furthermore, the communication management system is responsible for producing a pedagogically sound and aesthetically pleasing training session. After several iterations, the system produces a final training script that indicates the type, length, location, and begin/end times for each display (Figure 2.6).

From the previous discussion, it is clear that communication knowledge consists of rules that tell the system how to communicate task-relevant information to the student. It also consists of heuristics that designers use to assemble the correct interaction devices with the correct interaction styles and communication styles (Figure 2.7). For time-varying, multitask problems, like teaching someone how to operate a space shuttle, the designer needs to consider several additional factors. For example, a format for an individual display must not only provide information about a specific task, it must also blend with other displays that are presented simultaneously on the screen. It is becoming increasingly common for a format to be a member of a larger set that is stored in software and presented on demand in different display areas (Ripley, 1989). Consequently, the designer must make some provision for a smooth transition between formats as the different instructional events unfold. A poorly designed format will either fail to communicate critical information or demand more processing time than the student has available. The problem of constraining the design of a multimedia training system that uses simultaneous displays in a learner-controlled environment is the subject of the next section.

DESIGNING COMMUNICATION KNOWLEDGE

The creation of a student-centered communication management system requires special skills, special system capabilities, and special tools. The task is further complicated by the introduction of multimedia, multi-interactive, and simultaneous displays. A third problem relates to the human communication barriers that exist among those responsible for creating the training system — the psychologist, the computer programmer, and the instructional designer. Although these problems may appear to be

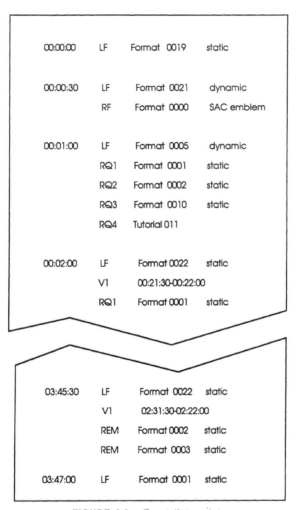

FIGURE 2.6. Event list script.

overwhelming, one rather obvious solution is to develop a tool that will organize and systematize the development of a complex training system.

Traditional computer science research has long suggested the importance of using software engineering tools to significantly improve the structure of programs and assist programmers with their problem-solving tasks. Researchers argue that a design methodology can provide a focus and structure for solving computer problems (Boehm, 1981). A design methodology is an artificial language that enables the programmer (and

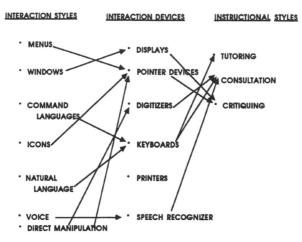

FIGURE 2.7. Communication style.

any other member of the design team) to describe a particular idea at a conceptual, rather than implementation, level. A design methodology also encourages a consistent design that can be shared among all the members of the team, including the psychologist, instructional designer, and the programmer. Finally, a design methodology fosters dialogue independence and permits the implementation of specific communication styles. As a result, it is possible to explicitly represent and test various communication styles because the methodology can be replicated under different conditions and with different domains. The problem, of course, is selecting a design tool that properly describes the computer's actions and reactions to a student's inputs. In short, the design tool needs to represent a communication process that often appears to be nondeterministic.

One way to distinguish between the various design methodologies is to classify them according to the *declarative* and *procedural* paradigms. Procedural representations are used to describe knowledge about how to perform a task. In contrast, declarative systems are used to represent descriptive information. In some ways, the tension between the declarative and procedural representations has made it difficult to propose a design methodology for ITSs. Most designers of ITS systems believe that both the storage and retrieval of expert knowledge is best facilitated by the frame/object orientation, a declarative approach (Clancey, 1987). Yet, when researchers wish to describe how their systems actually work, they use a procedural approach to explain the student–computer interaction (Clancey, 1987). A procedural representation more closely resembles the communication act. A procedural representation can best describe how one process activation is often dependent on the outcome of another.

The majority of the languages used to specify human–computer interfaces emphasize procedural information. Although these procedural methodologies go by different names — state transition diagrams (Ling, 1982), Petri Nets (Jentzen, 1980), and augmented data flow diagrams (Kuo & Karimi, 1988) — they all present a formal design model that looks very similar to a directed graph. In every case, nodes are used to represent the completion of events, whereas arcs represent transitions from one event to another. Different system responses are shown on the arcs and may involve an invocation of another part of the graph. Thus, the designer can represent both the conceptual and detailed structure of the student-computer interaction. In addition, a designer can represent a student's exploration of a single state by drawing an arrow from a node to itself.

An example of the use of a procedural methodology to describe the OM student–computer interaction is presented in Figure 2.8. As previously mentioned, the OM tutor allows students to discover relationships between orbital elements and ground tracks. The student initiates a discovery activity by changing one or more orbital parameters and generating a ground track. After investigating the effects of changing different parameter values for different ground tracks, students can advance to the *prediction* window where they can make a hypothesis regarding the shape of a particular ground track. Students test their hypotheses by selecting options from the menu and comparing the inputs to the expert's conclusions. After making several successful predictions, students enter the *orbit prediction* environment voluntarily, which is designed to check students' mental states by asking them to perform a task in the reverse order of the one previously described. Students are shown a specific ground track and asked to enter orbital descriptors that match the ground track displayed on the screen. In this manner, students explore the orbital mechanics microworld. Figure 2.8 describes this interaction and shows how students advance through the program.

There are many compelling reasons for using this methodology to construct student-centered environments. There are also a number of reasons why another design tool might be more appropriate. It is obvious, for example, that flow diagrams are cumbersome for specifying highly interactive environments (Jacob, 1983). Higher level, more directly exe-

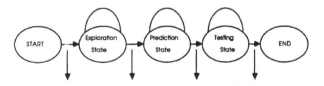

FIGURE 2.8. Procedural knowledge for OM.

cutable, specification languages would free the designer of the low-level details. Yet it is also obvious that a design methodology helps support knowledge abstraction and computational primitives at the architectural level. Such a methodology permits the knowledge engineer to cooperatively develop systems using a shared language of conceptual constructs rather than a set of problem-specific primitives. A design methodology for a learner-controlled environment is especially important because this form of problem solving is considered more complex than other types of tutors.

In contrast to the procedural methodology, the object-oriented paradigm provides a more declarative approach for representing communication knowledge and is exemplified by systems such as Bonar's bite-sized architecture (see chap. 3, this volume) and Woolf's Primitive Tutors (see chap. 6, this volume). The event-based nature of object orientation is effective for representing asynchronous dialogues and for representing the behavior of specific features regardless of their context. The capability for dynamic binding, hierarchical definition with inheritance of attributes and procedures, and communication by message passing work together to support shared, reusable code. These features are clearly demonstrated by Bonar's system that excels at representing graphical types of learning environments. However, one of the disadvantages of object orientation is the tendency to obscure temporal relationships and high-level sequencing behavior (Hartson & Hix, 1989). Using an object-oriented representation makes it difficult, from the instructional designer's point of view, to demonstrate the lesson's communication style.

It is obvious from this discussion that a single design methodology for communication knowledge management is yet to be discovered. In particular, what is needed is a holistic approach that would serve to complement the development of intelligent tutors. This approach needs to emphasize interface management as an integral part of the design process and should clearly show how the interface drives the rest of the system. At the present time, there are only suggestions that a methodology will exist. The current emphasis on instructional planners that adapt to different student responses (McMillan, Emme, & Berkowitz, 1988), bite-sized architectures that specify basic elements (Bonar, see chap. 3, this volume), and tutoring primitives that manage instructional domains (see chap. 6, this volume) seem to indicate that a coherent and cohesive methodology will eventually emerge.

EVALUATING COMMUNICATION KNOWLEDGE

Although a common methodology allows us to better describe communication knowledge, there remains the problem of determining whether the communication is effective. A review of the literature on student-centered environments reveals only a few studies that contain hard data on the effectiveness of their instruction (Hoecker & Elias, 1986; Shute & Glaser, 1986). Although many current AI systems emphasize the interactive and exploratory nature of learning, it is not clear whether systems using these principles are effective (Sebrechts & Deck, 1986). The evaluation of ITSs has always been predicated on behavioral experiments that determine whether one treatment is better than another treatment. The typical methodology is to construct a system, and then to use the system with multiple subjects and multiple trials to obtain reliable measures on the effectiveness of a treatment (Baggett, 1988). These experiments are usually difficult, costly, and time consuming to conduct. These experiments become even more difficult to perform as researchers develop training systems that use a variety of different media and interactive styles in conjunction with AI techniques. Trying to characterize the behavior of programs with stochastic elements can be quite difficult due to the nondeterministic nature of the output. That is, the same type of input from students may not necessarily produce the same output each time the tutor is run. Consequently, measuring the tutor's performance over its input domain can require an extensive, even prohibitive number of test cases.

A few evaluation studies attempt to discover which features of a tutoring system most affect individual users (Shute & Glaser, 1986). It is expected that this information can be used to predict the behavior of individual users engaged in complex problem-solving tasks. The factors that affect user behavior are quite complex and interact extensively with one another. Thus, information that predicts how an individual student reacts to an exploratory environment should help us produce more effective training systems.

Another approach to the evaluation issue is to determine patterns of behaviors that characterize different groups of student interactions. Thus here, the emphasis shifts from predicting individual behavior to predicting group behavior. For example, two groups of students enrolled in the Undergraduate Space Training School at Lowry Air Force Base were asked to use the OM tutors. Subjects were classified as either beginners (students in their first week of the program) or experts (students in their last week of the program). Subjects belonging to the two different skill levels were told how to use the system and then asked to interact with the system in a self-paced manner. A data collection program recorded all student–computer interactions. The data collection phase began after the students entered their first input and continued for no more than 15 minutes. Twenty subjects served in this experiment, 12 experts and 8 beginners.

An analysis of the subjects' interactions was performed using the Reitman and Rueter algorithm (McKeithen, Reitman, & Rueter & Hirtle,

1981), which clusters individual responses into groups of responses that always appear contiguously, regardless of order. The Reitman and Reuter algorithm is a measure of the similarity of two trees and is based on the number of nontrivial chunks the two trees have in common. By dividing the number of common chunks by the total, it constructs a proportion in common. Distance is then given by 1 — similarity. Using this particular analysis, the evidence showed that expert subjects demonstrate a greater variety and depth of interaction (see Table 2.1). The expert students used more on-line tools and used them in a more consistent manner. Further analysis suggests that, as a group, the expert subjects were more similar to each other than they were to their beginner counterparts. The expert subjects tended to pursue goals in a very planned and prescribed manner (Swigger, in press). The beginner students showed no similarity to each other, and tended not to pursue any clear goals.

This particular study shows that there is a correlation between expertise and knowledge organizations. This idea has already been confirmed by other studies on expertise (Engle & Bukstel, 1978; Larkin, McDermott, Simon, & Simon, 1980). This study also suggests that we can use this type of information to identify different patterns of skills that should, in turn, help us to build better communication management systems. As indicated by this study, the critiquing communication style did not improve beginning students' explorations of the microworld. More specifically, they did not demonstrate more effective problem-solving skills as they proceeded through the activities. As suggested in a previous section of this chapter, the critiquing style of communication is probably inappropriate for beginning students. A more sophisticated communication management system would have recognized the "beginner student" pattern and then shifted to a different communication style. Pattern matching is one of the standard themes in AI literature, so it seems appropriate to think that intelligent tutors can characterize group behavior. Identifying and adapting the communication style should become standard practice in ITSs.

TABLE 2.1
Expert — Beginner Interactions

	Average Distance Between Subjects	
	Experts	*Beginners*
Experts	.51	.72
Beginners		.81

RESEARCH OPPORTUNITIES

Visions of future ITSs suggest research in many different areas within computer science, instructional design, psychology, and engineering. In the near future, interface support environments will become integrated into the operating system. Indeed, the interface will be the operating system. Also, the trend will continue to be away from the commonly used keyboard input and frame-oriented, screen-at-a-time, question-at-a-time displays toward more dynamic displays, unusual devices, and different communication media (Mackay & Davenport, 1989). Stereo three-dimensional graphics projected on walls or inside of helmets will allow students to experience alternative realities (Fischer & Lemke, 1988). Development methodologies and tools will have to accommodate the different devices, interaction styles, and communication styles we cannot now imagine. As a result, a number of short- and long-term research opportunities seem obvious and a discussion follows.

Short-Term Goals

There are several immediate goals that researchers can accomplish in the next 5 years.

One short-term goal is to develop and then validate a methodology for the design of communication knowledge. The methodology might be similar to those models proposed in this chapter, or it might include other types of design tools. The methodology, at the very least, should be able to represent communication knowledge. More likely, the methodology will represent the entire system (Tanner & Buxton, 1984). It is becoming increasingly obvious that the interface defines the knowledge for both the expert module and the student model. Thus, any proposed methodology should include all the activities of the software life cycle with varying levels of automation. The methodology needs to be iterative, dialogue-independent, and capable of accommodating an evergrowing list of physical devices.

A second goal is to develop a nationwide database that classifies existing media according to its content and cognitive function. This country, as well as other nations, have produced a large number of films and videodiscs. An extensive database that contains information about films, videos, and other graphic material would allow us to extract different media selections in order to enhance existing instruction. However, experience from the document retrieval world has taught us that the key to the success of an information retrieval system is a proper index of the material. The short-term challenge will be to develop an indexing schema that correctly categorizes multimedia material for both instructional and information purposes.

A third goal that we can accomplish in the next 5 years is to expand the definition of student-centered environments to include interfaces that facilitate computer-supported cooperative environments. Cooperative problem solving refers to the shared, systematic behaviors displayed by two or more people as they work toward the solution of a single problem. As we begin to explore the issue of cooperative work environments (Stefik et al., 1987), we might also ask whether people know how to use these cooperative work environments for group decision making. If this is not the case, then we need to develop systems that teach people how to become more effective problem solvers in a computer-supported environment. The goal of this research would be to develop broad-based educational and training systems that can be used to teach people how to work together to solve a common goal. It has been observed that the need for such skills occurs frequently in this society. Yet rarely do we teach people how to develop cooperative skills, nor do we provide proper tools for them to communicate in this mode. As such, research is needed that will provide insight and software tools to achieve this goal.

Long-Term Goals

The achievement of long-term goals, to some extent, will depend on the technological advances that occur in the next few years. If the past is any indication of the future, then we can expect to be overwhelmed by the new media. Some of these devices will be capable of displaying three and even four dimensions. As a result, it will be possible to achieve some of the following goals.

Interfaces will adapt to their users. Some of the advances in machine learning suggest that we can build interfaces that bridge the gap between the user's model of the information and the system's organization of the data (Boose, 1985). Our initial success indicates that we can use these types of techniques to alter interfaces in order to conform to different communication styles. For example, chapter 1 of this text briefly describes how many students lack the basic skills necessary to perform minimal tasks. In the future, adaptable interfaces that conform to users' varying skill levels will permit both the expert and the novice to obtain valuable instruction and information from the same system.

Design methodologies for intelligent tutors will generate the code for ITSs. Automated support tools for programming languages already exist, and interest in them is increasing, especially within larger programming languages such as ADA and COBOL (Buxton & Druffel, 1984). However, almost all the automated tools associated with programming languages support the developer in the coding phase of software production, not the interface design stage. Both Kuo and Karimi (1988) and Bonar (see chap. 3, this volume) are correct in suggesting that interface development is one of the major bottlenecks in the design of intelligent systems. This implies that what is needed is an automated tool to generate both the graphics and the communication style for the system. Research in this direction has already started (Hartson & Hix, 1989), but much more needs to occur before there is a realistic automated tool.

Researchers will formulate a science that can be used to predict students' communication styles. Such a science will match a learner's cognitive style to the appropriate communication style. It will also examine a student's cognitive functions and the effects of attention, memory, gender, spatial ability, and so forth on performance. Although recent discoveries about the brain have had an impact on the fields of biology and psychology (Urbanczyk, Angel, & Kennelly, 1989), these ideas have yet to influence the design of instructional systems. Intelligent tutors must begin to model and represent basic human responses such as attention, memory, and anxiety. This type of information will be crucial to our understanding of how students learn and understand information and will be included in future systems.

SUMMARY

Many concepts and ideas in the field of communication management for ITSs have been presented here, among which include a definition of communication, a proposed methodology, and a means for evaluation. The need for such concepts are especially relevant as more student-directed learning environments are developed that require dynamic output displays, asynchronous dialogue, and concurrency. However, it is important to remember that both communication style and communication management remain more art than science. Indeed, this is why AI has been used in instructional systems. The challenge of the future will be to blend the art with the science.

REFERENCES

Anderson, J., & Reiser, B. (1985). The LISP Tutor. *Byte, 10,* 159–175.

Baggett, P. (1988). The role of practice in videodisc-based procedural instructions. *IEEE Transactions on Systems, Man, and Cybernetics, 18,* 487–495.

Bateson, G. (1951). Information and codification: A philosophical approach. In J. Ruesch & G. Bateson (Eds.), *Communication: The social matrix of psychiatry* (pp. 168-211). New York: Norton.

Boehm, B. (1981). *Software engineering economics.* Englewood, NJ: Prentice-Hall.

Boose, J. H. (1985). A knowledge acquisition program for expert systems based on personal construct psychology. *International Journal of Man-Machine Studies, 23,* 495-525.

Bork, A. (1981). *Learning with computers.* New York: Digital Press.

Brown, J. S., & Burton, R. (1982). Pedagogical, natural language and knowledge engineering techniques in SOPHIE I, II, III. In D. Sleeman & J. S. Brown (Eds.), *Intelligent tutoring systems* (pp. 227-279). New York: Academic Press.

Buchanan, B., & Shortliffe, E. (1984). *Rule-based expert systems: The MYCIN experiments of the Stanford heuristic programming project.* Reading, MA: Addison-Wesley.

Burton, R. R. (1982). Diagnosing bugs in simple procedural skill. In D. Sleeman & J. S. Brown (Eds.), *Intelligent tutoring systems* (pp. 157-184). New York: Academic Press.

Burton, R. R., & Brown, J. S. (1982). An investigation of computer coaching for informal learning activities. In D. Sleeman & J. S. Brown (Eds.), *Intelligent tutoring systems* (pp. 79-98). New York: Academic Press.

Buxton, J. N., & Druffel, L. E. (1984). Rationale for STONEMAN. In D. R. Barstow, H. E. Shrobe, & E. Sandewall (Eds.), *Interactive programming environments* (pp. 535-545). New York: McGraw-Hill.

Carroll, J., & McKendree, J. (1987). Interface design issues for advice-giving expert systems. *Communications of the ACM, 30,* 14-31.

Clancey, W. (1987). *Knowledge-based tutoring.* Cambridge, MA: MIT Press.

Dumas, J. S. (1988). *Designing user interfaces for software.* Englewood Cliffs, NJ: Prentice-Hall.

Ehrlich, R. W., & Hartson, H. R. (1981). DMS—an environment for dialogue management. *Proceedings of COMPCON81,* 121-125. New York: IEEE Computer Society.

Engle, R., & Bukstel, L. (1978). Memory processes among bridge players of differing expertise. *American Journal of Psychology, 91,* 673-689.

Fischer, G., & Morch, A. (1988). Crack: A critiquing approach to cooperative kitchen design. *Proceedings on Intelligent Tutoring Systems,* 176-185. New York: Association for Computing Machinery.

Fischer, G., & Lemke, A. (1988). Construction kits and design environments: Steps toward human problem domain communication. *Human-Computer Interaction, 3,* 105-160.

Goldstein, I. P. (1982). The genetic graph: A representation for the evolution of procedural knowledge. In D. Sleeman & J. S. Brown (Eds.), *Intelligent tutoring systems* (pp. 51-78). New York: Academic Press.

Hartson, H. R., & Hix, D. (1989). Human-computer interface development. *ACM Computing Survey, 21,* 1-91.

Hill, R. D. (1987). Event-response systems: A technique for specifying multi-threaded dialogues. *Proceedings of the ACM CHI + GI'87,* 241-248. New York: Association for Computing Machinery.

Hoecker, D., & Elias, G. (1986). User evaluation of the LISP intelligent tutoring system. *Proceedings of the Human Factors Society,* 182-185. Santa Monica, CA: The Human Factors Society.

Hutchins, E. L., Hollan, D., & Norman, D. A. (1986). Direct manipulation interfaces. In D. A. Norman & S. W. Draper (Eds.), *User centered system design* (pp. 230-260). Hillsdale, NJ: Lawrence Erlbaum Associates.

Jacob, R. J. (1983). Using formal specifications in the design of the human-computer interface. *Communications of the ACM, 26,* 259-264.

Jentzen, M. (1980). Structured representation of knowledge by Petri nets as an aid for teaching and research. In W. Brauer (Ed.), *Net Theory of Processes and Systems* (pp. 537-542). Series—*Lecture Notes in Computer Science No. 84.* Berlin: Springer-Verlag.

Kuo, F., & Karimi, J. (1988). User interface design from a real time perspective. *Communications of the ACM, 31,* 1456-1473.

Larkin, J., McDermott, J., Simon, D. P., & Simon, H. (1980). Expert and novice performance in solving physics problems. *Science, 208,* 1335-1342.

Ling, M. (1982). Designing data entry programs using state diagrams as a common model. *Proceedings of the 6th International Conference on Software Engineering,* 296-308. New York: IEEE Computer Society.

Mackay, W. E., & Davenport, G. (1989). Virtual video editing in interactive multimedia applications. *Communications of the ACM, 32,* 802-810.

McKeithen, K., Reitman, J., Rueter, H., & Hirtle, S. (1981). Knowledge organization and skill differences in computer programmers. *Cognitive Psychology, 13,* 307-325.

McMillan, S. A., Emme, D., & Berkowitz, M. (1988). Instructional planners: Lesson learned. In J. Psotka, L. D. Massey, & S. A. Mutter (Eds.), *Intelligent tutoring systems: Lessons learned* (pp. 229-256). Hillsdale, NJ: Lawrence Erlbaum Associates.

Newcomb, T. (1953). An approach to the study of communicative acts. *Psychological Review, 60,* 393-404.

Ripley, G. D. (1989). DVI—A digital multimedia technology. *Communications of the ACM, 32,* 811-822.

Rogers, E.,, & Kincaid, D. L. (1981). *Communication networks: Toward a new paradigm for research.* New York: Free Press.

Sebrechts, M., & Deck, J. (1986). Techniques for acquiring computer procedures: Some restrictions on interaction. *Proceedings of the Human Factors Society,* 275-279. Santa Monica, CA: The Human Factors Society.

Shneiderman, B. (1983, August). Direct manipulation: A step beyond programming languages. *IEEE Computer,* Vol. 16, 57-69.

Shneiderman, B. (1987). *Designing the user interface: Strategies for effective human-computer interaction.* Reading, MA: Addison-Wesley.

Shute, V., & Glaser, R. (1986). An intelligent tutoring system for exploring principles of economics. (Tech. Rep.) Pittsburgh: University of Pittsburgh, Learning Research and Development Center.

Soloway, E. M., & Johnson, W. L. (1984). Remembrance of blunders past: A retrospective on the development of PROUST. *Proceedings of the Sixth Cognitive Science Society Conference,* 57-60. Hillsdale, NJ: Lawrence Erlbaum Associates.

Stefik, M., Foster, G., Bobrow, D., Kahn, K., Lanning, S., & Suchman, L. (1987). Beyond the chalkboard: Computer support for collaboration and problem solving in meetings. *Communications of the ACM, 30,* 32-47.

Stevens, A. L., & Collins, A. (1977). The goal structure of a Socratic tutor. *Proceedings of the National ACM Conference,* 256-263.

Stevens, A. L., & Roberts, B. (1983). Quantitative and qualitative simulation in computer-based training. *Journal of Computer-Based Instruction, 18,* 16-19.

Swigger, K. (in press). An evaluation of the Orbital Mechanics tutor. *International Journal of Man-Machine Studies.*

Swigger, K., Burns, H., Loveland, H., & Jackson, T. (1987). An intelligent tutoring system for interpreting ground tracks. *Proceedings of AAAI-87,* 72-76. Los Altos, CA: Morgan Kaufman Publishers, Inc.

Swigger, K., & Holman, B. (1989). S-TRAINER: Script-based reasoning for mission assessment. In W. Mauer (Ed.), *Computer Assisted Learning* (pp. 552-559). Series—*Lecture Notes in Computer Science No. 360,* (pp. 552-559). Berlin: Springer-Verlag.

Tanner, P. P., & Buxton, W. A. (1984). Some issues in future user interface management system (UIMS) development. In *Seeheim Workshop of User Interface Management Systems* (pp. 224-230). Berlin: Springer—Verlag.

Tesler, L. (1981). The smalltalk environment. *Byte, 6,* 90-147.

Wenger, E. (1987). *Knowledge communication systems.* Los Altos, CA: Morgan Kaufmann.

Woolf, B. P., & McDonald, D. D. (1985). Building a computer tutor: Design issues. *AEDS Journal, 23,* 10-18.

Urbanczyk, A. A., Angel, C., & Kennelly, K. (1989). Hemispheric activation increases positive manifold for lateralized cognitive tasks: An extension of Stankov's hypothesis. *Brain and Cognition, 8,* 206-226.

Yazdani, M. (1987). Intelligent tutoring systems: An overview. In R. Lawler & M. Yazdani (Eds.), *Artificial intelligence and education 1* (pp. 183-202). Norwood, NJ: Ablex.

Interface Architectures for Intelligent Tutoring Systems

Jeffrey G. Bonar
GUIdance Technologies, Inc., Pittsburgh

The design of an intelligent tutoring system (ITS) is closely tied to how the ITS presents the domain to a student. Not only is the organization of domain knowledge based on the presentation, but so are teaching and diagnostic knowledge. Given the dominant role the student interface plays in organizing an ITS, we propose an ITS design methodology based on the notion of an interface to domain knowledge. This methodology organizes the interface based on a domain expert's view of the task domain. This proposal has the potential to give learners a much richer view of their task — a view explicitly based on the approach of domain experts. Furthermore, by organizing an intelligent tutor around a domain expert's conception of a domain, we facilitate the construction of that tutor by the domain expert. This means that the artificial intelligence (AI) wizard's role in ITS development can be reduced or even eliminated.

THE CENTRAL ROLE OF INTERFACES
IN CURRENT ITSs

In this chapter I propose that ITSs be designed explicitly around the interaction with the student, that is, designed around the interface. It is striking that almost every current ITS organizes its knowledge around how that knowledge is presented to the student. That is, the tutor's internal architecture and knowledge base are specifically designed to support a particular style of interaction with the student. Successful ITSs have resulted from careful crafting of knowledge around a particular effective interface approach. Tutors detect student bugs, infer underlying errors, and make corrections, but within elaborate and sophisticated interfaces that were carefully designed to highlight and draw attention to the domain knowledge the tutor was designed to teach. This may seem obvious; of course, an ITS needs a well-crafted interface for the student. This chapter suggests, however, that beginning with such an interface is the appropriate way to design an ITS. This suggestion should be viewed in contrast to the many proposals for ITS shells that allow domain knowledge to be "plugged in" to a domain-independent tutoring engine. Such proposals ignore the pervasive influence of user presentation on knowledge representation in a successful ITS. In particular, the domain knowledge component of a working ITS is never stored in a domain-independent formalism. This chapter starts from this observation, presents a framework for an interface-based ITS, and develops a methodology for explicitly designing an ITS around user presentation.

There are many examples of an implicit interface orientation in successful ITSs. PROUST (Johnson, 1986), for example, is a tutor for beginning programmers. PROUST takes a student program and analyses that program with an intelligent parser that looks for buggy or correct implementations of standard programming subtasks (called *plans*). The knowledge base of PROUST—a large catalog of descriptions for correct and buggy implementations of the subtasks—is directly tied to the tutor's interaction with the student.

Another tutor for beginning programmers, the LISP Tutor (Reiser, Anderson, & Farrell, 1985), coaches a student through the specific steps in coding particular LISP functions. The knowledge base consists of a set of production rules that accomplish the task given to the student and simulate common student errors. As students work, they are explicitly directed by the knowledge base. Each of the students' steps is tracked by invoking either a correct or errorful rule. Errorful rules include associated remedial text. Clancey's tutors, developed on medical knowledge bases (e.g., Clancey, 1983) began with the premise of using rules from an existing expert system knowledge base. During the course of his work, however, he has completely rewritten the rules so that they could be used to effectively present medical knowledge to a student. Finally, consider the Intelligent Maintenance Training System (Towne & Munro, 1988), a tutor to teach troubleshooting of complex systems. Systems are represented with screen-based simulations containing faults that must be discovered by the student. The knowledge base is represented in terms of the components of the simulation including both normal and fault states for those components. Students work by interacting with a simulation where one or more components are faulty.

In each of the cases cited, the knowledge base is organized around the particular style of presentation and pedagogy used by the tutor. When discussing how a tutor presents things to the student, we mean more than merely what is on the screen. The presentation includes the key elements — the conceptual vocabulary — used by experts when they talk about and solve problems within the domain. This vocabulary is a crucial part of the expertise that must be imparted to the student. The right vocabulary allows an expert to cut up a problem into the right pieces, and organizes those pieces into the right order for a solution. This vocabulary need not be words; programmers have standard subtasks like "search an array for a value," electrical engineers have circuit schematics, and so forth.

What is suggested here is that the vocabulary, diagrams, and conventions — that is, the interface used by experts, is exactly what must be acquired by novices. If we can build an ITS around interfaces directly, not only have we focused on the key issues of concern for a novice, but we have also made the acquisition of expert knowledge much simpler, because the ITS is designed around how the expert views the knowledge. In particular, now we can have skilled teachers, who are not AI experts, design the knowledge bases for ITS.

This chapter proceeds as follows. We begin with a discussion of the kinds of expertise that must be acquired from a domain expert to build an ITS and how that expertise must be delivered to the student by means of the ITS. Based on the notion of expertise developed here, an ITS architecture is proposed that is based on knowledge components called *plans* and an interface framework for organizing and manipulating plans. The next section describes design principles for creating pedagogical plans. The BRIDGE programming tutor is presented as an illustration of an ITS designed around a plan-based interface. The MATISSE system is introduced as a general tool for creating an interface-based ITS. The chapter concludes with an assessment of short- and long-term opportunities afforded by this work.

Two Key Tasks in an ITS

Previously, it was proposed that we guide ITS development by focusing on how the ITS presents the tasks, that is, the interface between the student and the task. In this section some details of that proposal are developed. The discussion is organized around the two key tasks in building an ITS: getting the expert knowledge into the system and then getting that knowledge back out to the student.

Getting Expert Knowledge into an ITS

What is the expertise that we want to capture in an ITS, and how does an interface-focus help us to capture that knowledge? We have identified three kinds of expertise that need to be captured. This three-component analysis of expertise derives from a body of cognitive science research that studies learning in technical domains such as basic math, physics, computer programming, and so forth (see Resnick & Omanson, 1987). The three components are discussed here.

Concepts. These are the abstract conceptual elements known by experts in a field. These are the ideas that experts use to think about tasks in their domain. Resnick and Omanson (1987) pointed out that in mathematics, even beginners must reason about objects that exist only as abstractions. One can, for example, point to 3 chairs, or even the numeral 3, but there is no "number 3" that can be pointed to. Number is an abstract conceptual element. In computer programming, a "loop" is similarly abstract, as is "voltage" in electrical circuits, "force" in mechanics, and "intercept vector" in air traffic control.

Traditionally, curriculums are organized around the attainment of such abstract concepts — for example, a textbook chapter on each concept or on a related group of concepts. Such an approach is incomplete. The next two components focus on aspects of expertise that are not clearly delineated in most standard curriculums.

Representations. These are the syntax, notations, and computational mechanisms used by an expert. They may be embodied in diagrams, standard forms, standard procedures, or algorithms. These are mechanical in nature, providing efficiency of operation while sacrificing some generality or formal properties. In mathematics the notational system consists of the standard numerals, symbols, a syntax, and various algorithms for rearranging elements of the notational system. In computer programming, the notational system is the programming language itself. Other disciplines have their own notational systems like free-body diagrams in mechanics, electric circuit schematics, chemical bond diagrams, and so forth.

Whereas these representations are not the domain, per se, comfort and facility with a representation is typical of expertise. The representations support algorithms in which basic operations can be performed with little or no understanding of the underlying concepts. Whereas experts do understand those concepts and use their understanding to make the notations, representations, and algorithms less brittle in their application, a novice often does not understand the concepts. There is a large body of work about how novices tend to learn representations with little understanding of the underlying concepts and get themselves into trouble by doing so (see, e.g., Chi, Feltovich, & Glaser, 1981; Gentner & Gentner, 1983; Gentner & Stevens, 1983; Larkin, 1983; Resnick, 1983). That is, novices try to apply the notations, representations, and algorithms without reference to the concepts, making errors in the process, errors they cannot detect. This notion of the different forms of expertise combining effectively is developed in more detail.

Rules for Referring to Situations in the World.   These rules allow the expert to apply concepts and representations to actual situations in the world. This aspect of expertise refers to the practical experience and well-trained sensibilities that an expert brings to a task. These rules allow the expert to extract neat, well-defined tasks from the complexity and fuzziness of the real world. The rules allow an expert to interpret a situation in the world in terms of the abstractions, represent that situation with standard representations, and make predictions or solve problems. So, for example, experts at basic arithmetic know how to apply arithmetic representations and concepts to the task of determining the most economical size laundry detergent at the supermarket. Similarly, an expert in basic electricity recognizes the circuits created in the way an automobile battery's negative pole is attached to the frame whereas the positive terminal is attached through switches and wires to the car's various electrical devices that are also attached to the frame. Finally, a programming expert is able to use standard loop constructs to represent all the different kinds of repetition found in the world.

Part of what makes people expert is their facility with all three aspects of expertise. When beginning a task, rules of reference allow the expert to interpret the situation at hand in terms of the concepts. These concepts are represented with a representation that then can be manipulated freely. The representation gives considerable cognitive efficiency because it operates without the constraints that would be induced by a constant, detailed attention to mapping back to the actual world situation. When needed, however, the expert is able to constrain and guide the notational operations with theoretical principles from the abstractions and practical limitations imposed by the situations in the world.

How does this approach help a domain expert get knowledge into an ITS? This section has cast the task of building an ITS as the task of building a work environment for a domain expert (Collins, Brown, & Newman, 1989). This work environment includes a representation of key conceptual elements, embedding that conceptual vocabulary in a notation or diagram, and having the notation use metaphors that tie the conceptual vocabulary to real-world situations. This task is considerably easier than the tasks required of an ITS builder today. The proposed approach requires that a domain expert (a) develop an environment that supports their performance on a task. The more standard approach to ITS development requires (a) and additionally requires, (b) routines that can reason about that performance. Providing software to support (a) is much simpler than providing software to support (b). Later in this chapter a specific proposal for (a) is discussed.

Learners Acquiring the Expertise in an ITS

The first half of this section discusses the kinds of expertise that an ITS must acquire from an expert and how that expertise might be acquired directly from a domain expert. Once the expert knowledge is inside an ITS, how does an interface orientation, based on the three kinds of knowledge discussed, facilitate the student in learning to solve domain problems? To answer, this occurs in various ways:

1. The interface is explicitly built on the three elements of expertise that are most important for a novice to learn. The important concepts and abstractions have some explicit, manipulable form, tied to notational conventions, and, through metaphor, related to applicable situations in the world. The student is embedded in the problem-solving environment of the expert. Of course, no expert would need an environment as explicit or detailed as that created for a student. Although overly detailed from an expert's point of view, the environment still reflects the expert's view of the task: The view we wish the student to acquire.

2. The interface can offload computations that might distract a student from the main lessons. In BRIDGE (Bonar, Cunningham, Beatty, & Weil, 1988), for example, much of the detailed semantics of the programming is handled for the student. Similarly, students using the geometry tutor do not need to do the detailed symbol manipulation required to apply theorems. In some ways this is cheating, the student is shielded from the full complexity of the task. The missing complexity, however, is the part that we as domain experts have judged as secondary or trivial. In fact, Anderson and Jeffries (1985) showed that this sort of trivial complexity can account, through working memory loading, for many errors in novice performance. In allowing the student to focus on the salient tasks and ignore the minor details, learning can be both more efficient and more satisfying.

3. The interface can highlight the most salient tasks or features. In the real world, for example, the broken part rarely changes color and starts to blink. There is no way to isolate key elements or subsystems if those elements or subsystems are physically intertwined.

AN INTERFACE-BASED FRAMEWORK
FOR UNDERSTANDING AND DESIGNING
ITS DOMAIN KNOWLEDGE: PLANS

How does one design an interface-based domain knowledge component for an ITS? In particular, we desire an architecture organized around how the domain looks to an expert, and yet, is accessible to a novice using the ITS. This section presents plans as a building block for such an architecture. Plans provide a tool for describing the educational process needed to move from novice to expert conceptions of a task. Furthermore, plans do this in a way that is explicitly available to the learner. Our architecture is based on two key components:

1. A detailed analysis of the domain knowledge concepts and formal operations needed to move from a novice conception of a task to an expert conception. This analysis is represented with a network of plans.

2. A visual interface that supports presenting those plans embedded in computer-based versions of standard notations and diagrams, suggesting metaphors that tie the plans and surrounding notations to situations in the world.

The MATISSE system, discussed at the end of the chapter, supports both components.

Plans: Organizing the Conceptual Aspect of Expertise

The interface-based ITS architecture is built around a set of icons that represent the abstractions or conceptual vocabulary for addressing problems in a particular domain. Each icon represents an important concept or formal operation that a novice must learn to apply to domain tasks. We call these concept–operation elements plans. A plan-set provides a set of tools for attacking a domain task. In addition to the plans, there are a few simple links that allow plans to be tied together in various ways (see Figure 3.1). This notion (and Figure 3.1) should be viewed as a high-level caricature — the details of the task domain specialize the links and visual appearance in some way particular to the application. For example, imagine a trouble-shooting task where each plan represents a test to be performed, and links represent the ordering of the tests as well as the information to be

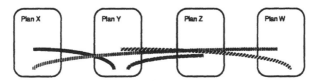

FIGURE 3.1 Plans representing the domain knowledge for an ITS. The plans represent important concepts or formal operations in the domain. The links describe how those plans are put together to perform a particular task in the domain.

communicated between tests. The key idea is creating visual elements to represent the key concepts or formal operations and a simple set of underlying links that support the basic interactions between those elements.

How is such a system expanded to include and teach expertise? We propose that each of the plans can be "opened up," revealing a whole new set of plans linked together in such a way that they enrich, deepen, or explain the top-level plan. That is, the plans at the top level actually are a high-level summary of some collection and organization of lower-level plans. This plan hierarchy goes on for many levels (see Figure 3.2). Moving down a level in the plan hierarchy is viewed from two perspectives:

1. When you open a plan up to show the lower-level set of plans that implement the original plan, you are requesting an explanation of how the top-level plan works.

2. Simultaneously, you are stating your willingness to confront the additional detail, additional complexity, or deeper abstraction inherent in the lower-level set of plans.

It is important to note that traveling down a level corresponds to exactly one new idea that must be understood by the student. The hierarchy of plans should reflect a concern for sensible curriculum, not for formal relationships. Plan P is a subpart of Plan X because, although relevant to the same kinds of tasks, it represents "one idea's worth" of information more than X.

Good teachers build elegant scaffolds through the complexity of their subject matter domain. The student is led with care, avoiding complexities that are not useful for the task at hand. Good teachers carefully select examples that are complete and accurate, as far as they go, but leave out important details that are irrelevant for that example. That is, the instructor designs the curriculum so the student only sees problems that are the right level of challenge for the student's current understanding. So, for example, elementary school students learning division begin with pairs of numbers that yield whole number results (e.g., 36/6), leaving remainders for later lessons.

Questions for Building a Plan Hierarchy

As far as it goes, the previous proposal is interesting, but not at all complete. There are many key questions to be answered before it is of any practical use in building an ITS. These questions are:

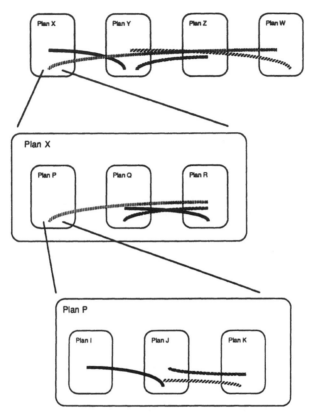

FIGURE 3.2 An abstract hierarchy of plans representing the domain knowledge for an ITS. The plans represent important concepts or formal operations in the domain. The links describe how those plans are put together to perform a particular task in the domain. Opening a plan up corresponds to a deeper, more sophisticated, or more complete view of the plan. Plans at the lower levels of the hierarchy combine to form the plans at the higher levels.

1. How do you cut up the task domain? What are the manageable pieces? How does one factor the many concepts and abstractions that make up any interesting domain into the various plans and links?

2. What do you put at each level of the hierarchy? For a given domain, what should be the highest level plans and what should be put in each successive layer? Is there one consistent layering, or do different task foci cause radical changes to the decisions about the layers to be presented?

3. What are the semantics of the plan icons? Exactly what semantics should be supplied to the plans? What of their internal structure is visible

before the plan is "opened up." What kinds of knowledge can be specified in plans and how should that knowledge be represented? How is the knowledge applied to a particular task?

4. What are the semantics of the links between plans? What do the connections mean? How many kinds of connections should there be? What do the links mean when working on a particular task?

In this chapter, we focus on Questions 1 and 2 (the semantics of the plan icons and links, Questions 3 and 4, are discussed in Bonar & Liffick, 1990): How do we design a plan hierarchy? We propose to make decisions about plan contents on pedagogical grounds; that is, "what's the simplest useful concept" and "what's the single abstraction that provides the next level of capability for the student." The next section describes four design rules to support the pedagogical design of ITS plans.

HOW TO DESIGN PLANS

This section discusses how to design the plans presented earlier. The design process is guided by the following concerns:

Representing Expertise. The plans are each supposed to represent a particular conceptual component of expertise. That is, each plan provides one particular thing or capability that is known by an expert.

Accomplishing Specific Tasks. In addition to representing expertise, we want the plans to represent a capability to accomplish a specific task. That is, a plan is a kind of tool that is good for certain domain tasks. Part of the expertise inherent in a plan is knowing which tasks it is good for and knowing how, in detail, to apply the plan to that task. This tool metaphor gives rise to the notion that each plan is represented by a particular icon.

Usable by a Novice. Plans should be usable by a novice. Plans are provided at many levels of expertise, so this means that for any user there must be a level of plans that is natural and familiar.

Facilitate Becoming an Expert. In addition to being usable by a novice, the plans must facilitate the development of expertise. Therefore, plans immediately below the familiar level should be learnable with a specific and relatively small amount of extra effort. This means that expertise can be acquired when the user is ready and interested; the cost involved in understanding the next level of plans can be gauged and evaluated as the need for more knowledge becomes apparent.

These are general concerns. The rest of this section uses these general concerns to frame the following four guidelines for plan-based interfaces:

- Plans should represent the three kinds of expertise discussed earlier: abstractions, notations, and references to situations in the world.
- An interface cannot capture a complete domain.
- Interfaces should be based on situations in the world.
- Yoking between representations is essential.

Although not highly specific, these guidelines are intended to provide direct support to a designer creating a plan curriculum. As each plan is proposed or sketched, these principles are intended as criteria against which to measure the new plan.

Plan Design Principle:
Plans Should Represent Three Kinds of Expertise

Why is it that we cannot simply teach Peano's axioms and expect fourth- and fifth-grade students to understand all of basic arithmetic? There is far more to a complete understanding than the formalization used by experts. A plan curriculum must attend to all aspects of expertise.

Previously we identified three kinds of expertise that need to be captured by plans:

1. Concepts.
2. Representations.
3. Rules for referring to situations in the world.

How exactly do these three kinds of expertise map on to an interface orientation for ITS domain knowledge? The interface needs to embody all three aspects — that is, provide the integration that is natural in an expert's performance. An interface should provide some concrete way to visualize an abstract concept, relate directly to standard representations, and refer to situations in the world. For example, White and Horwitz (1987) presented a series of microworlds designed to teach successively richer models of mechanics. Each model included a physical representation of concepts like velocity and acceleration based on the movements of a ball on the computer screen. The physical representation was also designed to suggest certain standard notational approaches. Similarly, the conceptual elements in Anderson's geometry tutor (Anderson, Boyle, & Yost, 1985; Anderson, Greeno, Kline, & Neves, 1981), provides a set of tools for managing proof subgoals and available theorems, and also uses standard geometry notation to label those subgoals. Finally in BRIDGE (Bonar, Cunningham, Beatty, & Weil, 1988), a tutor for teaching beginning programming, each programming concept has a distinctively shaped icon and syntax rules suggested by how different icons can fit together.

The previous discussion suggests that what makes a good interface is how effectively it collapses the three elements of expertise. Experts do not explicitly use the three aspects. Instead, they effortlessly move between the three aspects in an interaction with a domain problem. A good interface has the same characteristic; appropriate kinds of expertise are facilitated as needed. An ideal interface for an intelligent tutor presents a conceptual vocabulary, tied to standard notational conventions, with metaphors, pictures, and labels that tie the vocabulary elements to applicable situations in the world. This is the intent behind an iconic plan, viewed as both a tool and an encapsulation of more detailed expertise.

Plan Design Principle:
A Plan Interface Cannot Capture a Complete Domain

According to the second design principle, it is impossible to create a plan that captures more than a fraction of an interesting domain. Plans are, of necessity, small components. If domains of expertise were easily represented in small components, those domains would never have required highly trained experts. By definition, an expert is someone with a rich and subtle set of plans for describing their domain of expertise. A particular plan is designed to highlight one narrow distinction in the domain of interest.

This principle seems obvious but is quite difficult to formalize. Consider a practical example. Researchers frequently suggest ways to extend the power of the plan icons in the BRIDGE programming tutor. These suggestions take the form of "if you add Graphical Feature X to the plan on the screen, you can now have that plan also represent Concept B of the abstract domain in addition to Concept A which it already represents." Unfortunately, this can only be done at the cost of muddying the representation of some other feature, Y, or confusing a metaphor that refers to situations in the world. Practical experience recommends that a particular plan representation—a kind of loop construct that repeats some fixed number of times, for example—lends itself to a certain subset of the concepts. Any attempt to add more functionality—adding arbitrary expressions to the slot that hold the number of times the loop is to repeat, to continue the example—results in more muddled mapping to the concepts. Because adding a new feature to a microworld abstracts from the obvious real-world connections implied by the microworld, the microworld becomes pedagogically less powerful.

This chapter argues that microworlds can only capture a fixed portion of a target domain. Where are the natural division points of the target domain that allow pieces to be captured in a microworld? That is the subject of the next design principle.

Plan Design Principle: A Plan Interface Should Be Based on Situations in the World

A plan can only capture a small fixed portion of an expert domain, thus that portion should be based on a particular situation in the world. Researchers in cognitive science have spent considerable time distinguishing important interpretations for situations in the world that are captured with standard formal domains. For example, the dominant interpretations for integer addition and subtraction, are change, combine, and compare (Resnick & Omanson, 1987). Ohlsson (1988) found 12 interpretations for fractions including, for example, part–whole, ratio, division, and measure. Each of these interpretations results in particular rules, conventions, admissable operations, and so forth. In computer programming, a set of programming plans (Bonar & Soloway, 1985) were developed around the most common programming tasks (situations in the world). These plans were used to organize a programming tutor.

Designing plans based on particular situations in the world provides a natural starting point for the curriculum designer. For example, a particular concept rooted in real-world situations is a natural starting point for the design of screen objects that represent a plan. The situations in the world suggest the kinds of objects and the operations to be provided. Furthermore, basing plans on situations in the world makes pedagogical sense. For example, it is widely known that word problems (story problems) are one of the most difficult aspects of elementary mathematics. It has been observed that student difficulties with word problems relate to the difficulty students have in relating the mathematical ideas and notations to situations in the world, particularly when those ideas and notations apply in different ways for different situations (Resnick & Omanson, 1987). By creating plans based on particular situations in the world, one supports students in understanding the relationship between formal mathematics and its application.

Plan Design Principle: Yoking Between Representations Is Essential

In order for students to understand the connections between concepts, representations, and situations in the world, it is important that they see the mappings between these three kinds of expertise. There must be a way for the student to see how actions in one representation influence a second representation. In particular, it is important for students to see how concepts and world situations can be viewed in terms of standard notation. After Resnick and Omanson (1987) we call these connections *yoking* between representations. Yoking schemes should simultaneously display two or more aspects of the plan in such a manner that if a change is made in one aspect, corresponding changes are automatically made to the others.

Creating effective yoking is a more difficult task than might be imagined. In our plans for computer programming, there is a difficult question about how to yoke to variables inside a loop. Variables inside a loop stand for a sequence of values, consequently it is not clear whether those variables should be yoked to particular values over time, a growing sequence of values, or a static sequence of values. This is further complicated because the actual running version of the variable will only have one value at a time.

Peled and Resnick (1987) discussed an environment that makes extensive use of yoking in elementary arithmetic. In designing fraction microworlds, Ohlsson, Nickolas, and Bee (1987) needed to yoke particular concrete screen representations with numerical notations. A "strips and tiles" representation of fractions was developed. Unit rectangles are divided into equally sized sections (see Figure 3.3). The student controls the number of section divisions and can color individual sections. The colored sections represent a fraction's numerator whereas the total number of sections represent the denominator. A first question is exactly what is yoked to what. Concrete representations often do not have canonical

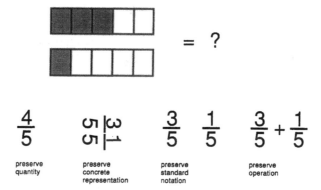

FIGURE 3.3 When designing plans that provide yoking, you must confront problems of what exactly to yoke. In this example there are four reasonable approaches to yoking a "strips-and-tiles" representation of fractions to the standard numerical notation.

forms, so there are several different aspects that can be yoked. The following are some possibilities:

- One quantity with another — Determine the value of the concrete representation, whatever form is actually used to represent that value, and yoke that to the representational system. For example, a student might have used two strips to represent the fractions ⅕ and ⅗, placing the strips close together. In this case, the representational yoke would show ⅘.

- One screen object with another — Preserve the integrity of the concrete representation forms, even if that produces an odd representational form. Continuing the example with strips and tiles, representing the fractions ⅕ and ⅗ with two strips, the yoke would produce a representational element that looks something like: $\frac{3}{5}\frac{1}{5}$ but with the fractions turned on their sides. This approach preserves the form of the concrete representation rather than the conventions of the standard representation.

- Objects from the representational domain with objects from the microworld — In this case, conventions of the standard representation are preserved rather than the form of the concrete representation. Using the previous example, the system would keep the two separate fractions far apart and distinct: $\frac{1}{5}$ $\frac{3}{5}$

- Regions on the screen imply operations — in this approach, screen regions are used to imply operations. Strips in different parts of the screen are treated as different fractions and strips near to each other are treated as implying an addition operation.

There are pedagogical uses for each of the different possible yoking relationships. As there is no mathematically "correct" choice, the question becomes "which mapping is most helpful for the learner?"

This section has presented four principles for the design of plans and interface-based ITS. The next section presents an extended example of such an ITS.

EXAMPLE OF PLAN-BASED ITS:
THE "BRIDGE" INTELLIGENT TUTOR
FOR TEACHING PROGRAMMING

Research into how novices learn programming reveals that understanding the semantics of standard programming languages is not the main difficulty of novice programmers. Instead, success with programming seems to be tied to a novice's ability to recognize general goals in the description of a task, and to translate those goals into actual program code (see, for example, Eisenstadt, Laubsch, & Kahney, 1981; Mayer, 1979;

Rist, 1986; Shneiderman & Mayer, 1979; Soloway & Ehrlich, 1985). In BRIDGE we built a programming environment that supports a novice in working with plans that describe the goals and subgoals typical of programming tasks. By using plans that describe programming goals, BRIDGE allows for initial novice conceptions of a problem solution that are informal and sketchy. The BRIDGE environment features an iconic-plan programming language with editor facilities to control execution and support debugging. A complete discussion of BRIDGE can be found in Bonar and Cunningham (1988) and Bonar and colleagues (1988).

BRIDGE supports a novice in the initial informal statement of a problem solution, subsequent refinement of that solution, and final implementation of the solution as standard programming language code. This is accomplished in three phases, discussed in detail in the rest of this section. To illustrate BRIDGE use, we discuss a student working on the ending value averaging problem:

> Write a program which repeatedly reads in integers until it reads in the integer 99999. After seeing 99999, it should print out the CORRECT AVERAGE without counting the final 99999.

Each of the phases is summarized, followed by a discussion of how that phase fits into the framework described earlier.

Phase 1: Informal Natural Language Plans

The first phase of BRIDGE involves an informal statement and refinement of the goals for the code. Empirical evidence (Biermann, Ballard, & Sigmon, 1983; Bonar, 1985; Bonar & Soloway, 1985; Kahney & Eisenstadt, 1982; Miller, 1974, 1981) suggests that novice programmers base their initial understanding of programming on a collection of programming-like plans formed from everyday experience with natural language procedural specifications. These plans come from experience with step-by-step instructions like "check all the student scores and give me an average" or "see that hallway, if any doors are open close them." These informal plans, however, are often extremely difficult for novices to reconcile with the more formal plans used in standard programming languages. Note, for example, that both example phrases involve an iteration without any specific mention of a repeated action. These informal plans represent the BRIDGE approach to basing plans on situations in the world.

In Phase 1, we provide a plan language based on simple natural language phrases typically used when people write step-by-step instructions for other people. For example, a student can construct the phrase ". . . and so on . . . until 99999 is seen." Figure 3.4 shows an example with several such phrases. Such phrases represent the highest level at which a student can express intentions to the system. Because of the ambiguity in such phrasings, BRIDGE must understand the student's intentions based on several possible naive models of programming. For example, a common naive model of looping allows a student to construct a loop with a description of the first iteration followed by the phrase "and so on." Based on the particular phrasings constructed by the student, BRIDGE infers a particular naive model.

BRIDGE supports three different naive models of programming loops. (See Soloway, Bonar, & Ehrlich, 1983, for a discussion of looping in novice programs.) Each of the models is illustrated with phrasing that might be used on the ending value averaging problem.

- Declarative restatement—The loop is not explicitly mentioned at all. All reference to values assumes that they are available as needed: For example, "compute the sum divided by the count," or just "compute the average."
- Aggregate Operator—The looping operations are subsumed by operators that act over entire data structures: For example, "add all the integers and divide by how many there were."
- And-So-On Loop—Mention is made of getting individual data values, as opposed to the aggregate values at the aggregate operator level. A looping construct is also mentioned, such as "continue until 99999 is seen." At the and-so-on level, however, the solution does not specify detailed coordination among the individual steps within the loop. Very characteristic is a specification of the first iteration of the loop followed by the phrase "and so on," or something similar to this.

```
Get the numbers
Compute the average
Output the average


Get the numbers
Add the numbers
Count the numbers
Compute the sum divided by how many numbers
Output the average


Read in an integer
Add the integer to running total
Count the integer
And so on until 99999 is seen
Compute the sum divided by how many numbers
Output the average
```

FIGURE 3.4 Informal language phrases making up a BRIDGE Phase 1 solution. These phrases capture BRIDGE's approach to basing plans on situations in the world.

Based on our empirical work (Bonar & Soloway, 1985), these models subsume most of the misconceptions novices have about simple programming loops. Although there are many different English phrases used by novices, a simple pattern-matching approach to parsing the phrases is sufficient for distinguishing among the three models for each of the different plans.

BRIDGE's task is to teach programming, thus detection of such a naive model results in a tutorial suggestion from BRIDGE. The architecture underlying BRIDGE could as easily respond to the user's naive model directly without attempting to teach the user the "correct" specification. In this more advisory mode, the system would insist on a more fully developed model only when the user's specification was incomplete or lacking key details.

In terms of the multilevel plan approach discussed previously and illustrated in Figure 3.1, the first phase of BRIDGE is an implementation of the highest level of plans. Each plan stands for the kinds of operations and mental models normally expressed in English-language step-by-step specifications written by nonprogrammers. These operations are vague and include significant implicit knowledge about the objects being operated on. Only a limited set of links are possible between the plans' ordering and nesting. Data communication links between the plans are implicit, reflecting the structure of natural language specifications.

Phase 2: Iconic Programming Plans

In the second phase of BRIDGE, a programming student refines the informal description of Phase 1 into a series of semiformal iconic programming plans. Figure 3.5 shows the BRIDGE plans used by a student working in Phase 2. In this phase the plans are schemalike structures that describe how goals are transformed into actual programming code (see Bonar, Weil, & Jones, 1986; Soloway & Ehrlich, 1985 for a detailed discussion of these plans).

Plans have various elements that interrelate with the elements of other plans. For example, a counter plan has to initialize, increment, and use elements, each with a particular relationship to the loop containing the counter. This interaction of elements often results in the plan implementation in standard programming constructs being dispersed across the program. A running total, for example, is implemented in PASCAL with four statements, dispersed throughout a program: a variable declaration, an initialization above a loop, an update inside that loop, and a use below the loop. Difficulties in translating from plans to programming language code account for many student errors (Spohrer, Soloway, & Pope, 1985).

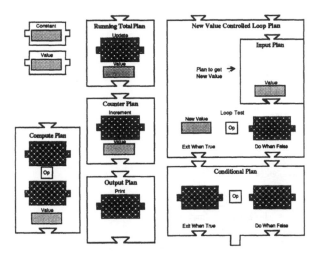

FIGURE 3.5 The BRIDGE system Phase 2 plans. These plans must be connected together to produce a solution based on the informal language description produced in Phase 1.

In the second phase of BRIDGE students focus on relating various plan elements, but without compromising the fundamental plan structure and introducing the syntactic complexity required by standard programming code. Figure 3.6 shows a typical Phase 2 solution to the ending value averaging problem. Each plan is represented by a single icon. There are two kinds of links between the plan elements. Control flow links are expressed by attaching puzzle tabs to puzzle slots. Data flow links are expressed by moving the small tiles with "ears" from the data source to the data destination. Such a data flow link is being constructed in Figure 3.6: The result of the Running Total plan is being connected to the average computation in the Compute plan.[1]

The plan icons shown in Figures 3.5 and 3.6 are a good illustration of our notion of shielding the student from the full complexity of the task. Whereas the plans assume the reader is a programming student, they are designed to skirt various tricky technical issues that should be the problem of the compiler designers, not the problem of novice programmers.

For example, the New Value Controlled Loop plan does not

---

[1]A problematic design issue arises with the data value tiles. We would like to show the data flow graphically, but found the screen too cluttered when a wire was drawn from each data source to each data destination. Although we experimented with approaches that showed these links only when requested by the student, graphical data links were ultimately abandoned in favor of overall simplicity.

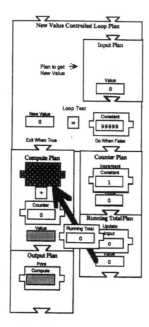

FIGURE 3.6 A typical Phase 2 solution in BRIDGE. The student is connecting the results of the Running Total plan to an input for the Compute plan.

explicitly specify the order of the new value fetch, the test of that new value, and the body below "Do Inside of Loop." Although this is an immediate concern to most experienced programmers, it never comes up with beginning programmers. Nonprogrammers have a very well-developed model of a loop that gets a data item, checks its applicability, and then proceeds only if the data item is usable (see Bonar & Soloway, 1985). There are good reasons most programming languages do not provide such a construct, but these reasons do not make sense when we can present novices with a library of plans adapted to their needs.

Whereas Phase 1 of BRIDGE represents the highest level plans, closest to the understanding of a nonprogrammer, Phase 2 represents a lower level of plan. The transition from Phase 1 to Phase 2, then, represents an implementation of "opening up" top-level (Phase 1) plans. In the current BRIDGE system the student must complete a Phase 1 plan specification and then must "open up" that specification to implement a Phase 2 elaboration of the original specification. As the student works in Phase 2, links back to Phase 1 are always available. In a nontutorial situation, the Phase 2 plan language would allow for refinement of the informal plans specified in Phase 1, but without requiring the complexity of a specification of the actions actually performed by the machine. The links in Phase 2 express potential connections between elements of the plans, as described earlier. Also, note that the Phase 2 plans are executable and can be run by students using the BRIDGE tutor. (See Brown, 1987, for a detailed discussion of program animation.)

Phase 2 illustrates the plan design principles discussed earlier. The Phase 2 plans represent all three kinds of expertise: concepts like looping, standard programming notations, (which will be fully developed in Phase 3), and, through shape and the jigsaw puzzle metaphor, reference to situations in the world. Each plan is narrowly focused; we do not try to create general purpose programming constructs. Consistent with this principle of not trying to capture an entire domain, we have resisted the suggestions of experienced programmers who would collapse various plans into more abstract constructs. The design of these plans comes from our experience with the kinds of world situations that must be implemented in standard programming constructs. Finally, Phase 2, in conjunction with Phase 1 and eventually Phase 3, show several complementary representations for the same information. In BRIDGE the yoking is over time, for example, Phase 1 gets translated into Phase 2, but the students explicitly use the connections between the phases.

Phase 3: Pascal Code

The third phase requires the BRIDGE student to translate the plan-based description of Phase 2 into actual PASCAL code. The yoking from Phase 1 to Phase 2 is now completed with a yoke to Phase 3. Furthermore, the tie from situations in the world is completed. World situations are most completely captured in Phase 1, less apparent in Phase 2, and disappear entirely in Phase 3.

Students are provided with a PASCAL structure editor (much like that of Garlan & Miller, 1984), and an interpreter with a stepping mode. In this phase, the user drops from the world of plans into a standard programming language. In a nontutorial version of the interface, this phase would be omitted.

Diagnosis in a Plan-Based Tutor

Any ITS needs to infer user intentions from user behavior. In particular, the system must infer all mental activity from the actual actions performed by the user. In tutoring programming, for example, a standard ITS must reconstruct the student's entire mental activity between seeing a program specification and actually entering code in the machine. Such a reconstruction must account for both the correct and incorrect knowledge used by the student during design and implementation.

A tutor's reconstruction of a student's program is based on at least two kinds of knowledge. First, there must be a way for students to break the high-level goals of the problem statement into lower level goals. Second, there must be knowledge about how to translate low-level goals into program code. Within the tutor we can represent these two kinds of knowledge as operators that transform one kind of structure into another. In addition to correct versions of these operators, the tutor must contain buggy versions representing common student misconceptions.

Using the knowledge base of correct and buggy operators, in principle, a tutor can use search techniques to reconstruct plausible accounts for errorful and ambiguous student specifications. This approach has been powerfully demonstrated in the programming tutor PROUST (Johnson, 1986). Although the approach works, it is very costly in terms of both search time and knowledge engineering. The accomplishments of PROUST must be weighed against the large cost in knowledge engineering time — several hundred hours per problem tutored (according to Johnson, 1986). This knowledge engineering is not particularly cost-effective because the student sees so little of the results. That is, almost all of the knowledge engineering that has gone into capturing operators that describe how to apply programming knowledge is never seen by the student. Inside of PROUST, these operators are optimized for the search task. They are not available in a form that could be presented to students or used to assist students as they work toward a solution.

BRIDGE uses a different approach in reconstructing the student's intentions. Instead of attempting to reconstruct a student's entire reasoning from problem statement to final code in one step, BRIDGE has the student prepare intermediate solutions in plan languages that correspond to particular levels in the process of moving from problem specification, to goals, to code. This alleviates many of the difficulties of the PROUST approach. The search is more manageable because it has been broken up into a series of much smaller searches. In each of the smaller searches, there are fewer relevant operators to try, and less reasoning "distance" to span between the user's surface behavior and the solution the tutor is trying to reconstruct. In addition, the BRIDGE approach simplifies the knowledge engineering. The fewer operators in each search correspond to a smaller overall catalog of operators to be specified. In addition, the smaller search spaces make it easier to tell when the space of possible correct and errorful versions has been covered.

BRIDGE as an Example of an Interface-Based ITS

BRIDGE provides a fairly detailed example of what I mean by an interface-based ITS. In particular:

- BRIDGE is built around plans.
- Plans are selected and designed based on pedagogical concerns, not formal concerns.
- Plans are arranged in a hierarchy, revealed to a student over the course of instruction.

BRIDGE also illustrates the gaps in the approach. Nothing about BRIDGE's presentation in the three phases is suggested by the architecture. Furthermore, the specific design for each phase must be created independently of the architecture. In general, nothing discussed to this point provides any help to the ITS designer in constructing an interface. Although the architecture and principles discussed earlier point toward an interface-based approach, they provide no support for developing a specific interface for a domain to be taught. In particular, trying to established notations, suggesting relevant metaphors, and capturing conceptual elements as tools that can be applied to problems, must all be implemented from scratch. The next section discusses MATISSE, a language for easily creating specific interfaces for use in an interface-based ITS.

MATISSE: CREATING INTERFACES
FOR AN INTERFACE-BASED ITS

The ITS discussed in this chapter feature highly interactive interfaces whose screen elements can be pointed to, dragged, and manipulated with the mouse as if those elements were actual physical objects. Literally, students can grapple with a quasi-physical representation of the knowledge they are to learn. For example, in BRIDGE students can manipulate the contents of programming plans, attach them together, and execute the results.

In this section we describe a programming environment that simplifies the creation of ITSs like BRIDGE. Most importantly, the environment supports the definition of plan, both the specific knowledge contained within the plan and the graphic interface by which the plan presents itself. The programming environment is called MATISSE[2] and has the following design goals:

---

[2]The name honors the paper cut-outs produced by Matisse. These cutouts suggest the modular plan components central to the ITS development environment. They also point toward the dynamics and vibrancy I hope to achieve with the programming environment.

- It should allow the ITS designer to tie to established notations, suggest relevant metaphors, and capture conceptual elements as tools that can be applied to problems.
- It should naturally support the notion of plans that can be linked and arranged in a hierarchy. (See Miller, 1982, for an early attempt to support this planning in an educational environment.)
- It should be usable by educators who are not programmers. The environment hides the programming complexities inherent in developing interface-based ITS. (See di Sessa, 1985, for a complete discussion of computer-based educational environments intended for nonprogrammers.)
- It should support the design, implementation, and delivery (in a classroom) of interface-based tutors. The systems designed with MATISSE must be efficient enough to work with students without reimplementation in standard languages (e.g., C, BASIC).

Note that the MATISSE system is not yet implemented. The following description should be viewed as an illustration of the evolving design approach; many details still need to be worked out.

In BRIDGE, each interface element — for example, the natural language phrases in Phase 1 and the jigsaw puzzle Phase 2 plan components — is hand coded by a skilled programmer. The specification of the behavior or the screen element was separate from the specification of the semantics of that element. Furthermore, the specification of the tutoring knowledge associated with that screen element was in yet a third place. The critical goal with MATISSE is to put all aspects — screen behavior, formal specification of behavior, and domain knowledge — into one specification.

To illustrate MATISSE, I present a design for a strips-and-tiles interface for teaching fractions. This is the interface referred to in Figure 3.3 (see Ohlsson et al., 1987, for more details). In this interface, students are given a concrete representation — *strips-and-tiles* — of fractions. The curriculum consists of problems in fraction arithmetic to be solved. Students use the strips-and-tile objects in activities, such as representing fractions with the screen objects, performing arithmetic operations by manipulating the screen objects, and translating screen objects back into standard notation. A MATISSE specification is built around objects that appear on the students' screen. Each of these objects corresponds to a plan, that is, a component of expertise. These objects should be designed based on the four guidelines discussed in earlier sections:

1. Objects should represent the three kinds of expertise: abstractions, notations, and references to situations in the world. In fact, the objects should, collapse these three components. That is, they should represent an abstraction, suggest a standard notation, and refer to

experience from the world. This is not as hard as it might seem. For example, strips-and-tiles fractions provide an ideal representation: combining the abstraction of fractions with a concrete representation and an obvious linkage to part–whole situations in the world.

2. An interface cannot capture a complete domain. Although the objects in a MATISSE description should include abstractions, notations, and situations in the world, the object need only capture a narrow part of the domain being addressed. For example, strips-and-tiles fractions are an ideal representation of part–whole situations as they are themselves a part–whole object. Strips-and-tiles simplify the addition and subtraction algorithms. This works well because part–whole situations in the world typically require addition and subtraction. Strips-and-tiles do not help much with multiplication and division of fractions. This is also consistent in that proportions, the kinds of fractions that are typically multiplied or divided, are poorly represented by strips-and-tiles, and better represented by a concrete representation based on slope. In summary, the strips-and-tiles interface is only good for certain kinds of fractions representing certain kinds of situations in the world.

3. Interfaces should be based on situations in the world. As discussed earlier, the screen elements should lend themselves to a particular set of situations in the world. In fact, the strips-and-tiles were designed to represent part–whole fractions.

4. Yoking between representations is essential. An essential part of the student's activities with the screen elements is mapping those elements to and from the standard notation. As is shown in the example elements that follow, maintaining a standard notation is an important part of a MATISSE specification.

Note that the strips-and-tiles example does not lend itself to a hierarchy of plans. Effective representation of a plan hierarchy is addressed in detail in Shahidi and Bonar (1989). The focus with MATISSE and the strips-and-tiles example is the specification of complex interface behaviors. The Shahidi and Bonar work discusses how a hierarchy of such specifications can be related.

An Example of MATISSE Design

This strips-and-tiles world has the following basic screen objects:

- A window to contain the strips-and-tiles microworld.
- Blank unit strips that can be subdivided into equally sized sections.

- Sets of lines that evenly divide a unit strip into some number of equally sized sections.

- Shaded sections, corresponding to one of the sections in the current set of dividers. Each section may or may not be shaded. All shaded divisions may or may not be pushed together at one end of the unit strip.

- Pen used to indicate shading of a section.

- Eraser used to indicate unshading of a section.

- Stockpile of blank unit strips.

- Dividing tool use to indicate divisions.

- Fractions in standard notation.

- A notebook window showing a fraction in standard notation. This window is the same size and shape as the strips-and-tiles window. Fractions in this window are placed in the same relative position as the strips whose values are represented.

A MATISSE description of this microworld consists of descriptions of each of those objects. Actually, a prototypical version of each object is described. All microworld elements are implemented as an instance of a prototypical component. A prototype indicates the screen appearance, properties, and relationship to instances of other prototypes. All instances of a particular prototype have unique values for internal properties but share the behavior specified in the prototype. So, for example, all unit strips share the operation that allow their division, but each instance of a unit strip can have a different number of divisions.

Continuing with the example, the unit strip has the following properties:

- Picture — In this case the picture is selected from a library of building blocks. One of the standard building blocks is a rectangle. The microworld designer can adjust the height and width of the rectangle, and the thickness of the outer line.

- Division Kind — A rectangle can be divided into sections with horizontal or vertical divisions. For the strips-and-tiles microworld the Division Kind property specifies vertical divisions. Other kinds of pictures have other kinds of divisions. For example, Circles can have pie-shaped divisions as well as horizontal and vertical divisions. All closed figures can be divided with a grid.

- Division Count — This property of the rectangle specifies how many divisions there should be.

- Value — The unit rectangles have a value that is a function of the number of divisions and how many of those divisions are shaded. The value can be expressed either of two different ways, depending on the desires of the microworld designer.

- An ordered pair consisting of the number of divisions and a count of the shaded divisions.
- A rational number created by dividing the number of divisions by the number of shaded divisions.
- Position — The location of the unit strip on the containing window.

Each of the unit strip properties can be specified with a library element — some predefined object available in the MATISSE library, a value — a number, text string, or geometric figure — or as a constraint equation. Constraint equations allow the microworld designer to express relationships that are to be maintained at all times. To continue the example, the properties of the unit strips have the following values:

- Picture — library: rectangle (1in,3in)

This specifies a 1-inch by 3-inch rectangle to be used as the picture for the unit strip.

- Division Kind — library: vertical divisions, shadable

This tells MATISSE to allow vertical divisions in the rectangle, and provide for the shading of those divisions.

- Division Count — value: 0

This is an initial value. This field can (and will) be changed by user actions

- Value — constraint:
  Ordered Pair (Shaded Division Count, Division Count)

This constraint equation says that the value of the unit strip is an ordered pair made up of the count of the divisions that are shaded and the number of divisions. Actually, no constraints are introduced at this point, except that this value, and any values that depend on this value, are updated automatically whenever the Shaded Division Count and the Division Count change.

- Position — value: Screen Position (StartingX, StartingY)

This is an initial value for the screen position. StartingX and StartingY can be replaced by some particular values. Note that the operator Screen Position is really a kind of ordered pair, specialized for representing screen position.

Now that the properties are specified, we must specify the behaviors for those properties that have a behavior:

- Division Count
  - always   Division Count is $< = 12$

This behavior enforces a constraint that the division count must be less than or equal to 12. This is required because the screen cannot resolve anything smaller.

- whenever   Left Button of Mouse is Down
  - and   Type of Cursor is Division Tool
  - and   Location of Cursor is Strip
  - then   Ask User "How many divisions?"
  - and   Division Count becomes User's answer

This MATISSE behavior specifies that the user can set the division count by picking up the Division Tool (how that is done is specified as part of the behavior for the Division Tool), and clicking it over the unit strip.

- Position
  - always   Position of Strip inside Microworld Window

This MATISSE behavior says that the strip must stay inside the micro-world window. That is the entire specification for the unit strips. A number of other objects need to be specified as well, but to simplify this exposition, only a few of those descriptions are shown here.

- Pen
  - whenever   Left Button of Mouse is Down
  - and   Type of Cursor is Normal
  - and   Location of Cursor is on Pen Icon
  - then   Cursor becomes Pen Cursor

  - whenever   Left Button of Mouse is Down
  - and   Type of Cursor is Pen Icon
  - and   Location of Cursor is Division of Strip
  - then   Shade Division of Strip

- Stockpile
  whenever Left Button of Mouse is Down
     and   Type of Cursor is Normal
     and   Location of Cursor is on Strip Stockpile
     then   Cursor becomes create new Strip

  whenever Cursor is Strip
     and   Left Button of Mouse is Down
     and   Location of Strip is in Microworld Window
     then   Location of Strip becomes Location of Cursor
            Cursor becomes Normal Cursor

- Fractions in standard notation
  whenever Yoking is on
     and   new Strip is created
     then   create new Fraction
            always Location of new Fraction
               becomes Location of new Strip
            always Value of new Fraction
               becomes Value of new Strip

CONCLUDING REMARKS:
NEXT STEPS AND FUTURE VISIONS

A crucial next step for ITS development is to put that development in the hands of domain experts who are not AI experts. A crucial next step with the work discussed here is to implement the MATISSE environment. There are several important steps:

- Development of a direct manipulation interface development tool. GUIdance Technologies Corporation is building CHOREOGRA-PHER(tm) for this purpose. CHOREOGRAPHER is designed to vastly simplify the work involved in creating interactive screen elements. CHO-REOGRAPHER provides primitives like "is next to," "is connected," "is currently pointed to by the mouse," and so forth. The point is to provide an environment that manages the low-level details of a highly graphical user–computer interaction.
- Using the interface tool, implement a version of MATISSE. MATISSE must be built on top of an environment like CHOREOGRA-PHER. Current programming environments are too low-level for building an environment as sophisticated and interactive as MATISSE.
- Extend the MATISSE model to include plan hierarchies. Using CHOREOGRAPHER, Anoosh Shahidi, a graduate student at the Univer-

sity of Pittsburgh, is developing a formal representational system for implementing plan hierarchies and then mapping those hierarchies onto the graphical capabilities of CHOREOGRAPHER. Using the full MATISSE system, Shahidi plans to build an ITS for spreadsheets. Building the full MATISSE system requires extensive testing and development with computer naive domain experts.

With a full MATISSE system, several longer term goals can be attacked:

• We expect development of MATISSE libraries to become an important issue. Different domains will need different kinds of "default" graphical objects to be available to the computer-naive domain expert. Over time, we expect large libraries of components to become necessary for the development of cost-effective intelligent tutoring systems.

• It is important to build large, realistic plan hierarchies — projects on the scale of the entire repair manual set for a jet fighter. Although much of such a project properly remains as text, much is best represented as interactive block diagrams. We see such a large-scale project, even a beginning on a small piece, as important to really understand the power and problems of the architecture discussed here. For example, as libraries become larger and the system is used to attack larger domains, there will need to be tools for managing the resulting complexity. Much of the current work on HYPERTEXT (see Conklin, 1987) and navigation in large HYPERTEXT networks becomes relevant. The framework presented here, in fact, could provide some direction for building better HYPERTEXT navigation tools.

This chapter proposes that we should start building an ITS based on how an expert views a domain, that is, based on the interface we would build for an expert working in the domain. Students cannot be expected to understand the full expert view from the beginning so we should construct a series of plans that gives students small, manageable steps up to the full expert view. The plans that make up these steps are cast in terms of the user interface components that a student can manipulate. The advantage to students is that they are always solving problems in a similar way to experts. The advantage to the ITS designer is that knowledge engineering becomes much more manageable, organized around how an expert acts and how an expert would tell a student to act. The tools and design principles discussed in the chapter are a first step toward realizing this proposal.

ACKNOWLEDGMENTS

Work reported here was supported by the Office of Naval Research under contract numbers N00014-83-6-0148 and N00014-83-K0655 and by the

Air Force Human Resources Laboratory under contract number F41689-84-D-0002, Order 0004. Any opinions, findings, conclusions, or recommendations expressed in this report are those of the author, and do not necessarily reflect the views of the U.S. Government.

There are many people who provided support and direction for the research presented here. Susan Chipman and Valerie Shute, the contract officers on the above contracts, were consistantly supportive and challenging. Hugh Burns, Carol Luckhardt, and James Parlett provided many helpful comments on earlier drafts of this paper. Robert Cunningham implemented Bridge and designed many of its features. Stellan Ohlsson and Stewart Nickolas designed the strips and tiles microworld.

GUIdance Technologies, Inc. provided extensive support for the creation of this paper. GUIdance Technologies has been formed to develop the Choreographer interface development environment that supports direct manipulation interfaces and runs on standard hardware using standard software. Choreographer will be used in the implementation of MATISSE.

Choreographer is a trademark of GUIdance Technologies, Inc.

REFERENCES

Anderson, J. R., Greeno, J. G., Kline, P. J., & Neves, D. M. (1981). Acquisition of problem-solving skill. In J. R. Anderson (Ed.), *Cognitive skills and their acquisition*. Hillsdale, NJ: Lawrence Erlbaum Associates.

Anderson, J. R., Boyle, C. F., & Yost, G. (1985). The geometry tutor. In A. Joshi (Ed.), *Proceedings of the Ninth International Joint Conference on Artificial Intelligence* (pp. 1–7). Los Altos, CA: Morgan Kaufman.

Anderson, J. R., & Jeffries, R. (1985). Novice LISP errors: Undetected losses of information from working memory. *Human-Computer Interaction, 1*, 107–131.

Biermann, A. W., Ballard, B. W., & Sigmon, A. H. (1983). An experimental study of natural language programming. *International Journal of Man–Machine Studies 18*, 71–87.

Bonar, J. (1985). *Understanding the bugs of novice programmers*. Unpublished doctoral dissertation, University of Massachusetts, Amherst.

Bonar, J., & Soloway, E. (1985). Pre-programming knowledge: A major source of misconceptions in novice programmers. *Human-Computer Interaction, 1*, 133–162.

Bonar, J., Weil, W., & Jones, R. (1986). *The Programming Plans Workbook* (Technical Report). Pittsburgh: University of Pittsburgh, Learning Research and Development Center.

Bonar, J., & Cunningham, R. (1988). BRIDGE: Tutoring the programming process. In J. Psotka, L. Massey, & S. Mutter (Eds.), *Intelligent tutoring systems: Lessons learned* (pp. 409–434). Hillsdale, NJ: Lawrence Erlbaum Associates.

Bonar, J., Cunningham, R., Beatty, P., & Weil, W. (1988). *BRIDGE: Intelligent tutoring with intermediate representations* (Technical Report). Pittsburgh: University of Pittsburgh, Learning Research and Development Center. (Available by writing to GUIdance Technologies, 800 Vinial St., Pittsburgh, PA, 15212.)

Bonar, J., & Liffick, B. (1990). A novice visual programming language. In S. K. Chang (Ed.), *Principles of visual programming systems* (pp. 326–365). Englewood Cliffs, NJ: Prentice-Hall.

Brown, M. H. (1987). *Algorithm animation*. Cambridge, MA: MIT Press.

Chi, M., Feltovich, P., & Glaser, R. (1981). Categorization and representation of physics problems by experts and novices. *Cognitive Science, 5,* 121–152.

Clancey, W. (1983). The Epistemology of a rule-based expert system — A framework for explanations. *Artificial Intelligence, 20,* 215–251.

Collins, A., Brown, J. S., & Newman, S. E. (1989). Cognitive apprenticeship: Teaching the crafts of reading, writing, and mathematics. In L. B. Resnick (Ed.), *Knowing, learning and instruction. Essays in honor of Robert Glaser* (pp. 453–494). Hillsdale, NJ: Lawrence Erlbaum Associates.

Conklin, J. (1987). HYPERTEXT: An introduction and survey. *IEEE Software, 12,* 17–41.

diSessa, A. (1985). A principled design for an integrated computational environment. *Human-Computer Interaction, 1,* 1–47.

Eisenstadt, M., Laubsch, J., & Kahney, H. (1981). Creating pleasant programming environments for cognitive science students. In *Proceedings of the Third Annual Cognitive Science Society Conference.* Berkeley, CA: Cognitive Science Society.

Garlan, D. B., & Miller, P. L. (1984). GNOME: An introductory programming environment based on a family of structure editors. In *Proceedings of the Software Engineering Symposium on Practical Software Development Environments.* New York: Association for Computing Machinery.

Gentner, D., & Gentner, D. R. (1983). Flowing waters or teeming crowds: Mental models of electricity. In D. Gentner & A. L. Stevens (Eds.), *Mental models* (pp. 99–129). Hillsdale, NJ: Lawrence Erlbaum Associates.

Gentner, D., & Stevens, A. L. (Eds.). (1983). *Mental models.* Hillsdale, NJ: Lawrence Erlbaum Associates.

Johnson, W. L. (1986). *Intention-based diagnosis of novice programming errors.* Palo Alto, CA: Morgan Kaufman.

Kahney, H., & Eisenstadt, M. (1982). Programmers' mental models of their programming tasks: The interaction of real world knowledge and programming knowledge. *Proceedings of the Fourth Annual Conference of the Cognitive Science Society,* Ann Arbor, MI: Cognitive Science Society.

Larkin, J. H. (1983). The role of problem representation in physics. In D. Gentner & A. L. Stevens (Eds.), *Mental models.* Hillsdale, NJ: Lawrence Erlbaum Associates.

Mayer, R. E. (1979). A psychology of learning BASIC. *Communications of the Association For Computing Machinery, 22*(11), 589–598.

Miller, L. A. (1974). Programming by non-programmers. *International Journal of Man-Machine Studies, 6,* 237–260.

Miller, L. A. (1981). Natural language programming: Styles, strategies, and contrasts. *IBM Systems Journal, 20,* 184–215.

Miller, M. (1982). SPADE-0: A structured planning and debugging environment for elementary programming. In D. Sleeman & J. Brown (Eds.), *Intelligent tutoring systems.* New York: Academic Press.

Ohlsson, S. (1988). Mathematical meaning and applicational meaning in the semantics of fractions and related concepts. In J. Hiebert & M. Behr (Eds.), *Number Concepts and operations in the middle grades* (Vol. 2, pp. 53–92). Hillsdale, NJ: Lawrence Erlbaum Associates.

Ohlsson, S., Nickolas, S. E., & Bee, N. V. (1987, December). *Interactive illustrations for fractions: A progress report* (Technical Report KUL-87-03). Pittsburgh: Learning Research and Development Center, University of Pittsburgh.

Peled, I., & Resnick, L. B. (1987). Building semantic computer models for teaching number systems and word problems. In J. Bergeron, N. Herscovics, & C. Kiernan (Eds.), *Proceedings of the Eleventh International Conference of the Psychology of Mathematics Education* (Vol. 2, pp. 184–190). Montreal: University of Montreal Press.

Reiser, B., Anderson, J., & Farrell, R. (1985). Dynamic student modelling in an intelligent tutor for LISP programming. In A. Joshi (Ed.), *Proceedings of the Ninth International Joint Conference on Artificial Intelligence* (pp. 8–14). Los Altos, CA: Morgan Kaufman.

Resnick, L. (1983). A new conception of mathematics and science learning. *Science, 220,* 477–478.

Resnick, L. B., & Omanson, S. F. (1987). Learning to understand arithmetic. In R. Glaser (Ed.), *Advances in instructional psychology* (Vol. 3, pp. 41–95). Hillsdale, NJ: Lawrence Erlbaum Associates.

Rist, R. S. (1986). Plans in programming: Definition, demonstration, and development. In E. Soloway & S. Iyengar (Eds.), *Empirical studies of programmers* (pp. 28–47). Norwood, NJ: Ablex.

Shahidi, A. K., & Bonar, J. (1989). *Novice/expert planning language system* (Technical Report) Pittsburgh, PA: GUIdance Technologies.

Shneiderman, B., & Mayer, R. (1979). Syntactic/semantic interactions in programmer behavior: A model and experimental results. *International Journal of Computer and Information Sciences, 8*(3).

Soloway, E., & Ehrlich, K. (1985, November). Empirical studies of programming knowledge. *IEE Transactions of Software Engineering,* SE-10, 595–609.

Soloway, E., Bonar, J., & Ehrlich, K. (1983, November). Cognitive strategies and looping constructs: An empirical study. *Communications of the ACM 26* (11), 853–860.

Spohrer, J., Soloway, E., & Pope, E. (1985). A goal/plan analysis of buggy PASCAL programs. *Human–Computer Interaction, 1,* 163–207.

Towne, D. M., & Munro, A. (1988) The intelligent maintenance training system. In J. Psotka, L. Massey, & S. Mutter (Eds.), *Intelligent tutoring systems: Lessons learned* (pp. 479–530). Hillsdale, NJ: Lawrence Erlbaum Associates.

White, B., & Horwitz, P. (1987). Thinker tools: Enabling children to understand physical laws (Report No. 6470). Cambridge, MA.: BBN Laboratories

Design of a Domain-Independent Problem-Solving Instructional Strategy for Intelligent Computer-Assisted Instruction

Harold F. O'Neil, Jr.
University of Southern California

Dean A. Slawson
University of California, Los Angeles

Eva L. Baker
UCLA Center for Technology Assessment

This chapter is organized into five sections. Section 1 is included to provide background and context. Section 2 contains the domain-independent instructional strategy and documents the evolutionary changes in our thinking on this strategy. Section 3 provides an overview of the instructional rules. Section 4 provides instantiations of the rules in a troubleshooting context. In Section 5, implementation issues are discussed and future research and development is suggested.

BACKGROUND AND CONTEXT

The ideas for this chapter were derived from a program of research in the area of intelligent computer-assisted instruction (ICAI) with which we were associated. We view the application of ICAI as one way of increasing the cost-effectiveness of future education and training systems. We prefer the term ICAI to intelligent tutoring systems (ITSs) because we view tutoring as only one of many possible instructional strategies. ICAI also offers a technology to implement one-on-one tutoring, which Bloom (1984) suggested is the most effective educational intervention. In particular, we are interested in designing and developing software tools that would make the design and development process of ICAI more efficient and effective. From our viewpoint in the instructional arena, we originally thought that this would provide both domain-independent and domain-dependent instructional strategies. Thus, each strategy would be instantiated in the domain of interest. These strategies would collectively teach the subject matter in question. This chapter briefly discusses ICAI and then focuses on what we consider the key technical issues.

Intelligent Computer-Assisted Instruction

ICAI is the application of artificial intelligence (AI) to computer-assisted instruction. Artificial intelligence, a branch of computer science, is defined as making computers smart in order to (a) make them more useful and (b) to better understand human intelligence (Winston, 1977). Topic areas in AI have included natural language processing, vision, knowledge representation, spoken language, planning, and the development of expert systems.

Expert system technology is the branch of AI that, at this point, is most relevant to ICAI. ICAI systems use approaches from AI and cognitive science to teach a range of subject matters. Representative types of subjects include: computer programming in PROUST (Johnson & Soloway, 1983, 1987) or the LISP-tutor (Anderson, Boyle, & Reiser, 1985), rules in ALGEBRA (McArthur, Stasz, & Hotta, 1987), and diagnosis of infectious diseases in GUIDON (Clancey, 1979, 1987), rules in troubleshooting (Johnson, Hunt, Duncan, & Jeffrey 1988; Miller, 1989). Representative research in ICAI is described by Fletcher (1989), O'Neil, Anderson, and Freeman (1986), and Wenger (1987).

Progress in cognitive science has been made in the following areas: identification and analysis of misconceptions or "bugs" (Clement, Lockhead, & Soloway, 1980), the use of learning strategies (O'Neil & Spielberger, 1979; Weinstein & Mayer, 1986), the nature of expertise as expert versus novice knowledge (Chi, Glaser, & Rees, 1982), the role of mental models in learning (Kieras & Bovair, 1983; Konoske & Ellis, 1986), and the role of self-explanations in problem solving (Chi, Bassok, Lewis, Reimann, & Glaser, 1987).

The key components of an ICAI system are: (a) the *knowledge base,* that is, what the student is to learn, i.e., the expert model that represents the relevant knowledge in the domain and that can solve problems as an expert, based on this knowledge; (b) a *student model,* in which a model is constructed by comparing the student's performance to the computer-based expert's behavior on the same task; and finally (c) a *tutor,* that is, instructional techniques for teaching the declarative or procedural knowledge. This final component represents the teacher and must be able to apply the appropriate instructional tactics at the appropriate times. It should model the desirable properties of a human tutor. In general, the tutor must know what to say to the learner and when to say it. In addition, it must know how to take learners from one stage of skill to another and how to help learners, given their current state of knowledge. In general, there are few extant examples of complete ICAI systems.

Although suggestive evidence has been provided by Anderson, Boyle, and Reiser (1985) and Baker, Bradley, Aschbacher, and Feifer (1985), few of these ICAI projects have been evaluated in any rigorous fashion. We have not yet found complete examples of the explicit use of formative evaluation. In a sense, they have all been toy systems for research and demonstration. Nonetheless, these projects have generated a good deal of excitement and enthusiasm because they indicate that ICAI systems can be effective instructional environments.

Still, few instructional design considerations (e.g., Ellis, Wulfeck, & Fredericks, 1979; Park, Perez, & Seidel, 1987; Reigeluth, 1987) are reflected in ICAI tutors. An exception is the work of Baker and colleagues (1985) that suggests instructional strategies to improve existing ICAI programs. This chapter reports a systematic attempt to provide an instructional framework for the design of an ICAI system. In particular,we have struggled with the specifications of domain-independent instructional strategies and domain-dependent instructional strategies.

Conceptual Issues

A particularly knotty problem associated with developing the framework for domain-independent instructional strategies has been determining the boundaries of concepts such as *domain* and *independent*. We believed that a domain-independent set of instructional knowledge would be critical to obtaining any leverage of effort from a knowledge-based approach.

What is a *domain?* In cognitive science, "domain" usually refers to a subject matter area (e.g., math) or a process within a subject matter area (e.g., use of math formulae). Domain is often used synonymously with application area (e.g., equipment maintenance). Furthermore, within an application area the focus has often been on the task level (e.g., diagnose and troubleshoot an electrical system). Instructional researchers, however, tend to use domain to refer to performance outcomes (e.g., the learning of procedures). Thus, domain could legitimately refer to subject matter, application area, task, or performance outcome. As we believe it is essential to be specific, explicit, and consistent in our meanings of critical terms, we will use domain to refer either to *task* or *subject matter area*.

What is *independent?* Given the diversity of definitions of domain, independent can have a number of interpretations. Independent can mean "other than" or "as well as" the target domain. Domain-independent instructional strategies could mean strategies that are independent of the subject matter (i.e., strategies independent of math), or independent of the performance outcome (i.e., strategies appropriate both to concept learning and to problem solving), or both. In other words, the problem of domain independence is a problem of degree of transfer or generalizability.

Our solution to this issue is based on two key assumptions: (a) it is mandatory for instructional practices to specify for the designer the outcome or objective of the learning (e.g., problem solving); and (b) various outcomes (e.g., problem solving or principle learning) have specific learning conditions, that is, instructional strategies. (The second assumption was adopted from the framework of Bob Gagné (Gagné, 1985) and David Merrill (Merrill, 1987).) These learning conditions are dependent on outcome (e.g., problem solving), but are independent of domain or task as we are using it (e.g., diagnose and troubleshoot the electrical system). These learning conditions or strategies are also thought to be independent of subject matter or application area. Nonetheless, these conditions (or strategies) must be instantiated for a particular domain.

What is *dependent?* Reflecting the issue of independence is the issue of domain dependence. Our analysis suggests that domain dependence indicates a design feature that is exclusive or unique to the particular task area, with no generalizability across either subject matter or types of performance outcomes.

The next set of discriminations involves distinguishing between instantiations of domain-independent instructional strategies and domain-dependent instructional strategies. After considerable effort to develop counterexamples, we have agreed that we have found no domain-dependent instructional strategies that could not just as well be called domain-specific instantiations of domain-independent instructional strategies. This finding may counter some work on problem solving in cognitive science. However, we believe that whereas task requirements differ enormously, task-specific instruction is best conceived of as instantiations of domain-independent instructional strategies rather than as domain-dependent instructional strategies unique to the particular domain. In fact, the differences between domain-independent and domain-specific instantiations of strategies are not hard and fast, and, undoubtedly, share space on the same continuum. A review by Alexander and Judy (1988) provides an excellent source of literature on this issue.

With respect to our rule classification as domain-dependent or domain-independent, we have decided to operationally define independent in terms of a strategy's appropriateness to a particular class of learning outcomes, specifically, problem solving.

Implications for Instructional Knowledge Base Design

Our appraisal of the knowledge-base design goal suggested that we should develop a research-informed set of instructional strategies that were logically independent of task or subject matter area. Uninstantiated rules could then be derived for each outcome class, using standardized formats and common data definitions, yet preserving the domain independence of the strategies. The uninstantiated rules would reference the content of instruction by class only and avoid unnecessary dependencies, thus they could be reused in various applications and would be easy to maintain.

For the practitioner, it would become a relatively simple task to derive instantiations of strategies that have already been extracted and encoded, bypassing a reinvention from primary sources. There are two reasons to expect this: First, consider the ready accessibility of strategies in "runnable" form. The attributes of the instructional content relevant for encoding would be uniquely identified by the classes of conditions or premises of the rules. Second, efficiency derives from the inheritance characteristics of the knowledge system, whereby attributes from domain-independent strategies are automatically applied to instantiations.

Linking the Art and Science of Instruction

Beyond the several potential efficiencies for the ICAI instructional designer, there are more far-reaching implications for the relationship between instructional development and theory. According to a typical ISD model, the development of conventional instructional systems proceeds in the following manner: 1. from instructional goals and needs assessment relevant to a specific project; 2. by conducting an instructional analysis through development of performance objectives, specification of entry behaviors and characteristics, test items, instructional strategies; 3. through the development and selection of instructional materials (Dick & Carey, 1985). Formative evaluation accompanies development, which is followed by revision and then summative evaluation. Instructional theory is applied in this effort, particularly in the development and selection of materials, but theory validation is not the focus of design or evaluation in systems development. Formative and summative evaluation focus on the "engineering" questions (e.g., "Does it work?" or "How might it work better?"). The key point is that instructional *strategies* are not validated in the development of conventional applications—their *instantiations* are.

By avoiding entanglement among instructional strategies and other application-specific knowledge, the use of domain-independent strategies could encourage a closer link between the science of instruction and the practice of building applications. The explicit separation of generic and instantiated strategies and the use of common definitions make it possible to test and revise instructional theory in the form of rules by comparing effects within and between applications. The division of strategies within an application is thus accompanied by a unification of strategies in the world of theory. Theory is expressed in terms that are meaningful to the applications, application generators, instructional designers, and instructional scientists. A common language for theory and practice means that strategies are operationalized in a form that is reliably replicable and immediately testable. The most significant outcome of developing domain-independent instructional strategies may be that the validation of theory and applications can occur on common ground.

The costs associated with eliciting and codifying instructional strategies may be excessive overhead for most instructional systems developers, but this need not be a hindrance. Optimistically, there might arise new specializations, perhaps instructional knowledge *creators, elicitors,* and *instantiators,* that would be interconnected by a "marketplace of canned ideas." Ultimately we might see entrepreneurial processors of research data that would link systems developers—who would browse and select from libraries of instructional strategies—with researchers looking for test cases that run on a few standard platforms.

A Model: Instructional Development with Domain-Independent Strategies

It is possible to synthesize the results of our conceptual analysis and a traditional development approach (Gagné, Briggs, & Wager, 1988). Table 4.1 is a first-cut instructional systems development model incorporating the use of domain-independent instructional strategies. As in the Dick and Carey model (1985), the suggested process is initiated with the identification of systems goals, followed by the elicitation or identification of subject matter. Subsequently, terminal and enabling objects are identified and classified by performance types. The selection or development of domain-independent rules follows. Next, these rules are instantiated for a specific application. Finally, formative evaluation, revision, and summative evaluation are conducted.

The model is not specific to any particular system architecture and may require additional steps dependent on the implementation. For example, elicitation and testing of student errors for an error catalogue is not mentioned because diagnostic approaches vary. Furthermore, the sequence of steps is not absolute; for example, some elicitation of subject matter knowledge may be required before objectives can be fully identified. Yet, detailed content elicitation in practice will be constrained by the scope of the application, which may be undefined at that juncture.

TABLE 4.1
Knowledge-Based Approach to Instructional Systems Development

1. Identification of system goals
2. Elicitation of subject matter knowledge
3. Identification of performance objectives
4. Identification of enabling objectives
5. Classification of objective performance types
6. Identification of available domain-independent rules to teach identified types of objectives
7. Elicitation of unavailable domain-independent rules needed to teach identified types of objectives
8. Instantiation of domain-independent rules for specific application
9. Iterative formative evaluation and revision of instantiations
10. Summative evaluation fed back to domain-independent knowledge sources for theory validation

With respect to more traditional development processes, the unique features of this approach are: (a) the efficiencies obtained by structured development using existing domain-independent rule-sets as the basis of instructional strategies, and (b) the potential facilitation of instructional strategies research via the communication of runnable theories. The creation of sets of rules is obviously prerequisite to even the most direct application of this model. The remainder of this chapter is based on our attempt to create such domain-independent strategies, put them in the form of rules, instantiate them for an application, and begin the process of validation.

Methodology

Instructional science is multidisciplinary, incorporating elements of learning theory, human factors, and motivation, to name a few. Within any of these fields, there is often disagreement about the nature of the phenomena, let alone the proper application of knowledge. Our approach was to synthesize well-established instructional theories with expert assistance in order to create a framework for presenting and sequencing instructional events. This framework was then used to structure the selection of supplemental instructional knowledge derived from current research. Selected strategies would need to elaborate the framework or, minimally, avoid inconsistencies with it. Instantiations were created using an interview process with experienced teachers of the course for which our instruction was destined as a test case. Validation consisted primarily of expert reviews and paper simulations to determine consistency and completeness. A complementary view of this issue is provided by Wiggs and Perez (1988). The major steps in the process are summarized in Table 4.2.

TABLE 4.2
Development of Domain-independent Instructional Strategies, Rules, and Instantiations

1. Synthesize Instructional Theories Based on Expert Knowledge

   Gagné, Briggs, and Wager's (1988) instructional theory is well established and comprehensive but not well articulated with respect to
   specific instructional strategies (Reigeluth, 1987). Gagné's personal
   assistance was sought to apply the events of instruction for
   problem solving (Gagné, 1985) to the selected domain. David Merrill's
   (1987) Component Display Theory was integrated with Gagné's
   revised strategies to provide the next level of detail (i.e., microstrate-
   gies). Both systems derive from attempts to synthesize instructional
   science research into prescriptive models. Minor modifications of sequence were made to the strategies to render them consistent with
   actual practice in teaching the course for which instantiations were
   to be developed.

2. Create Draft Elicitation Protocol and Knowledge Formats

   A draft elicitation protocol was developed for use in interviewing
   course instructors to answer questions about the course structure
   and instructional methods used, student background, and prerequisite skills. A review of project-related software functions and modules (e.g., curriculum-syllabus database) for the application and
   prototypical rules derived form Gagné's example lesson resulted in
   a more or less generic production-rule format and classification
   system for the knowledge base. Following feedback, the elicitation
   protocol was revised (see Step 4).

3. Derive Draft Rule Set

   Instructional strategies were abstracted from research articles
   selected in a series of library database searches. Rules were derived
   by understanding implications of the research and formulating
   results of relevant, high quality studies using the format defined in
   Step 2. Other instructional experts were consulted for a general
   review of the strategies and rules, and for additional rules to teach
   subordinate skills. An initial pass was made to assure standardization of terminology, to classify the rules into instructional and remedial categories, and to group them into consistent sets. The need
   for additional rules was identified.

4. Elicit Instantiations

   The elicitation protocol was revised to focus on instantiations and
   expert instructors were asked to provide examples of the rules actually used in instructing the subject matter of the appropriate performance outcome class. In addition to instantiating primary strategies,
   alternate and remedial strategies were elicited and compared with
   the generic instructional strategies. In some cases, instances were
   developed for rules that had not been anticipated in the original
   derivation of rules from strategies. However, in all such cases, rules
   and domain-independent strategies could be inferred from the instantiations and traced back to the research base or framework.
   Prepared course and content documents were also a source for additional instantiations consistent with the instructional strategy.

(continued)

TABLE 4.2 (continued)

5. Validate and Revise

> Reviews were conducted by independent instructional design experts and domain experienced teachers. Rule sets were checked again for consistency and for completeness and revised accordingly. An additional troubleshooting task was analyzed and it was determined that the task strategies differed in some respects but that the instructional strategies were equally applicable. A more generic version of the instructional strategy was induced to demonstrate its generalizability.

DOMAIN-INDEPENDENT INSTRUCTIONAL STRATEGY

For our own work we have chosen problem solving as it is appropriate for ICAI technology and is considered a domain-independent strategy. *Problem Solving* (a Gagné term) is roughly equivalent to Merrill's *Using Principles*. The domain-independent instructional strategies (or, in Gagné's terms, learning conditions[1]) for problem solving are shown in Table 4.3.

The instructional strategy in Table 4.3 is clearly at a very general level. For our research program our area of interest is troubleshooting. Troubleshooting is a concept that comprises many activities; one activity is problem solving. Technicians are confronted with a malfunction that shows itself in certain "symptoms." They must then use their knowledge of the system, the tools available for diagnosis, and troubleshooting strategies to find the source(s) of the malfunction. Each malfunction with its set of symptoms constitutes a new problem to be solved by a thinking process. The more rational and informed the thinking can be, the more efficient the procedure of locating the trouble.

Carrying out troubleshooting in this area involves following procedures of several kinds. Sometimes the trouble can actually be found by following a fixed sequence of steps (this is one end of a continuum of complexity of troubleshooting tasks). More often, though, procedures are simply parts of the whole activity that is required. There are procedures for identifying the location of parts of the system, procedures for taking apart equipment components, and procedures for using test equipment. Technicians must know all of these procedures, or they will be impeded in their main task — thinking out the solution of a problem.

It should be emphasized that this knowledge is predominantly what is called *procedural*. However, *declarative* knowledge (such as the equipment

---

[1]These conditions are in Gagné's terminology *instructional events*, which distinguish the teaching of problem solving from teaching other types of learning outcomes.

TABLE 4.3
**Domain-independent Instructional Strategy (Learning
Conditions) to Teach Problem-solving Outcomes
(from Gagné, 1977)**

1. Retrieval of relevant rules and concepts
2. Successive presentation of novel problem situations
3. Demonstration of solutions by student

"lore" of the veteran) is useful as an aid to the encoding and the retrieval of the procedures themselves.

Table 4.4 presents an elaboration of an instructional strategy to teach troubleshooting. It was generated by Robert Gagné (cited in O'Neil, Slawson, & Baker (1987), revised by an Army subject matter expert in troubleshooting, and further edited by the lead author. Entries 1, 2, and 3 are domain-specific instantiations of the learning condition "retrieval of relevant rules and concepts" (see Table 4.3). Entry 4 is the "successive presentations of novel problem solutions" (see Table 4.3). And Entry 5 is the "demonstration of solutions by student" (see Table 4.3).

In summary, the instructional outline in Table 4.4 presents a domain-independent instructional strategy (Entries 1–5) for teaching the domain-dependent problem-solving task strategy (e.g., split-half) of electrical troubleshooting. We view the teaching of these task strategies as "using principles": Tasks would be taught using a modified version of Merrill's Component Display Theory (Merrill, 1987). These tasks are taught using domain-specific instantiations of domain-independent instructional strategies. In Table 4.4, the domain-independent instructional sequence is provided in list format because this is clearer and more efficient than rule format for communicating macrosequences. The rules that sequence items in this list are "housekeeping" — not instructional — and would be devised by the implementor. This chapter provides a first cut of the instantiations of these strategies by providing instantiations of the domain-independent instructional strategies in troubleshooting the electrical faults of a particular vehicle. Furthermore, in Table 4.5, we have induced a generalized domain-independent instructional strategy to test diagnostic problem-solving based on a refinement of Table 4.4.

INSTRUCTIONAL STRATEGY RULES

This section presents selected examples of instructional strategy rules. The terminal objective of the rule sets is for the learner to acquire and apply the two task strategies: (a) fault search based on malfunction probability and (b) fault search based on change cost. Rules for the Remediation of the task

TABLE 4.4
Domain-Independent Instructional Strategy for Electronic Troubleshooting

To teach domain-independent troubleshooting, using several malfunctions of the Improved Tow Vehicle (ITV) turret systems as instances of domain-independent strategies:

1. Communicate that electrical troubleshooting consists of using techniques and strategies to verify data or signal flow in a device in order to find and replace faulty Line Replaceable Units.

2. Communicate a description of the sample system as a whole to identify schema having the following components:

   a. Present an orientation that typically includes demonstration and hands-on experience with the system in full operation including operational controls or inputs and ways in which failures are indicated on the device.

   b. Use of concept of line replaceable units (LRUs) and reference designators. Briefly present names, locations, and functions (generally) of specific LRUs to be used in this instruction — using block diagrams, technical manuals, etc. Require the student to identify the parts by function by pointing to them. In this context, present concepts of how things are caused in the system by major subsystem functions and data/signal flows.

   c. Present concepts of schematic representations of systems and methods of illustrating physical/schematic mapping to be used, with examples.

   d. Teach detailed operation and function (how the system works in terms of inputs, controls, component functions, causal flows, and outputs) of major activating and intermediary components, with reference to schematics and physical layout diagrams.

3. Confirm or teach subordinate skills.

4. Describe and demonstrate the troubleshooting task strategies. These are taught in the order of typical use or most likely frequency of use, except that split half is taught first because the other strategies are frequently combined with this "default" strategy.

   a. split half (basic strategy for determining efficient fault search in series circuits).

   b. malfunction probability (test likely failed components first).

   c. change cost (e.g., perform easiest tests first).

   d. necessary and sufficient factors (using logic and knowledge of normal parameters to localize and identify faults).

   e. commonality of fault (using principle that concurrent symptoms with common component imply the common component is faulty).

5. Provide practice, using a variety of novel problems requiring the strategies taught and provide feedback and corrections.

strategies plus Rules for use of selected concepts and facts is also provided. The next section provides an instantiated instructional interaction to illustrate their function. The rules and, thus, the instantiations are sequenced to demonstrate a hypothetical path through the course of

TABLE 4.5
Revised Domain-Independent Instructional Strategy to Teach Diagnostic
Problem Solving

1. Define diagnostic problem-solving family to be taught by describing problem-solving characteristics or events pertaining to the family.

2. Communicate a description of the appropriate sample device(s), as whole systems, and necessary concepts and principles of operation in the order prescribed:

   a. Present name and brief overall description of the device including operational controls or inputs and ways in which failures are indicated on the device with examples.

   b. Present concepts of how things are caused in the system (e.g., data/signal flow if electrical system, forces if mechanical, etc.).

   c. Present concepts of schematic representation and methods of illustrating physical/schematic mapping to be used; examples.

   d. Present concept and function of replaceable units—using block diagrams as needed—as examples. Require the student to identify the parts by pointing to them. (Teach top-level description first.)

   e. Teach operation and function (how the system works in terms of inputs, controls, component functions, causal flows, and outputs) of major activating and intermediary components, with reference to schematics and physical layout diagrams, taught by tracing causal paths through components on schematics and referencing physical locations. (Teach detailed operation and function using schematics after general function of replaceable units in previous presentation.)

3. Confirm or teach subordinate skills.

4. Describe and demonstrate appropriate diagnostic problem-solving strategies to be taught for this application.

5. Provide practice, using a variety of novel problems requiring the strategies taught and provide feedback and corrections.

instruction. Therefore, the rules for domain-independent instructional strategies are presented first, followed by instantiations for teaching two selected troubleshooting task strategies. Table 4.6 provides a "cross-walk" of the rules and their instantiations in this chapter. The task strategies are taught as an expert approach to troubleshooting an electromechanical fault in the turret system of the ITV.

However, rules are not included for pretesting, remediation of basic skills, initial teaching of subordinate skills, communication of a device model, posttesting, sequencing, and help. The remedial rules are invoked to address subordinate skills and knowledge that even an experienced troubleshooter might have difficulty in recalling or applying. Domain-independent instructional strategy rules are first listed in functional groups based on the domain-independent instructional strategy to teach troubleshooting (Table 4.4).

TABLE 4.6
Cross-Walk Among Rules and Instantiations

Rules and Their ID Numbers	Figure Number	Instantiation (Figure Numbers)
Use-Principles		
3107	4.1	4.15, 4.28
3108	4.2	4.16, 4.29
3114	4.3	4.17, 4.30
Use-Concept		
3411	4.4	4.18
3412	4.5	4.19
3413	4.6	4.20
3415	4.7	4.20
3416	4.8	4.21
3417	4.9	4.22
3419	4.10	4.23
3421	4.11	4.24
3422	4.12	4.25
3425	4.13	4.26

Domain-Independent Strategy Rules: Primary Instruction

The following rules are primary instructional rules of Use-Principle for Item 4 (Table 4.4). Each rule is provided as a figure with the following format conventions:

1. Rule identification number (Rule ID:)

2. Statement of the rule in English as an if . . . then condition action pair

3. A comment to provide an instructional design explanation ("Comment")

4. A reference to provide the best "evidence" reference (Ref) for a rule. In some cases the rule reflects a synthesis of several studies and thus several references are provided.

The Component Display Theory (CDT) prescriptions for teaching use-principles for the teaching of task strategies could be implemented in the forms of discovery, simulation, conversational tutorial, and expository tutorial (Merrill, 1987). This chapter specifies the rules for expository tutorial mode (rules 3107, 3108, 3114).

Some terminology from Merrill (1987) will assist the reader unfamiliar with Component Display Theory to interpret the rules: *Component*

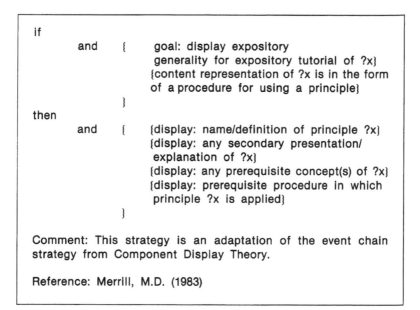

```
if
                {goal: apply Expository Tutorial for ?x}
    then
        and   {     {assert goal: display Expository Generality for
                      expository tutorial of ?x}
                    {assert goal: display Expository Instance for
                      expository tutorial of ?x}
                    {assert goal: display Inquisitory Instance for
                      expository tutorial of ?x}
              }
```

Comment: For use-level performance, the presentation should consist of an expository generality (rule) followed by a set of expository instances, followed by a set of previously unencountered inquisitory instances (practice).

Merrill, M.D. (1983)

FIGURE 4.1   Expository tutorial rule. Rule ID: 3107.

```
if
        and   {     goal: display expository
                    generality for expository tutorial of ?x}
                    {content representation of ?x is in the form
                     of a procedure for using a principle}
              }
    then
        and   {     {display: name/definition of principle ?x}
                    {display: any secondary presentation/
                     explanation of ?x}
                    {display: any prerequisite concept(s) of ?x}
                    {display: prerequisite procedure in which
                     principle ?x is applied}
              }
```

Comment: This strategy is an adaptation of the event chain strategy from Component Display Theory.

Reference: Merrill, M.D. (1983)

FIGURE 4.2   Expository generality rule. Rule ID: 3108.

if

{goal: display Expository Generality for expository
tutorial of ?x}

then   {highlight the concepts involved in the principle ?x}

Comment: Expository Generality elaboration can also appear in
the form of help (attention focus device), and prerequisite
information (related fact, concept, principle, procedure).

Reference: Merrill, M.D. (1983)

FIGURE 4.3   Expository generality elaboration. Rule ID: 3114.

Display Theory provides several useful distinctions in a performance-
content classification system and a set of instructional prescriptions tie to
the classification system. Merrill views content as consisting of facts (e.g.,
association between date and procedure), concepts (set of objects that share
common characteristics), procedure (set of steps to carry out an activity),
and principles (e.g., cause and effect relationships in a process). The
performance of a person is to either remember or use (apply a generality
to a specific case) or find content (find or invent new generality). A
generality (*rule*) is a statement of a definition, principle, or the steps in a
procedure. An instance (*example*) is a specific illustration of an object,
symbol, event, process, or procedure . . . *Expository* means to present, tell,
or show; *inquisitory* means to question, ask, or require practice. CDT also
makes the distinction between primary presentation forms (rule, recall,
example, practice) and secondary presentation forms that supplement
them and that may be attention focusing devices, prerequisite information,
alternative representations, or mnemonics.

Domain-Independent Strategy: Remediation

This subsection contains rules for remediation in recall and use of the task
strategy principles and subordinate concepts and facts. The rules are
provided as a figure with the same format conventions as the prior
subsection. Then particular rules are error or "bug" driven. The following
set of rules are used to teach using a concept (rules 3411–3425)

```
if        {goal: teach Use-Concept ?concept}

then
          and    {      {assert goal: display Expository Generality of
                         ?concept}
                         {assert goal: display one Expository Instance of
                         ?concept}
                         {assert goal: display Inquisitory Instance of
                         ?concept}
                 }
```

Comment: For Use-Concept level performance, the presentation should consist of an expository generality followed by a set of expository instances or examples, followed by a set of previously unencountered inquisitory instances (practice) consisting of several additional instances different from the instances used for the expository instances.

Reference: Merrill (1983, 1987).

FIGURE 4.4 Use-concept rule. Rule ID: 3411.

```
if        {goal: display Expository Generality of ?concept}

then
          and    {      {display: name of ?concept}
                         {assert goal: display definition of ?concept}
                 }
```

Comment: The Expository Generality should consist of the name and the definition of the concept.

References: Merrill (1983), Merrill & Tennyson (1977).

FIGURE 4.5 Expository generality of concept rules. Rule ID: 3412.

```
if              {goal: display definition of ?concept}

then
       and    {        {display: superordinate concepts of
                        ?concept}
                        {display: all the relevant attributes of
                        ?concept and relationship of attributes}
              }
```

Comment: The definition should include identification of the superordinate class, the relevant attributes that distinguish instances of this concept from coordinate concepts within the same superordinate class, and the relationship of these attributes to one another.

Reference: Merrill & Tennyson (1978).

FIGURE 4.6 Definition of concept rules. Rule ID: 3413.

```
if     {goal: display definition of ?concept}

then   {display: best example along with the definition of
       ?concept}
```

Comment: A best example should be presented along with the definition of the concept (Park & Tennyson, 1986). Merrill calls the best example the "Reference Example." In his sample lesson (Merrill, 1987, p. 212) the reference example is presented along with the definition.

References: Park and Tennyson (1986), Merrill (1987).

FIGURE 4.7 Best example of concept rule. Rule ID: 3415.

```
if      {goal: display Expository Instance of ?concept}

then    {display: example with a matched non-example}

Comment: This is the match rule in Component Display Theory.

Reference: Merrill (1983).
```

FIGURE 4.8   Match example of concept rule. Rule ID: 3416.

```
if
        and     {    {goal: display Expository Instance of
                      ?concept}
                      {the learner makes an error}
                      {there is more than one rational set}

                }
then                 {assert goal: display a concept in a different
                      rational set in Inquisitory Instance mode}
```

Comment: This rule defines the switch from Expository Instance mode to Inquisitory Instance mode. According to Park and Tennyson (1986), expository instances are always presented when learner makes a mistake in practice mode (except the best example). Thus, mode switch is necessary after student makes an error in expository instance mode. (See also Rule ID: 3418).

Reference: Park and Tennyson (1986).

FIGURE 4.9   Switch from expository instance to inquisitory instance rule. Rule ID: 3417.

```
if
        and     {       {goal: display Inquisitory Instance of
                        ?concept}
                        {it is the first time the goal is set for the
                        current concept}

                }

then                    {display: instance in a rational set with fewest
                        number of relevant attributes}
```

Comment: In concept teaching, one measure of difficulty is the number of relevant attributes for a concept. The concept with the least number of attributes is the one easiest to be classified. "A *rational set* provides examples that illustrate the variability of the irrelevant attributes of a production while sharpening focus on the relevant attributes of the production" (Tennyson & Park, 1980, p. 194).

Reference: Merrill and Tennyson (1978), Tennyson and Park (1980).

FIGURE 4.10   Display easier instance concept rule. Rule ID: 3419.

```
if
        and     {       {goal: display Inquisitory Instance of
                        ?concept}
                        {the learner answers the instance
                        correctly}
                        {the learner answers all the instances at
                        the
                        same difficulty level correctly}

                }

then
        and     {       {display: an instance from a rational set
                        different from the current one}
                        {display: the instance at a higher difficulty
                        level}

                }
```

Comment: An optional instance presentation sequence in Park and Tennyson (1986) works to present an inquisitory instance (interrogatory example) of any other concept in the rational set if the learner answers the current one correctly but the mastery level is not yet reached.

Reference: Park and Tennyson (1986).

FIGURE 4.11   Optional instance presentation of concept rule. Rule ID: 3421.

```
if
        and     {       {goal: display Inquisitory Instance of
                        ?concept}
                        {the learner answers the instance
                        incorrectly}

                }
then                    {assert goal: display an instance in the same
                        rational set in Expository mode}
```

Comment: Present another example of the same concept in an expository form if the learner's classification on a given interrogatory example is incorrect.

Reference: Park and Tennyson (1986).

FIGURE 4.12 Switch from inquisitory to expository instance of concept rule. Rule ID: 3422.

```
if
        and     {       {goal: display Inquisitory Instance of
                        ?concept}
                        {the number of instances that is already
                        presented is larger than 4}
                        {the learner's score is larger than the
                        criterion}

                }

then
        and     {       {the learner reached mastery level}
                        {instruction on the set of concepts is
                        completed}

                }
```

Comment: A minimum of four instances per concept is necessary before predicting mastery at any given criterion level (Tennyson, 1984).

Reference: Tennyson (1984).

FIGURE 4.13 Instances to predict mastery. Rule ID: 3425.

INSTRUCTIONAL INSTANTIATIONS

The format of presentation for the instantiations (Figures 4.14–4.30) is a sequential list consisting of: (a) assertions based on prior system actions or data (e.g., tutorial subgoals), (b) consequently triggered, instantiated rules, (c) resulting displays, and (d) learner responses. Goal-removing consequences of rules can be inferred in most cases and are not stated explicitly. The instructional goal is to teach a use-principle, describe, and then demonstrate a troubleshooting task strategy: malfunction probability (Item 4b in Table 4.4). The content is electronics troubleshooting and the content representation of the malfunction probability task strategy is in the form of a procedure for applying a principle.

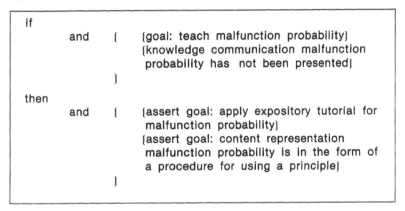

FIGURE 4.14 Instantiation of rule ID. Table 4.4 strategy.

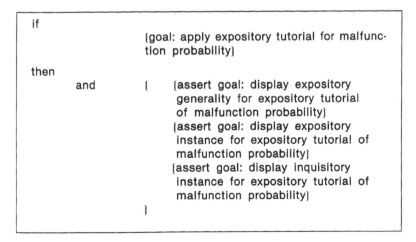

FIGURE 4.15 Instantiation of rule ID: 3107.

```
if
        and    {      {goal: display expository generality for
                       expository tutorial of malfunction
                       probability}
                       {content representation of malfunction
                       probability is in the form of a procedure for
                       using a principle}
               }

then
        and    {      {display: name/definition of principle
                       malfunction probability}
                       {display: any secondary presentation/
                       explanation of malfunction probability}
                       {display: any prerequisite concept(s)
                       of malfunction probability}
                       {display: prerequisite procedure in which
                       principle malfunction probability is
                       applied}
               }
```

FIGURE 4.16 Instantiation of rule ID: 3108.

if

       {goal: display expository generality for expository
       tutorial of malfunction probability}

then

       {highlight the concepts involved in the principle
       malfunction probability}

DISPLAY:

Name/Definition for Entry 4b "Malfunction Probability"

*Finding a fault based on malfunction probability or failure rate
means looking first for LRUs that tend to fail most frequently.*

*Secondary Presentation/Explanation for Entry 4b "Malfunction
Probability"*

*A part with a high failure rate is one that fails frequently, and is
therefore the most likely cause of the symptom. A good
strategy for quickly and efficiently locating circuit faults is to
look first for components that tend to fail most frequently. All
else being equal, it is better to test the components that are
most likely to fail before the components that are less likely to
fail. This strategy, called "finding the fault based on the failure
rate," tends to reduce the number of tests you must perform to
make a diagnosis.*

*Secondary Presentation/Prerequisite Concept of Ways to Deter-
mine Failure Rate Information for Entry 4b, "Malfunction
Probability."*

*In addition to these general rules, you can learn from others
and from your own experience which parts have a high failure
rate in general or on a particular device. You may also have
access to logistical and other field data sources available on
failure rates. When you examine a circuit for evidence of physical damage (e.g. burnt components, worn or torn insulators),
you are also gathering evidence of the likelihood that a component is not functioning.*

*Once you have determined which components are most likely
to have caused the symptoms, you may begin to test them and
see if your hypothesis is correct.*

FIGURE 4.17 Instantiation of rule ID: 3114.

```
if        {goal: Use-Concept Failure Rate}

then
          and    {       {assert goal: display Expository Generality
                          of Failure Rate}
                          {assert goal: display Expository Instance
                          of Failure Rate}
                          {assert goal: display Inquisitory Instance
                          of Failure Rate}
                 }
```

FIGURE 4.18 Instantiation of rule ID: 3411.

```
if        {goal: display Expository Generality of Failure Rate}

then
          and    {       {display: name of Failure Rate}
                          {assert goal: display definition of Failure
                          Rate}
                 }

DISPLAY:

  "Review of Concept: Malfunction Probability"
```

FIGURE 4.19 Instantiation of rule ID: 3412.

```
if        {goal: display definition of Failure Rate}
then
          and    {    {display: superordinate concepts
                        of Failure Rate}
                       {display: relevant attributes
                        of Failure Rate}
                       {display: best example of Failure Rate}
                 }
```

DISPLAY

Malfunction probability or failure rate reflects the likelihood that failure of a component will occur in a situation. Malfunction probability is determined by both component types and situation characteristics.

Certain kinds of components tend to fail more frequently than others. Also, components in certain situations tend to fail more frequently. High or low failure rate components can appear in high or low failure rate situations, but certain combinations of components and situations are especially trouble prone. The highest malfunction probability or failure rate will be found when high failure rate components happen to be found in high failure rate situations.

The tables below list relevant attributes (component types and situations) that are likely to result in failure:

High Failure Rate Component Types

Most frequent: Electromechanical components (e.g. switches, motors, solenoids, relays, controls), especially if they have a high rate of operation cy les or if they interface with humans (e.g. a mechanical switch which is opened and closed frequently).

Next most frequent: Electronics-only components. Active devices (e.g. transistors) are more likely to fail than passive devices (e.g. capacitors).

Less frequent: Wiring harnesses,

Also, a component through which large currents flow (e.g. 1 amp or more for electronics components) is more likely to fail than a component through which small currents flow.

High Failure Rate Situations

Exposure to elements (e.g. moisture, dust or dirt, very high or low temperatures or rapid temperature changes).

Exposure to wear and tear (e.g. wiring harness in the path of travel of crew, frequently flexed wires, etc.)

An example of a worst case scenario (high failure rate) would be an electromechanical component (these tend to wear out), in a situation exposed to the wear and tear of elements: for example, an electromechanical relay in a poorly sealed control panel box.

FIGURE 4.20   Instantiation of rule IDs: 3413 and 3415.

```
if        {goal: display Expository Instance of Failure Rate}

then
          {display: example with a matched non-example}

DISPLAY:

   Example:   high probability of failure — switch (mechanical)
              low probability of failure — resistor (passive
              electronics)
```

FIGURE 4.21 Instantiation of rule ID: 3416.

```
if
          and    {    {goal: display Expository Instance
                       of Failure Rate}
                       {the learner thinks s/he understands the
                       concept}
                       {there is only one rational set}

                  }

then                   {assert goal: display a concept in the
                       same rational set at the same difficulty
                       level in Inquisitory Instance mode}
```

FIGURE 4.22 Instantiation of rule ID: 3417.

```
if
          and    {    {goal: display Inquisitory Instance
                       of concept}
                       {it is the first time the goal is set
                       for the current concept}

                  }

then                   {display: the instance in a rational set with
                       fewest number of relevant attributes}
DISPLAY:

   Which is more likely to fail, a switch or a wiring harness?
CORRECT LEARNER RESPONSE: A switch.
```

FIGURE 4.23 Instantiation of rule ID: 3419.

```
if
        and     {       {goal: display Inquisitory Instance of
                        Failure Rate}
                        {the learner answers the instance
                        correctly}
                        {the learner answers all the instances at
                        the same difficulty level correctly}

                }

then
        and     {       {display: an instance from a rational set
                        different from the current one}
                        {display: the instance at a higher difficulty
                        level}

                }

DISPLAY:

    Which has a higher failure rate?

    1) proximity detector (exposed, electronic)
    2) panel switch (exposed, electromechanical)
INCORRECT LEARNER RESPONSE: 1) proximity detector
```

FIGURE 4.24 Instantiation of rule ID: 3421.

```
if
        and     {       {goal: display Inquisitory Instance
                        of Failure Rate}
                        {the learner answers the instance
                        incorrectly}

                }

then                    {assert goal: display an instance in the
                        same rational set in Expository mode}
DISPLAY:

    A panel switch is more likely to fail than proximity switch since
    both are exposed but the panel switch is subject to operator wear
    and tear and is electromechanical whereas proximity detector is
    electronic.
```

FIGURE 4.25 Instantiation of rule ID: 3422.

```
if
        and     {       {goal: display Inquisitory Instance of
                        Failure Rate}
                        {the number of instances that is already
                        presented is larger than 4}
                        {the learner's score is larger than the
                        criterion}
                }

then
        and     {       {the learner reached mastery level}
                        {instruction on the set of concepts is
                        completed}
                }
```

FIGURE 4.26   Instantiation of rule ID: 3425.

```
if
        and     {       {goal: teach change cost}
                        {knowledge communication change cost
                        has not been presented}
                }

then
        and     {       {assert goal: apply expository tutorial
                        of change cost}
                        {assert goal: content representation of
                        change cost is in the form of a procedure
                        for using a principle}
                }
```

FIGURE 4.27   Instantiation of rule ID: Table 4.4b Strategy.

```
if
            {goal: apply expository tutorial of change cost}
then
    and    {    {assert goal: display expository generality
                 for expository tutorial of change cost}
                 {assert goal: display expository instance
                 for expository tutorial of change cost}
                 {assert goal: display inquisitory instance
                 for expository tutorial of change cost}

           }
```

FIGURE 4.28   Instantiation of rule ID: 3107.

```
if
    and    {    {goal: display expository generality for
                 expository tutorial of change cost}
                 {content representation of change cost
                 is in the form of a procedure for using
                 a principle}

           }

then
    and    {    {display: name/definition of principle
                 change cost}
                 {display: any secondary presentation/
                 explanation of change cost}
                 {display: any prerequisite concept(s)
                 of change cost}
                 {display: prerequisite procedure in which
                 principle change cost is applied}

           }
```

FIGURE 4.29   Instantiation of rule ID: 3108.

if
> {goal: display expository generality for expository tutorial of change cost}

then {highlight the concepts involved in the principle change cost}

DISPLAY:

Name/Definition for Entry 4c "Change Cost"

Finding a fault based on change cost means first performing the tests which are least time consuming, expensive, etc. and saving harder to perform checks or tests to do later, only if they are needed. [SMEs for this system use swapping as diagnostic procedure—other systems might use "test cost" concept.]

Secondary Presentation/Explanation for Entry 4c "Change Cost"

A part with a high change cost is one that is difficult to test, and is therefore less desirable to test initially. A good strategy for quickly and efficiently locating circuit faults is to look first for components that are easiest to test. All else being equal, it is better to test the components that are easiest to test before the components that are harder to test. This strategy, called "finding the fault based on the change cost," tends to reduce the time and effort you spend to make a diagnosis.

Secondary Presentation/Prerequisite Concept of Test Procedure Change Costs for Entry 4c

You will need to be able to estimate the change cost of components which may be faulty. Change cost is determined by a number of factors which you must weigh subjectively to come up with the best estimate. You should rank all of the candidate LRU's by weighing all these factors. When considering these factors, ask yourself "Which would be easiest to test?" Doing the easy tests first saves time, effort, cost, and risk. Below is an example of different kinds of tests, ranked in order of change cost:

Cost of Performing Tests Which Involve Various Factors:

1	2	3	4	5
very low	low	average	high	very high

No removal, e.g.: switch setting or using meter on already connected breakout box; unlug a connector; remove a component; remove a component requiring hydraulics bleed down determine if a cable has an intermittent fault

FIGURE 4.30 Instantiation of rule ID: 3114.

DISCUSSION AND RESEARCH DIRECTIONS

With Rules in Figures 4.1–4.3, students would be taught electronics troubleshooting task strategies using the instructional strategy found in Table 4.4 (Entries 1, 4, and 5). Because our application is to teach troubleshooting task strategies, a pretest would be needed to screen out any students who do not have the prerequisite facts, concepts, procedures, and skills (Table 4.4, Entries 2 and 3). Students experienced in troubleshooting the ITV should get a perfect pretest score, barring error. The pretest is not part of the instructional rules or instantiations for teaching the trouble-shooting task strategies, and so is not included in our designed knowledge base. Likewise, rules for remediation of basic skills posttesting and sequencing are not included. However, we have provided instantiations of instructional strategies for the communication of selected troubleshooting task strategies (e.g., presentation of the principles with examples and practice). In addition, remediation to correct misunderstanding or misapplication of the task strategies themselves, plus a few deficiencies common to even experienced troubleshooters were selectively provided.

An implementor would note the implicit macrosequencing information in Table 4.4. Concepts or principles are taught in the order in which they appear. Microsequencing for teaching the task strategies is indicated in specific rules. At a microlevel, the presentation of each troubleshooting task strategy is followed by practice on the strategy just taught and instruction and practice on synthesizing the new knowledge with any previously taught strategies.

Future Developments

Following are some specific areas in which additional work is needed for the researcher and for the implementor.

Alternate and Parameterized Strategies

One of the requirements for a researcher is to be able to modify and try out variations of the domain-independent instructional strategies (i.e., the provision of "knobs and dials"). For example, the researcher might vary (a) the degree or kind of learner control; (b) the immediacy, amount, or kind of feedback (e.g., guided practice option); (c) performance criteria or branching options after learner performance evaluation (e.g., if fail then ignore/retry/kick out); or (d) the amount or kind of tutorial help or explanations available when requested by learner.

Any of these options could be implemented in a variety of ways. For example, learner control could be optionally "off," "on," or "automatic" (i.e., under control of the tutor). With or without control by the researcher, the default or "automatic" selection of alternative strategies must be specified by metarules that determine the active rule sets.

Review Techniques

In addition to the areas of knowledge base refinement indicated in the previous comments, general refinement of the knowledge communications, rules, and rule classifications are needed. Depending on the degree to which an application is to be developed (i.e., the courseware issue), further work may also be required in specifying rules that are specific to a learner interface. The rules will have to undergo more extensive validation in the areas of consistency and completeness.

Validation is incomplete as we did not implement the rule set. We did, however, check for completeness, consistency, and correctness of the rules. Simulations (via people, not computer software) of rule firing under error-free instruction resulted in rule changes. Furthermore, the knowledge communications were revised so that they now have labels for their constituent parts. These labels would allow the domain-independent sequencing rules to reference displays indirectly, and the instantiations with explicitly coded sequencing of presentations would be eliminated. Our check for consistency and completeness also turned up some inadequate rules, rule conflicts, and misclassifications, that were resolved and resulted in a modified rule set.

Comments on the Experience

The neatly rational description presented here belies an iterative, often stumbling attempt to codify complex decisions in a loosely constrained decision space. In fact, the focus on domain independence may be an oversimplification of the degrees of knowledge structure and implementation independence required to realize any of the anticipated benefits. The kinds of remedial rules that would be worthwhile in our application, for example, depended on the frequency of error types and the kinds of information available to the tutoring module from the diagnostic module. The possibilities for presentation rules, in practice, would be constrained by the user interface. In fact, it is surprising how much we needed to know before we could begin to design a "domain-independent" knowledge base! It must be kept in mind that domain independence is a necessary but not sufficient condition for implementation independence. Any attempt to share strategies among systems builders or researchers at the rule or instantiation level will require a degree of *platform* standardization that does not appear imminent.

Where Are We Now?

We have made a good "first cut" of a domain-independent instructional strategy to teach troubleshooting of an electrical system. Moreover, we have a reasonable rule set to teach aspects of domain-specific task strategies. Our next step is to implement and test our design.

ACKNOWLEDGMENT

The research reported herein was supported in part by the Air Force Human Resources Laboratory, Army Research Institute for the Behavioral and Social Sciences, Office of Naval Research/Defense Advance Research Project Agency, Navy Training Systems Center, and Advance Design Information, Inc. However, the views, opinions, and/or findings contained in this report are the authors' and should not be construed as an official Department position, policy, or decision, unless so designated by other official documentation. The authors wish to thank Dr. Azad Madni for his ongoing intellectual stimulation on the Knowledge Acquisition Project.

REFERENCES

Alexander, P. A., & Judy, J. E. (1988, Winter). The interaction of domain-specific and strategic knowledge in academic performance. *Review of Educational Research, 58*(4), 375–404.

Anderson, R. J., Boyle, C. F., & Reiser, B. J. (1985). Intelligent tutoring systems. *Science, 228,* 456–462.

Baker, E. L., Bradley, C., Aschbacher, P., & Feifer, R. (1985). *Intelligent computer-assisted instruction (ICAI) study.* Los Angeles: UCLA Center for the Study of Evaluation.

Bloom, B. S. (1984, June/July). The 2 sigma problem: The search for methods of group instruction as effective as one-to-one tutoring. *Educational Researcher, 13*(6), 4–15.

Chi, M. T. H., Bassok, M., Lewis, M. W., Reimann, P., & Glaser, R. (1987). Self-explanations: How students study and use examples in learning to solve problems (Tech. Rep. No. 9). Pittsburgh, PA: University of Pittsburgh, Learning Research and Development Center.

Chi, M. T. H., Glaser, R., & Rees, E. (1982). Expertise in problem solving. In R. J.

Sternberg (Ed.), *Advances in the psychology of human intelligence* (Vol. 1, pp. 7–76). Hillsdale, NJ: Lawrence Erlbaum Associates.

Clancey, W. J. (1979). *Transfer of rule-based expertise through tutorial dialogue.* (Report No. CS-769). Stanford, CA: Stanford University, Computer Science Department.

Clancy, W. J. (1987). *Knowledge-based tutoring The GUIDON program.* Cambridge, MA: MIT Press.

Clement, J., Lockhead, J., & Soloway, E. (1980). Positive effects of computer programming on students' understanding of variables and equations. In *Proceedings of the National Association for Computing Machinery Annual Meeting,* (pp 97–99). Nashville, TN.

Dick, W., & Carey, L. (1985). *The systematic design of instruction* (2nd ed.). Glenview, IL: Scott, Foresman.

Ellis, J., Wulfeck, W. H., & Fredericks, P. S. (1979). *The instructional quality inventory: II. User's manual* (NPRDC SR 79-24). San Diego, CA: Navy Personnel Research and Development Center.

Fletcher, J. D. (1988). Intelligent training systems in the military. In S. J. Andriole & G. W. Hopple (Eds.), *Defense applications of artificial intelligence: Progress and prospects.* (pp. 174–189). Lexington, MA: Lexington Books.

Gagné, R. M. (1977). *The conditions of learning* (3rd ed.). New York: Holt, Rinehart & Winston.

Gagné, R. M. (1985). *The conditions of learning and theory of instruction* (4th ed.). New York: Holt, Rinehart & Winson.

Gagné, R. M., Briggs, L. J., & Wager, W. W. (1988). *Principles of instructional design* (3rd ed.). New York: Holt, Rinehart & Winston.

Johnson, W. B., Hunt R. M., Duncan P. C., & *Jeffrey* E. N. (1988, August). *Development and demonstration of microcomputer intelligence for technical training (MITT).* (AFHRL-TP-88-8). Brooks AFB, TX: Air Force Human Resources Laboratory.

Johnson, W. L., & Soloway, E. (1983). PROUST: Knowledge-based program understanding (Report No. 285). New Haven, CT: Yale University, Computer Science Department.

Johnson, W. L., & Soloway, E. (1987). PROUST: An automatic debugger for PASCAL programs. In G. P. Kearsley (Ed.), *Artificial intelligence: Applications and methodology.* Redding, MA: Addison-Wesley.

Kieras, D. E., & Bovair, S. (1983, March). *The role of a mental model in learning to operate a device* (Tech. Rep. No. 13 RZ/DP/TR-83/ONR-13). Tucson: University of Arizona, Department of Psychology.

Konoske, P. J., & Ellis, J. A. (1986, December). *Cognitive factors in learning and retention of procedural tasks* (NPRDC TR 87-14). San Diego, CA: Navy Personnel Research and Development Center.

Lesgold A., Lajoie, S., Bunzo, M., & Eggan, G. (1988, March). *SHERLOCK: A coached practice environment for an electronics troubleshooting job.* Pittsburgh, PA: University of Pittsburgh, Learning Research and Development Center.

McArthur, D., Stasz, C., & Hotta, J. (1987). Learning problem-solving skills in algebra. *Journal of Educational Technology Systems, 15*(3), 303–324.

Merrill, M. D. (1983). Component display theory. In C. M. Reigeluth (Ed.), *Instructional-design theories and models: An overview of their current status* (pp. 279–333). Hillsdale, NJ: Lawrence Erlbaum Associates.

Merrill, M. D. (1987). A lesson based on the component display theory. In C. M. Reigeluth (Ed.), *Instructional theories in action* (pp. 201–244). Hillsdale, NJ: Lawrence Erlbaum Associates.

Merrill, M. D., & Tennyson, R. D. (1977). *Concept teaching: An instructional design guide.* Englewood Cliffs, NJ: Educational Technology.

Merrill, M. D., & Tennyson, R. D. (1978). Concept classification and classification errors as a function of relationships between examples and nonexamples. *Improving Human Performance Quarterly, 7,* 351–364.

Miller, M. L. (1989, January). *A prototype intelligent maintenance tutoring system for troubleshooting the M16A1 automatic rifle.* Army Project No. 2P665502M770) Alexandria, VA: U.S. Army Research Institute for the Behavioral and Social Sciences.

O'Neil, H. F., Jr., Slawson, D. A. & Baker, E. L. (1987) First application's domain-independent and domain-specific instructional strategies for knowledge bases. Sherman Oaks, CA. Advance Design Information.

O'Neil, H. F., Jr., & Spielberger, C. D. (Eds.). (1979). *Cognitive and affective learning strategies.* New York: Academic Press.

O'Neil, H. F., Jr., Anderson, C. L., & Freeman, J. A. (1986). Research in teaching in the Armed Forces. In M. C. Wittrock (Ed.), *Handbook of research on teaching* (3rd ed.). New York: Macmillan.

Park, P., Perez, R. S., & Seidel, R. J. (1987). Intelligent CAI: Old wine in new bottles or a new vintage? In G. P. Kearsley (Ed.), *Artificial intelligence: Applications and methodology.* Reading, MA: Addison-Wesley.

Park, O., & Tennyson, R. D. (1986). Response-sensitive design strategies for sequence order of concepts and presentation form of examples for using computer-based instruction. *Journal of Educational Psychology, 78,* 153–158.

Reigeluth, C. M. (Ed.) (1987). *Instructional theories in action: Lessons illustrating selected theories and models.* Hillsdale, NJ: Lawrence Erlbaum Associates.

Tennyson, R. D., & Park, O. (1980). The teaching of concepts: A review of instructional design research literature. *Review of Educational Research, 50,* 55–70.

Weinstein, C. F., & Mayer, R. F. (1986). The teaching of learning strategies. In M. C. Wittrock (Ed.), *Handbook of research on teaching (3rd ed.)* (pp. 315–327). New York: Macmillan.

Wenger, E. (1987). *Artificial intelligence and tutoring systems.* Los Altos, CA: Morgan Kaufmann.

Wiggs, C., & Perez, R. S. (1988). The use of knowledge acquisition in instructional design. *Computers in Human Behavior, 4,* 257–274.

Winston, P. H. (1977). *Artificial intelligence.* Reading, MA: Addison-Wesley.

Woolf, B., Murray, T., Suthers, T., & Schultz, K. (1988, June). Knowledge primitives for tutoring systems. In *Proceedings of the International Conference on Intelligent Tutoring Systems,* Montreal, Canada.

5

Computer-Aided Instructional Design Systems

Peter Pirolli
University of California, Berkeley

Intelligent tutoring systems (ITSs) are, above all, artifacts for the purpose of instruction. They may be useful objects for scrutiny for scientific and engineering aims, but their ultimate utility will be determined by how well they teach. Therefore, research on ITSs must not only produce particular systems, but also develop systematic bodies of theory and principled methods that can be used to design effective teaching machines. But this is only part of the problem if our goal is to make ITSs a new and integral part of regular education and training. The theories and methods of designing ITSs must be transferred to the hands of the practitioners who design instruction in the public, private, and military sectors.

As Joseph Weizenbaum (1976) said, "the tool is much more than a mere device: it is an agent for change" (p. 18). His statement was part of a larger thesis: The computer is a tool that shapes people's imagination.[1] Here, I propose that computational tools can be used productively to disseminate new knowledge about the design of instruction, and to shape the imagination of practicing instructional designers. Toward this end, this chapter examines several recently developed computer-aided instructional design systems. These systems are computer environments in which users analyze instructional situations, instructional goals, and specify the structure of instructional interactions. Three systems are presented. The first is

---

[1]Weizenbaum was specifically arguing that computation could be used—to his dismay—to produce a mechanized view of man as an instrumental reasoner, to the exclusion of all other views. I am not concerned here with that aspect of his thesis, although it is an important one to ponder.

ISD Expert (Merrill, 1987), which is an expert system based on Merrill's component display theory (Merrill, 1983). The second is Expert CML (Jones & Wipond, in press; Wipond & Jones, 1988), that contains an expert system using knowledge acquired from expert instructional designers. The third system is the Instructional Design Environment (IDE) (Russell, Moran, & Jordan, 1988), which is an augmented hypermedia system for instructional design and development. These systems vary along many dimensions, including capabilities for providing advice, their intended users, and their modifiability. The systems chosen for discussion should illustrate the space of possibilities for computer-aided instructional design.

SIGNIFICANCE OF COMPUTER-AIDED INSTRUCTIONAL DESIGN

There are many who believe that we are in a dark age of education, and there are some who believe we may be on the verge of a renaissance, with computers as the tangible instruments of change (e.g., see recent discussion in Holden, 1989). In this light, it is interesting to reflect on the history of architecture, the most established of design professions, and the source of perhaps the most tangible and long-lasting products of the true Renaissance. In the middle of the 15th century, Leon Battista Alberti wrote a series of volumes, *On the Art of Building in Ten Books* (Alberti, 1450/1988), that many historians (Grayson, 1979; Rykwert, 1979) regard as the first modern treatise on architecture. Alberti was a true Renaissance man in every sense of that word, being well versed in a variety of humanities, arts, and sciences (Gadol, 1969). His work is remarkable because it is based on a reanalysis of ancient writings (in particular the work of the Roman engineer Vitruvius Pollio), the extraction of design principles from the classical Roman architecture that he observed throughout Italy, and the formulation of a theoretical basis for the practices of Brunelleschi and other contemporary builders at the beginnings of the Italian Renaissance. Alberti did more than collect a compendium of principles and practices; he developed a theoretical framework that rationalized the form of buildings based on contemporary notions of perspective, nature, and beauty.

Indeed, Alberti's work on the art of building was revolutionary because it described how buildings of the future *were to be* built, in contrast to earlier work that revered how buildings *had been* built (Rykwert, 1988). Alberti's framework was both systematic and generative and, more than any other work, was probably responsible for the rapid spread and evolution of Renaissance architecture (Raeburn, 1980). The essential aspects of Alberti's work remained a dominant view of architecture until at least the mid-19th century (Raeburn, 1980). If we seek to foster a technological renaissance in education, then we do not need discussions of how particular systems *were* built. Rather, we must have a systematic and generative theory of how tutoring systems *are to be* built.

Although the rapid spread of Renaissance architecture was facilitated by the availability of a systematic and generative theory of design, it also benefited from a wonderful new technology for disseminating knowledge: the printing press. In fact, Alberti's *On the Art of Building* was the first printed book on architecture, preceding the printed edition of the more ancient treatise of Vitruvius by a year (Rykwert, 1979). All of us are likely to agree that once again we have a wonderful new technology for disseminating knowledge at our doorstep: computational media. To workers in the field of ITSs, the idea that design practices can be disseminated using computers should not be foreign.

Thus, past history illustrates the importance of abstracting, systematizing, and disseminating principles of design. More recent history also shows how important this process is, as well as the importance of investing in the development of tools and design practices that insure the quality of the final products while increasing the efficiency of the design process. One of the major bottlenecks in the maturation of a technology is the transfer of engineering and production processes out of the research labs into mainstream industry. Research labs are simply not in the business of meeting the demands of the real marketplace. In the case of educational technology, the transfer issue is especially important. There is a long history indicating the ramifications of failing to make this transfer (Cuban, 1986). In the first third of this century, film and radio were touted as revolutionary approaches to instruction. In the second third of the century, it was television. In the last third, it is computers. In each case, the educational impact of the technology did not live up to the expectations of its proponents. Cuban (1986) argued that part of this failure is due to the ownership of the technology by researchers rather than members of the mainstream educational system. Practitioners' resistance to new technology was partly due to their perception that it did not fit their particular instructional problems, and often, practitioners did not have a deep understanding of the rationale for the new technology. Transferring educational technology out of the labs is important to its widespread acceptance.

So it is important that we develop and disseminate engineering methods and tools for building ITSs. Along these lines, there has been progress in work on development environments aimed at streamlining the software and knowledge engineering aspects of ITS development. Such work includes the development of ITS shells (Woolf, chap. 6, this volume), interface development environments (Bonar, chap. 3, this volume), and knowledge engineering tools tailored for ITSs (Clancey, 1987). One could argue that these tools provide the basic materials for constructing ITSs. However, whether designing buildings or instruction, one must have a well thoughtout plan in addition to the materials. Instructional design should provide the plans that structure the media of ITSs for efficient and effective communication of knowledge.

In this regard, it is worth noting an earlier evaluation of the PLATO computer-assisted instruction (CAI) system (see O'Shea & Self, 1983). PLATO development environments were disseminated to a large number of parties, and eventually about 3,000 authors contributed 8,000 hours of PLATO instruction. The evaluations were mixed, largely due to high variability in the quality and quantity of instructional design effort involved in the various pieces of PLATO instruction. Although software development environments may be necessary to the production of computer-based instruction, they do not appear to be sufficient to insure that the instruction is successful.

It seems apparent that an investment should be made in the development and dissemination of instructional design methods and tools that are tailored for building ITSs. One way to do this is to copy the approach taken to the development of software and knowledge engineering tools. Specifically, we could attempt to develop computational environments that support and streamline the instructional design process. The computer-aided instructional design systems discussed here are early developments along this path. In sum, (a) it is critical that the engineering and production processes for ITSs move out of the research labs into the field, (b) that instructional design is a necessary and crucial part of this process, and (c) that computer-aided instructional design systems are a potential conduit for moving the instructional design of ITSs out of the research labs, and furthermore, for increasing the effectiveness and efficiency of instructional design in general.

INSTRUCTIONAL DESIGN

Traditionally, instructional design theories attempt to specify the space of instructional *situations,* to identify the space of instructional *methods,* and to develop statements, called *principles* or *theories,* that link these spaces (Reigeluth, 1983). The analysis of instructional situations is taken broadly to include the effects of instructional methods, usually called instructional *outcomes,* and the *conditions* that affect the outcomes and use of those methods. Such conditions include the subject matter, the instructional setting, properties of the targeted learners, and the nature of the learning task.

Principles of instruction are taken to be those statements that characterize elementary building blocks for instructional methods. *Descriptive* principles are scientific statements about the effects of a particular method under given conditions. *Prescriptive* principles are the kind of statement used in design to identify the optimal method to use in a given situation. Instructional theories are systematically related sets of principles that deal with larger and more integrated sets of methods, describing outcomes and prescribing methods in given situations. Comprehensive instructional theories are intended to provide the knowledge base for solving the problems of instruction by providing the rules and constraints for forming efficient and effective instructional interactions.

Elsewhere (Pirolli & Greeno, 1988), we have looked at traditional views of the instructional world, such as work in the paradigm of Gagné and Briggs (1979), and asked how that view is expanding and changing with developments in ITSs and cognitive science. The analysis of instructional situations has been enhanced greatly by richer and more detailed characterizations of the knowledge to be acquired by students and of the cognitive states of students throughout an instructional process. For example, Anderson's (1988) review of kinds of expert modules in ITSs indicates the variety of ways of representing detailed knowledge targeted as instructional outcomes, including ways of representing declarative knowledge, procedural knowledge, and qualitative process models. Analysis of the conditions for instruction has been greatly enhanced by similarly rich and detailed student modeling techniques (VanLehn, 1988), that provide a means for tracking subtle changes in students' cognitive states during instructional interactions rather than broader characterizations of the student populations.

Commensurate with the evolution of more detailed ways of representing knowledge has been the evolution of techniques for the empirical analysis of behavior, largely deriving from work on verbal protocols (Ericsson & Simon, 1984; Kuipers & Kassirer, 1984). Research on interface design and tutoring strategies is expanding the space of instructional methods, and many authors (Anderson, Boyle, & Reiser, 1985; Towne & Munro, 1988) have attempted to formulate principles to prescribe their conditions of use. Finally, there are attempts to produce tighter couplings of theories of instruction to theories of learning, and to develop systematic accounts of social patterns of activity and their relations to the development of metacognition, epistemology, and social practice (Pirolli & Greeno, 1988).

It would be beneficial for practicing instructional designers to use these new ways of looking at instruction to structure their approaches to problem solving. The new analytic techniques more accurately capture knowledge acquisition, performance, and transfer (Singley & Anderson, 1989). In addition, the new instructional methods can achieve at least a standard deviation improvement in efficiency and effectiveness over traditional group-oriented instruction (Anderson, Boyle, Corbett, & Lewis, in press). Unfortunately, there are no broad integrative theories of instruction arising out of the new cognitive science perspective. However, given the variety of instructional problems addressed by ITSs, it may be absolutely necessary to forego general prescriptive theories and opt for methodologies tailored to specific classes of training and instruction.

Another way to characterize instructional design is to view the design process as problem solving (see Goel & Pirolli, 1989, for a discussion of design problem solving). At a very general level, instructional design could be characterized as a search in problem spaces. The states of the search process would mainly represent models of instructional conditions, desired outcomes, and instructional methods. In other words, the problem states would be partial developments of the instructional design. Operators in this search process would be mainly concerned with proposing, adding, removing, elaborating, modifying, and evaluating the elements that make up a particular design.

This very general characterization of design is, of course, overly simplistic; design is an ill-structured task, typically involving search in many problem spaces, and greatly influenced by available knowledge (Goel & Pirolli, 1989; Reitman, 1964; Simon, 1973). In design, typically there are many degrees of freedom or substantial lack of information in the problem definition. Consequently, design problems require substantial analysis, negotiation, and structuring. There is delayed or limited feedback from the world during problem solving, yet actions in the world have costs (e.g., time and money) and there are penalties for being wrong. This suggests that a substantial amount of performance modeling of the artifact must take place during problem solving. Furthermore, design problems tend to be large, complex, and require problem solving over the course of days, months, or even years. Consequently, the size and complexity of problems require management through problem decomposition and the correlated use of abstraction hierarchies in the specification of an artifact.

In a sense, instructional theories concern what constitutes a good blueprint for instruction. The design process involves problem solving that searches for those good blueprints for specific problems. To be effective, computer environments for instructional design should promote the creation of good blueprints and make the search task simpler and less effortful. The use of such environments should be structured in ways that support or constrain users in ways that usually result in good instruction, and the environments should include functionality that augments the limited capacities of the human problem solver.

COMPUTER-BASED INSTRUCTIONAL DESIGN SYSTEMS

Several computer-based systems for instructional design are under current development. Although none are in widespread use, it is useful to examine their form and function with an eye toward future possibilities. Three systems are discussed in some detail here. The first is ISD Expert (Merrill, 1987), which is the prototype for an expert system consultant for instructional developers. The second is CML Expert (Jones & Wipond, in press; Wipond & Jones, 1988), a prototype of an expert system that monitors and provides advice on curriculum and course development. The third system is the Instructional Design Environment (IDE), an augmented hypermedia system (Russell et al., 1988; Russell et al., 1989) that has been mainly used in technical training and foreign language instruction.

ISD Expert

ISD Expert (Merrill, 1987) is a prototype expert system intended for use as a consultation system by inexperienced instructional designers. It has been implemented in an expert system shell, and contains several hundred rules. Use of the system assumes that the user has already done some analysis involving the identification of student attributes, subject matter knowledge, and the goals of the instruction. The user enters into a dialog with the system, eventually producing an output consisting of a set of specifications and recommendations for a course design.

It is apparent that the model of instruction underlying ISD Expert (Merrill, 1987) derives from work in the Gagné and Briggs (1979) approach to instruction, and particularly on the more recent integrative theories of Merrill (1983) concerning instructional presentations for specific concepts, principles, and skills, and of Reigeluth and Stein (1983) concerning the organization of lesson modules and courses. Figure 5.1 illustrates the components of this model underlying ISD Expert. The inputs to the process are specifications of instructional goals, subject matter knowledge, and student attributes. Using these inputs, a *content structure* is constructed. A content structure is an organization of subject matter content. A particular organization will also depend on goals and student attributes. Based on the content structure, goals, and student

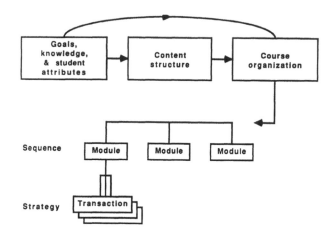

FIGURE 5.1 The model of instructional design underlying ISD Expert.

attributes, a *course organization* is constructed. This determines the paths a student may take through the components of instruction. This organization consists of *modules,* which are comprised of some *representation of content,* a set of *transactions,* and a set of *strategy rules.* Transactions are communicative actions or activities fulfilling some instructional function. *Sequencing rules* organize modules and strategy rules organize transactions.

ISD Expert is in part dependent on a frame-based representation of various types of content structures, course organizations, strategies, and transactions. ISD Expert also has a rule-based component used to select and refine particular frames given that other frames have been selected and partially or fully instantiated. Although a substantial amount of knowledge has to be acquired from a user in order to construct a particular design, there is also a substantial amount of knowledge that is embedded within the system. The source of this knowledge is based directly on instructional theory, as opposed to knowledge acquired from the study of practicing instructional design experts.

It is interesting to note that ISD Expert not only knows what methods will achieve which goals, but it can also recommend a space of alternative methods with graded degrees of confidence across the alternatives. This is basically an extension of the technique of accumulating certainty factors in diagnostic expert systems. For example, to provide an overview, the system (on a scale of −1 to +1) might recommend a synthesis transaction with a certainty of .40, a summary transaction with certainty of .30, and an exposition with certainty of .10.

Although ISD Expert is currently just a prototype for a consultation system, it has some interesting properties:

- It suggests that substantial amounts of knowledge about instructional design can be embedded in an expert system.
- Such knowledge can be used to drive designers through territory they are not familiar with, providing advice, suggestions, or even making decisions.
- The rationale for the design can be reconstructed by tracing through the expert system rules that were involved in the creation of a particular set of instructional specifications.

Expert CML

Jones and Wipond (in press; Wipond & Jones, 1988) have been engaged in the development of an expert computer-managed learning system (Expert CML) that has many similarities to ISD Expert. The Expert CML system is designed to have four main components, called *phases*. Phase 1 of Expert CML is a curriculum development environment. Phase 2 is a course development environment. Phase 3 is a system that manages students' progress through courses. Phase 4 is a component that deals with the evaluation of students, courses, and curricula. Here discussion is focused on Phases 1 and 2.

In contrast to ISD Expert, the knowledge base for Phases 1 and 2 of Expert CML was acquired from experts in curriculum and course development. Jones and Wipond (in press) report that these experts were university researchers and practitioners with many years of experience who were studied in structured interviews and in solving simple instructional design problems. Although none of the experts followed a single instructional model, they exhibited substantial agreement on a number of instructional design principles (Jones & Wipond, in press). Knowledge acquisition from experts was also augmented by a literature review of instructional design.

The audience for Expert CML is expected to vary in curriculum and course design expertise. The expert system component acts as a monitor that oversees the users' development activities. To meet variations in user expertise, the monitor is designed to provide sufficient guidance for novices, yet be unobtrusive enough to avoid hindering experts. The interaction is intended to be controlled by the user, rather than the expert system.

Curricula and courses are designed by specifying the entities from which they are built and the relationships among those entities. Such entities include things such as courses, modules within courses, the learning objectives that students will have to meet, and the learning activities that will take place. Like ISD Expert, these entities are represented in a frame-based scheme. A core set of frames is provided in Expert

CML. Each frame for an entity may have many attributes and may have default values for some attributes. Although the core entities cannot be changed by the user, new entities may be created as modifications of the core items. These new entities are connected to the core items by links that permit inheritance of features and default values from the core items.

At any point in the development process, the current design is represented as a collection of facts, that are instantiations of frames representing a curriculum. The rule-based component of Expert CML contains rules that match against this fact database and the current action performed by the user, and provides guidance concerning problems with the design specification, corrective actions, or the next steps to take. These monitoring activities of Expert CML are captured by *expertise* and *advice* rules. Expertise rules capture instructional design principles for curricula and courses. These rules basically appraise the quality of the instructional blueprints specified by a user and notify the user when rules are violated. When several violations occur, they are assigned dynamically computed priorities (Jones & Wipond, in press). Advice rules structure the problem solving in design by suggesting the next task to be carried out.

Expert CML encourages a top-down refinement scheme, although users are not constrained to progress in this manner. In Phase 1, *curriculum development,* the top-most level of the design concerns the specification of departments and programs within departments. The next level concerns the specification of a curriculum framework, which defines the basic entities that will make up the curriculum and relationships among those entities. A default framework is provided that can be modified by users in restricted ways (Wipond & Jones, 1988). The default framework includes entities that can represent courses within programs, topics and subtopics, modules and submodules, learning objectives, evaluation items (tests), and learning activities. Prerequisite and corequisite relationships among topics and modules can also be represented. The next level of refinement concerns the specification of course content, including the goals of courses, topics, and subtopics, time estimates, and prerequisite and corequisite relationships among topics and modules. Finally, specific modules are developed, with associated learning objectives, activities, and evaluation items.

An important component of Expert CML is the specification of taxonomies that are used to categorize module objectives, learning activities, evaluation items, and resources in ways that allow the system to determine the completeness of modules and the ordering of the curriculum. Some of these taxonomies are derived from the instructional design literature and include classifications for cognitive, affective, and psychomotor objectives. When objectives are specified for individual modules, the user includes specifications of the criteria that must be satisfied by some performance on the part of a student and the conditions under which the objective will be demonstrated. The system ensures that module objectives are complete and consistent using information specified in the taxonomies. In addition, the user can specify time estimates, difficulty rating, and criticality ratings for individual modules, and these can be used by the system to check that various constraints (e.g., the total duration of the course) are not being violated.

In phase 2, *course design,* the user selects portions of curricula developed in phase 1 to be delivered to some particular group of students over some specific time frame. The paths that students can take through the instruction is specified, along with scheduling constraints, and grading schemes. The user can also specify templates that will automatically create study guides for individual modules based on module specifications. The system can employ information about prerequisite and corequisite relationships to insure that the course structure selected by the user does not violate specifications developed in phase 1.

The Instructional Design Environment

In contrast to ISD Expert and Expert CML the Instructional Design Environment (IDE) centers on experienced users driving their way through the system. IDE (Russell et al., 1988; Russell et al., 1989) is a hypermedia system in which instructional designers can enter, edit, and manipulate their analyses and specifications. Information is entered into *notecards* and relations among notecards can be specified by *links* of various *link types.* Notecards are of a variety of *card types,* and with each card type is an associated *substance.* Substances are essentially different kinds of media, such as text, graphical browsers, sketches, animations, and so forth, each coming with its own set of editing operations, and perhaps default content (for example, a set of slots to be filled, or icons that act as buttons to generate sets of actions). Notecards and links can be organized in *notefiles,* and notecards may contain *cross-links* across notefiles.

Figure 5.2 presents a conceptual view of a possible notecard structure in IDE, with notecards represented by boxes and ovals, and links represented by lines and arrows. At the top of Figure 5.2 is an analysis of subject matter that organizes material around the functional decomposition of a device into subsystems and parts, and associated analyses of relevant concepts and tasks. At the bottom of Figure 5.2 is part of a maze representing an abstract view of the structure of a piece of interactive videodisc instruction.

IDE is not coupled to any particular design methodology and consequently exists in a variety of forms, each tailored to the specific needs

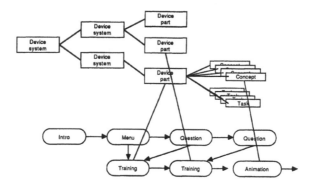

FIGURE 5.2 A heterogeneous mix of cards and links in IDE hypermedia analysis.

or interests of its users. Particular designers or groups of designers may tend to use specific ways of representing their analyses and specifications. To capture these regularities, new card types are developed. In a fairly compelling way, these task-specific card types are analogous to the frame-based representations used in ISD Expert and Expert CML. The card types are used to encode particular kinds of content representation (e.g., concepts, tasks, skills, device components) and various kinds of instructional presentations and organizations. These card types usually contain fields that the user is expected to fill in or that already contain default information. Sets of common actions, that can be captured by menus and action-generating buttons associated with particular card types are associated with particular representations. These common operations are analogous to the knowledge encoded in the rule-based component of ISD Expert. The construction of new card types and associated actions is available to designers through a relatively simple set of tools.

Basically, users of IDE create, organize, and manipulate complex networks of interlinked notecards. These notecard networks may be created in an unrestricted manner, or according to prespecified structures. For example, *component* cards linked together by *subcomponent* links can be used to represent the hierarchical structure of some device. Figure 5.3 shows two component cards. On the left of Figure 5.3 is a component card, with fields for information about the name of a machine part, its function, its part number, possible failure modes, and associated repair tasks. On the right side of Figure 5.3 is a component card that has been filled in. The icons enclosed by rectangles inside of the component card in Figure 5.3 are called *link icons*. These icons represent links to other notecards and, when activated (using a mouse), bring up a window containing the contents of the linked card. IDE tools created for such networks of component cards

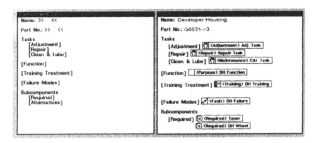

FIGURE 5.3 An unfilled (left) and filled (right) Component card.

can be used to generate parts lists or the expected failure rates based on other information specified in the component cards. Other kinds of networks may have other kinds of tools associated with them.

The component card in Figure 5.3 also contains several autolink buttons, which are enclosed in square brackets in the body of the card. These autolink buttons are usually specified in the definition of the various card types, and are inherited by any instantiation of such card types. When activated by the user (by using a mouse), an autolink button will generate new links of prespecified types that point to existing cards or new cards of prespecified types. Although the user is usually free to create and link cards of any types, the autolinks provide an implicit default structure and greatly speed up the creation of IDE card networks.

IDE also comes with capabilities for organizing related sets of card types and tools into *modes* that can be associated with the specific subtasks associated with design. For instance, in working with several instructional design groups (Russell et al., 1989), IDE developers structured IDE to have modes for (a) data collection, (b) task analysis/structuring knowledge, (c) sequencing, (d) delivery, and (e) evaluation. The data collection mode is meant to be used during the early stages of design when the main task is simply collecting incoming information and notes. The task analysis/ knowledge structuring mode supports the development of analyses of subject matter. The sequencing mode is used to organize the content with respect to the instructional goals and student attributes. The delivery mode is used to sketch out, or actually specify the particular instruction in the media of choice. The evaluation mode is used to collect feedback from the implementation of the course.

The basic card and link types provided in IDE can be extended in order to meet the representational demands of new design tasks. Card and link types are defined in an inheritance hierarchy and users can create new card types based on existing ones. This is very much like the kinds of extensions that were possible for the Expert CML hierarchy of frames.

Templates can be laid out within new card types to specify the various
fields, default values, and autolink buttons that will be associated with the
card types. When new cards of these new types are created, they will
contain all of the specified template information.

As suggested earlier, a variety of IDE tools have been created to
facilitate certain tasks associated with particular kinds of IDE card
networks. Perhaps the most commonly used tool is the *browser*. A browser
collects card types and link types specified by the user, from some source
node, and displays this network graphically. Figure 5.4 depicts an IDE
browser. Cards are represented by rectangular nodes and links are depicted
as lines between nodes. Browsers come with a set of editing tools that allow
the user to rapidly access, modify, and extend the depicted network
structure. The *search tool* can be used to find and collect cards meeting
certain conjunctive or disjunctive specifications of field information. This
tool acts very much like a database retrieval function that looks for cards
with specific internal structure. In contrast, the *collection tool* looks for cards
of a specific type that emanate certain kinds of links. This tool acts like a
database function that looks for cards with a specific external structure.

Cluster tools identify similar sets of cards according to some metric
provided by the user. Such tools are useful when analyses have been
performed by different designers who used idiosyncratic card types, link
types, field names, and field values. Cluster tools can be used to search
through the products of the different designers for common or distinct
network substructures. The *link follower* traverses a network along links of
a specified type, displaying encountered cards in the order that they are
encountered, and allowing the user to select among choices when the
network branches. This tool is especially useful when the designer wishes
to step through the frames that represent the specific pieces of instruction
in a complex branching structure that will be presented to students.
Finally, the laserdisc toolbox is a collection of tools that connect IDE to an
interactive videodisc. Using these tools, IDE can be used to access, create,
and modify segments of an interactive videodisc.

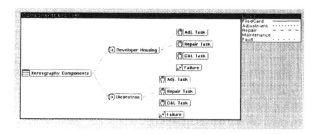

FIGURE 5.4 A browser for a network of component cards.

IDE has been used in the design of instruction for a variety of media, including text, interactive videodisc, and as a driver for an ITS. Russell (1988) described the ITS architecture (IDE-Interpreter) that can take as input a set of specifications output from IDE. Based on their experience, Russell and colleagues (1989) noted some interesting properties of IDE:

- Although hypermedia is too ill-structured to be used as a true database management system, it can act as a vast repository of heterogeneous information, and many kinds of queries can be answered through direct inspection or automatic search techniques tailored for specific tasks.
- Analyses, specifications, and other products are available in a shareable and inspectable form. In some cases, IDE collaborations have taken place across the country.
- Permanent storage of structured and inspectable designs permits the reuse of analyses and specifications, the modification of materials to meet changing needs, and reanalysis of existing designs to extract principles or identify problems.
- The creation of representation types and tools implicitly creates a design standard and allows a design methodology to evolve through time.

SUMMARY

The three computer-based instructional design systems can be contrasted along a number of dimensions. First, consider the intended audience for each system. ISD Expert was designed to be used by rank novices in instructional design. Such a system might be particularly useful for subject matter experts or programmers who seek to develop instruction. At the other extreme is IDE, which assumes an audience of sophisticated instructional designers. In between the extremes is Expert CML, that is intended to cater to users with various levels of expertise.

Commensurate with the intended audience is the degree of constraint and guidance used by the system to shape the designs of users. IDE provides some degree of implicit structuring by providing a set of default modes, which contain an implicit standard for representing instructional analyses and specifications. However, the user is given a great deal of freedom to change the existing representations. Furthermore, it is up to designers to include information concerning the rationale for their design, and to check that the design meets desired principles. Currently, IDE does not have mechanisms that check the quality of a user's instructional design.

In contrast, ISD Expert constrains the user to develop instructional specifications according to specific instructional principles. The expert system knowledge of ISD Expert guides the user through the design process, sometimes automatically making decisions, and also notifies the user of violations. The basic entities for representing instruction, and the rules that check the quality of the design are not open for modification by the user. Expert CML appears to be less constraining than ISD Expert. Expert CML uses its expert system knowledge to unobtrusively suggest both tasks to be performed and violations of instructional principles. However, the user can choose to ignore this advice and expertise. The basic representation scheme used in the design is open for some restricted modifications by the user, but the rules that advise on task sequencing and principle violations are not.

The knowledge bases for ISD Expert and CML Expert were constructed in very different ways. In ISD Expert, the knowledge base derives from instructional design theory. In Expert CML much of the knowledge was acquired from expert curriculum designers, although the literature on instructional theory was also consulted. There are probably costs and benefits to consider when deciding between theory-based or expert-based approaches for the development of knowledge bases for expert instructional design systems. Human experts may have many experience-based heuristics that sit outside of current instructional theory. They may also have substantial situation-specific knowledge that is much more efficient to use than knowledge consisting of very general principles. In addition, the way that experts think about the structure of the task may be more suitable for efficient human-computer interaction.

On the other hand, computers have different capacities than humans and could precisely deploy theory-based knowledge in ways that might prove unwieldy for even the best of experts. Heuristics, situation-specific knowledge, and the structuring of design tasks evolve in experts in reaction to their experience and the limitations of human information processing. Theory-based knowledge could possibly generalize to novel design problems and be deployed in ways that are impossible for humans to carry out with certainty. For instance, modern engineering theory behind bridge design has allowed us to go beyond the rules of thumb used even 100 years ago, and computers can perform stress analyses of complex structures much more accurately and speedily than the best of experts.

In organizations that have large, rapidly changing training requirements, such as large industries and the military, expert system approaches to design may be particularly useful. One of the major problems in such organizations is ensuring that instruction is designed under the same standards. This implies that design knowledge has been disseminated appropriately to instructional developers within the organization. For instance, in the early 1970s, the U.S. military began a massive effort in distilling and disseminating a systematic approach to instructional design.

These efforts produced the Instructional System Design (ISD) methodology. Despite many excellent training courses developed under ISD, there are indications that the methodology never quite lived up to its initial high expectations. For example, a report by the U.S. Army Training Board (U.S. Department of the Army, 1985, cited in Anderson, 1986) charges that most Army training products were not designed, developed, or validated scientifically — the precise purpose of the ISD approach. Anderson (1986) suggested that this failure was partly due to a lack of training and onsite guidance for the corps of professional designers employed by the military. A second factor was the lack of "enforcement" of ISD analysis and specification. The expert systems used in ISD Expert and Expert CML were developed specifically to address such problems of disseminating effective design knowledge and ensuring that it gets used.

However, Anderson (1986) suggested additional shortcomings in the deployment of the ISD methodology. One was the implicit assumption in ISD that tasks (that were the target of instruction) occurred in a stable environment, both across subunits of the organization and across time. Correlated with this was the assumption that these tasks were clearly articulated and defined. In reality, student populations varied with recruitment criteria; new technology and skills were continually being integrated into practice, and the jobs required of personnel varied greatly, depending on the inventory of equipment assigned to them, their missions, and coworkers. A related problem was the focus of ISD on training specific tasks, such as repair of a particular piece of equipment, rather than the basic knowledge and skills that permit continuous on-the-job training over a tour of duty. Although Anderson's critique is focused on ISD, these are problems that would be faced by any implementation of a new design methodology in a large, heterogeneous, rapidly changing work organization. In this light, the high degree of modifiability of IDE, permitting it to evolve through time in the hands of users, and to evolve into different versions appropriate for different kinds of instructional problems, is a highly desirable feature.

Neither ISD Expert or Expert CML use knowledge that directly addresses the design of ITSs — probably because instructional theory in that area is in its infancy and there are so few experts. Although IDE can be coupled to an ITS architecture, there has been very little experience with its use. Despite the lack of broad integrative design theories for ITSs, there are many important developments. Several researchers (e.g., Anderson et al., 1985; Towne & Munro, 1988) have suggested design principles for ITSs. Techniques for task analysis, based on artificial intelligence (AI) methods of knowledge representation, have been developed (Singley & Anderson, 1989; Kieras & Polson, 1985) and shown to be very good predictors of task learnability (Polson, Bovair, & Kieras, 1987) and across-task transfer (Pirolli & Bielaczyc, 1989; Singley & Anderson, 1989). For instance, Kieras and Polson (1985) developed a production system formalism for characterizing task-related knowledge and a generalized augmented transition network formalism for capturing device operations that can be useful in capturing man–machine interactions. Using these formalisms, they have had a great deal of success in predicting the learnability of text editors (Polson et al., 1987). Similar success has been achieved in the analysis of other cognitive skills such as computer programming, calculus, and geometry, and specifically in the context of instruction using ITSs (Pirolli & Bielaczyc, 1989; Singley & Anderson, 1989).

Protocol analysis techniques have played an important role in the study of cognition and the development of ITSs. The work of Means and Gott (1988) illustrates a protocol analysis technique that can be used even when the analyst knows very little about the subject matter area. The technique, called the two-expert method, basically involves having two experts develop problems and give them to each other. In the process, the expert gives verbal protocols of problem solutions, sketches relevant models, identifies relevant resources, and identifies alternative solution paths. Much of the work surrounds the development of a graphical representation of relevant portions of the problems space. Such techniques and associated graphical representations seem ideal for a computer-based medium.

In the field of ITSs, the selection and organization of instructional content has received less attention than the analysis of expert and student knowledge. There have been some interesting exceptions to this rule. For instance, Kieras (1988) began to develop heuristics for specifying the mental models of devices to be taught in association with particular tasks. Rational task analysis, domain experts, and relevant device documentation serve as background information. Then, the knowledge making up a mental model (how a device works) is selected based on its relevance to task goals, the accessibility of system components to inspection or manipulation, and explanations of critical procedures. In general though, the forte of traditional instructional design theory is its development of methods for developing larger-scale curricula and courses, an area that is only beginning to receive attention in the development of ITSs (e.g., Lesgold, 1988).

Thus, current computer-aided instructional design systems illustrate some of the ways that design knowledge can be represented and used. However, thus far these systems have been based on traditional theories of instructional design. We are also at a point when new design principles and methods are emerging from the fields of ITSs and cognitive science. Computer-aided design systems, integrating tools for knowledge engineering, software design, and a new way of instructional design, could well put

ITSs into the mainstream. As Leon Battista Alberti (1988/1450) wrote, "There is no reason why we should follow [the traditionalists] design in our work, as though legally obliged; but rather, inspired by their example, we should strive to produce our own inventions, to rival, or if possible, to surpass the glory of theirs" (p. 24).

ACKNOWLEDGMENTS

The writing of this chapter was supported in part by the Office of Naval Research, contract N0014-88-0233, and funding from the National Center for Research in Vocational Education. I would like to thank Dan Russell for many conversations about the ideas presented in this chapter.

REFERENCES

Alberti, L. B. (1988). *On the art of building in ten books.* (J. Rykwert, N. Leach, & R. Tavernor, Trans.). Cambridge, MA: MIT Press. (Original work published 1450)

Anderson, C. L. (1986). *Where did we go wrong? An analysis of the way Instructional Systems Development was mustered out of the Army.* Paper presented at the Annual Meeting of the American Educational Research Association.

Anderson, J. R. (1988). The expert module. In M. C. Polson & J. J. Richardson (Eds.), *Foundations of intelligent tutoring systems* (pp. 21–53). Hillsdale, NJ: Lawrence Erlbaum Associates.

Anderson, J. R., Boyle, C. F., Corbett, A., & Lewis, M. W. (in press). Cognitive modelling and intelligent tutoring. *Artificial Intelligence.*

Anderson, J. R., Boyle, C. F., & Reiser, B. J. (1985). Intelligent tutoring systems. *Science, 228,* 456–462.

Clancy, W. J. (1987). *Knowledge-based tutoring.* Cambridge, MA: MIT Press.

Cuban, L. (1986). *Teachers and machines.* New York: Teachers College Press.

Ericsson, K. A., & Simon, H. A. (1984). *Protocol analysis: Verbal reports as data.* Cambridge, MA: MIT Press.

Gadol, J. (1969). *Leon Battista Alberti, universal man of the early Renaissance.* Chicago: University of Chicago Press.

Gagné, R. M., & Briggs, L. J. (1979). *Principles of instructional design* (2nd ed.). New York: Holt, Rhinehart & Winston.

Goel, V., & Pirolli, P. (1989). Motivating the notion of generic design within information processing theory: The design problem space. *AI Magazine, 10,* 18–36.

Grayson, C. (1979). Leon Battista Alberti, architect. *Architectural Design, 49,* 7–17.

Holden, C. (1989, May). Computers make slow progress in class. *Science, 244,* 906–909.

Jones, M., & Wipond, K. (in press). Intelligent environments for curriculum and course development. In P. Goodyear (Ed.), *Teaching knowledge and intelligent tutoring.* Norwood, NJ: Ablex.

Kieras, D. E. (1988). What mental model should be taught: Choosing instructional content for complex engineered systems. In J. Psotka, L. D. Massey, & S. A. Mutter (Eds.),

Intelligent tutoring systems: Lessons learned (pp. 85–111). Hillsdale, NJ: Lawrence Erlbaum Associates.

Kieras, D. E., & Polson, P. G. (1985). An approach to the formal analysis of user complexity. *International Journal of Man–Machine Studies, 22,* 365–394.

Kuipers, B., & Kassirer, J. P. (1984). Causal reasoning in medicine: Analysis of a protocol. *Cognitive Science, 8,* 305–336.

Lesgold, A. (1988). Toward a theory of curriculum for use in designing intelligent instructional systems. In H. Mandl & A. Lesgold (Eds.), *Learning issues for intelligent tutoring systems* (pp. 114–137). New York: Springer-Verlag.

Means, B., & Gott, S. P. (1988). Cognitive task analysis as a basis for tutor development: Articulating abstract knowledge representations. In J. Psotka, L. D. Massey, & S. A. Mutter (Eds.), *Intelligent tutoring systems: Lessons learned* (pp. 35–57). Hillsdale, NJ: Lawrence Erlbaum Associates.

Merrill, M. D. (1983). Component display theory. In C. M. Reigeluth (Ed.), *Instructional-design theories and models* (pp. 279–333). Hillsdale, NJ: Lawrence Erlbaum Associates.

Merrill, M. D. (1987). An expert system for instructional design. *IEEE Expert, 2,* 25–37.

O'Shea, T., & Self, J. (1983). *Learning and teaching with computers.* Englewood Cliffs, NJ: Prentice-Hall.

Pirolli, P., & Bielaczyc, K. (1989). Empirical analyses of self-explanation and transfer in learning to program. In *Proceedings of the Annual Meeting of the Cognitive Science Society* (pp. 450–457). Hillsdale, NJ: Lawrence Erlbaum Associates.

Pirolli, P., & Greeno, J. G. (1988). The problem space of instructional design. In J. Psotka, L. D. Massey, & S. A. Mutter (Eds.), *Intelligent tutoring systems: Lessons learned* (pp. 181–201). Hillsdale, NJ: Lawrence Erlbaum Associates.

Polson, P. G., Bovair, S. & Kieras, D. (1987). Transfer between text editors. In J. M. Carroll & P. Tanner (Eds.), *Proceedings of the CHI '87 Human Factors in Computing and Graphics Interface Conference* (pp. 27–32). New York: Association for Computing Machinery.

Raeburn, M. (1980). *Architecture of the western world.* New York: Rizzoli.

Reigeluth, C. M. (1983). Instructional design: What is it and why is it? In C. M. Reigeluth (Ed.), *Instructional design theories and models: An overview of their current status* (pp. 3–36). Hillsdale, NJ: Lawrence Erlbaum Associates.

Reigeluth, C. M., & Stein, F. S. (1983). The elaboration theory of instruction. In C. M. Reigeluth (Ed.), *Instructional-design theories and models* (pp. 335–381). Hillsdale, NJ: Lawrence Erlbaum Associates.

Reitman, W. R. (1964). Heuristic decision procedures, open constraints, and the structure of ill-defined problems. In M. W. Shelly & G. L. Bryan (Eds.), *Human judgements and optimality* (pp. 282–315). New York: Wiley.

Russell, D. M. (1988). IDE: The interpreter. In J. Psotka, L. D. Massey, & S. A. Mutter (Eds.), *Intelligent tutoring systems: Lessons learned* (pp. 323–349). Hillsdale, NJ: Lawrence Erlbaum Associates.

Russell, D. M., Moran, T. P., & Jordan, D. S. (1988). The instructional design environment. In J. Psotka, L. D. Massey, & S. A. Mutter (Eds.) *Intelligent tutoring systems: Lessons learned* (pp. 203–228). Hillsdale, NJ: Lawrence Erlbaum Associates.

Russell, D. M., Burton, R. R., Jordan, D. S., Jensen, A. M., Rogers, R. A., & Cohen, J. (1989). *Creating instruction with IDE: Tools for instructional designers* (Tech. Rep. No. PS-00076). Palo Alto, CA: Xerox Palo Alto Research Center.

Rykwert, J. (1979). Inheritance or tradition? *Architectural Design, 49,* 2–6.

Rykwert, J. (1988). Introduction. In L. B. Alberti's, *On the art of building in ten books* (pp. ix–xxi) (J. Rykwert, N. Leach, & R. Tavernor, Trans.). Cambridge, MA: MIT Press. (Original work published 1450)

Simon, H. A. (1973). The structure of ill-structured problems. *Artificial Intelligence, 4,* 181–204.

Singley, M. K., & Anderson, J. R. (1989). *Transfer of cognitive skill.* Cambridge, MA: Harvard University Press.

Towne, D. M., & Munro, A. (1988). The intelligent maintenance training system. In J. Psotka, L. D. Massey, & S. A. Mutter (Eds.), *Intelligent tutoring systems: Lessons learned* (pp. 479–530). Hillsdale, NJ: Lawrence Erlbaum Associates.

VanLehn, K. (1988). Student modelling. In M. C. Polson & J. J. Richardson (Eds.), *Foundations of intelligent tutoring systems* (pp. 55–78). Hillsdale, NJ: Lawrence Erlbaum Associates.

Weizenbaum, J. (1976). *Computer power and human reason.* San Francisco: W. H. Freeman.

Wipond, K., & Jones, M. (1988). Curriculum and knowledge representation in a knowledge-based system for curriculum development. *Proceedings of the ITS-88,* (pp. 97–102). Montreal, Canada.

Representing, Acquiring, and Reasoning About Tutoring Knowledge

Beverly Woolf
University of Massachusetts

BUILDING A TUTORING SYSTEM

We have evolved a generic and consistent foundation for representing, acquiring, and reasoning about tutoring knowledge. The big payoff has been that we can now apply the framework and evolving theory to several domains. We are not invested in promoting a particular tutoring strategy, nor do we advocate a specific intelligent tutoring system (ITS) design. Rather, we build tools that allow for a variety of system components, teaching styles, and intervention strategies to be combined into a single framework. For example, Socratic tutoring, incremental generalizations, and case-based reasoning are just a few of the teaching strategies we have experimented with using this framework. Ultimately, we expect the machine to reason about its own choice of intervention method, to switch teaching strategies, and to use a variety of tactics and teaching approaches, while making decisions about the most efficacious method for managing one-on-one tutoring.

We are aided in our work by colleagues in three states who apply the tools we develop to new domains and new user groups.[1] For example, colleagues at San Francisco State University have sent us several carefully built physics simulations on top of which we placed the tutoring formalism described here. These colleagues help us evaluate the tutors. With their

---

[1] Participant institutions include San Francisco State University; San Francisco City College; Trinity College in Hartford, CT; and State University of New York at Plattsburgh, NY.

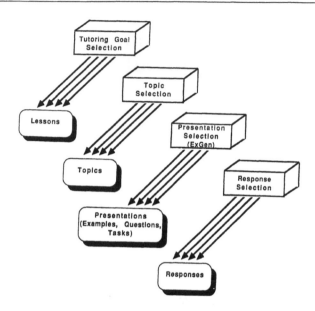

FIGURE 6.1   Representation and control in a tutoring system.

help, we have designed systems that tutor about statistics, thermodynamics, time management, statistics, genetics, algebra word problems, and explanations. In this chapter we describe an iterative methodology for developing these systems, along with the generic tutoring foundation.

Development Cycle
for Artificial Intelligence Systems

Development of an intelligent tutor, like development of any artificial intelligence (AI) system, requires several iterative cycles: Computer scientists and instructional designers first collaborate on the design and development of the system, additional collaboration is required to test the system with students, and then the original implementation is modified and refined based on information gained through testing. This cycle is repeated as time permits.

For example, a professor at City College of San Francisco used the statics tutor (discussed later) in a classroom and noticed weaknesses in the simulation's ability to inform the student. She augmented the system with verbal discourse, adding examples or explanations, making diagnoses, and clarifying system response. She gave us a list of her additional discourse moves to be incorporated into the next version of the tutor.

Representation and Control

AI programs require that a teaching expert define the knowledge to be used along with the control structures that define the way an interpreter will traverse that knowledge. Knowledge representation refers to how such knowledge is stored by a system to allow it to model the domain, human thinking, learning processes, and tutoring strategies. Knowledge bases might store concepts, activities, relations between topics, and other quantities needed to make expert decisions. In tutoring, they might store a variety of lessons, topics, presentations, and response selections available to the tutor (see Figure 6.1). Control refers to passage of an interpreter through those knowledge bases and its selection of appropriate pieces of knowledge for making a diagnosis, a prediction, or an evaluation. For tutoring, control structures might be specified at the four levels indicated in Figure 6.1, separately defining control for selection of lesson, topic, presentation, and response selection.

Currently, our control structures are motivated by specific instructional and diagnostic goals; thus, for example, one control structure produces a predominantly Socratic interaction and another produces interactions based on presenting incrementally generalized versions of new concepts or examples.

Acquiring and encoding this large amount of knowledge, or the knowledge acquisition process, is difficult and time consuming. We have built a number of tools that facilitate representing, acquiring, and reasoning about tutoring knowledge (see Figure 6.2). For three of the knowledge bases (topics, presentation, or response) we consider the nature of the knowledge that must be accessed, such as the examples or questions (from the presentation knowledge base), or the activity the tutor must engage in, such as to motivate or teach a topic, or to provide follow-up. We have built tools, shown at the bottom of Figure 6.2, to support most activities listed in the figure. Only a few such tools are described in this chapter, namely TUPITS, ExGen, Response Matrix, DACTN, and multiple views.

We divide the discussion into two parts. The first describes tools for representing tutoring primitives (lessons, topics, and presentations). The second discusses tools for representing discourse knowledge.

TOOLS FOR REPRESENTING
TUTORING PRIMITIVES

We define *tutoring primitives* as basic elements needed for communicating knowledge, such as topics to be taught, specific tutoring responses, and

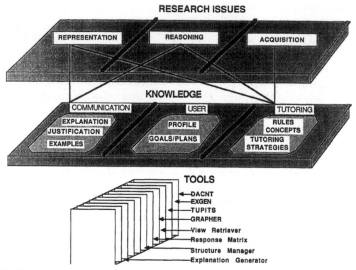

FIGURE 6.2 Tools for the representation and control of tutoring knowledge.

possible student errors. Our knowledge bases hold a variety of examples, knowledge types, tasks to be given to the student, and discourse states describing various human–machine interactions.

Examples of Tutoring Primitives

As an example of how tutoring primitives are used, we describe two tutors we have built in conjunction with the Exploring Systems Earth (ESE) Consortium[2] (Duckworth, Kelley, & Wilson, 1987). These tutors are based on interactive simulations that encourage students to work with elements of physics, such as mass, acceleration, and force. The goal is to help students generate hypotheses as necessary precursors to expanding their own intuitions. We want the simulations to encourage students to listen to their own scientific intuition and to make their own model of the physical world before an encoded tutor advises them about the accuracy of their choices. These tutors have been described elsewhere (Woolf & Cunningham, 1987; Woolf & Murray, 1987) and are only summarized here.

Figure 6.3 shows a simulation for teaching concepts in introductory

[2]San Francisco State University, the University of Massachusetts, and the University of Hawaii are members of the Exploring System Earth Consortium (ESE), a group of universities and industries working together to build intelligent science tutors. The consortium is supported by the Hewlett-Packard Corporation.

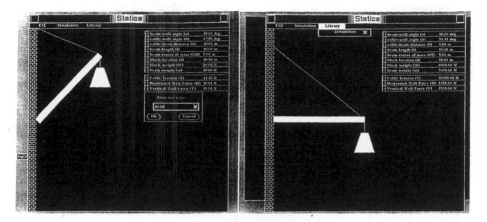

FIGURE 6.3 Statics tutor.

statics. In this example, students are asked to identify forces and torques on the crane boom, or horizontal bar, and to use rubber banding to draw appropriate force vectors directly on the screen. When the beam is in static equilibrium there will be no net force or torque on any part of it. Students are asked to solve both qualitative and quantitative word problems.

If a student were to specify incorrect forces, either by omitting force lines or by including the wrong ones, the tutor makes a decision about how to respond. Depending on the tutorial strategy in effect, there are many possible responses. The tutor might present an explanation or hint, provide another problem, or demonstrate that the student's analysis leads to a logical contradiction. Still another response would be to withhold explicit feedback concerning the quality of the student's answer, and to instead demonstrate the consequence of omitting the missing force; that is, the end of the beam next to the wall would crash down. Such a response would show students how their conceptions are in conflict with the observable world and help them visualize both an internal conceptualization and the science theory. In this example, the tutoring primitives are the topics, questions, and presentation used to represent knowledge. For statics, the primitives are topics such as compression, tension, and linear equilibrium. A presentation might be a graphic of the crane boom at 45° and a request to the student to find the force perpendicular to the boom.

A second tutor is designed to improve a student's intuition about concepts such as energy, energy density, entropy, and equilibrium in thermodynamics. It makes use of a very simplified but instructive simulated world (Figure 6.4) consisting of a two-dimensional array of identical atoms similar to that of Atkins, 1982. Like the statics tutor, the

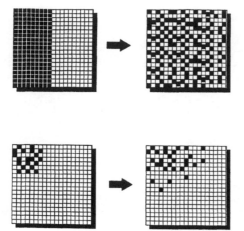

FIGURE 6.4 Thermodynamics tutor.

thermodynamics tutor monitors and advises students about their activities and provides examples, analogies, or explanations. In this simplified world the atoms have only one excited state; the excitation energy is transferred to neighboring atoms through random collisions. Students can specify initial conditions, such as which atoms will be excited and which will remain in the ground state. They can observe the exchange of excitation energy between atoms, and can monitor, via graphs and meters, the flow of energy from one part of the system to another as the system moves toward equilibrium. In this way, several systems can be constructed, each with specific areas of excitation. For each system, regions can be defined and physical quantities, such as energy density or entropy, plotted as functions of time. For this thermodynamics system, tutoring primitives includes topics such as energy, energy density, and equilibrium. A presentation consists of a specific display of excited and ground-state atoms and a number of regions within which the system measures energy or energy density.

Representing and Reasoning About Tutoring Primitives

For each domain, we represent topics, examples, explanations, and possible misconceptions in the four knowledge bases described in an earlier section. We use a network of Knowledge Units (KU) frames to express relationships between topics such as prerequisites, corequisites, and related misconceptions (Figure 6.5). It is important to note that the network is

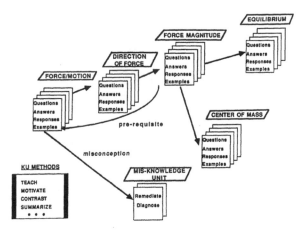

FIGURE 6.5 Hierarchy of frames.

declarative—it contains a structured space of concepts, but does not mandate any particular order for traversal of this space.

The network describes tutorial strategies in terms of a vocabulary of primitive discourse moves such as *teach, motivate, contrast,* and *summarize.* It is implemented in a language called TUPITS,[3] which was built as a framework to facilitate development of numerous tutors. It is an object-oriented representation language that provides a framework for defining primitive components of a tutorial discourse interaction. These components are then used by the tutor to reason about its next action.

As shown in Figure 6.5, each object in TUPITS is represented as a frame and each frame is linked with other frames representing prerequisites, corequisites, or triggered misconceptions. The primary objects in TUPITS are:

- Lessons, which define high-level goals and constraints for each tutoring session;
- Knowledge Units (KUs); which hold the following information for each topic;
- MIS-KUs, which represent common misconceptions, wrong facts or procedures, and other types of "buggy" knowledge;
- Examples, which specify parameters that configure an example, diagram, or simulation to be presented to the student;

---

[3]TUPITS (Tutorial discourse Primitives for Intelligent Tutoring Systems) was developed by Tom Murray and runs on both Hewlett-Packard Bobcats and Apple Macintosh IIs.

- Questions, which define tasks for the student and how the student's behavior during the task might be evaluated; and
- Presentations, which bind an example together with associated questions.

Mis-Knowledge Units (MIS-KUs) represent common misconceptions or knowledge "bugs" and ways to remediate them. Remediation is inserted opportunistically into the discourse. The tutoring strategy sets parameters for this aspect of KU selection by indicating whether such remediation should occur as soon as the misconception is suspected, or wait until the current KU has been completed.

Control is achieved through information associated with each object, which allows the system to respond dynamically to new tutoring situations. For instance, KUs, or topics represented as objects, have procedural methods associated with them that:

- teach their own topic interactively;
- teach their own prerequisites;
- explain knowledge didactically;
- test students for knowledge of that topic;
- summarize themselves;
- provide examples of their knowledge (an instantiation of a procedure or concept);
- provide motivation for a student learning the topic; and
- compare this knowledge with that of other KUs.

A specific tutoring strategy manifests itself by parameterizing the algorithm used to traverse the knowledge primitives network based on classifications of and relations between knowledge units. Several major strategies have thus far been implemented. For example, the tutor might always teach prerequisites before teaching the goal topic. Alternatively, it might provide a diagnostic probe to see if the student knows a topic. Prerequisites might be presented if the student does not exhibit enough knowledge on the probe. These prerequisites may be reached in various ways, such as depth-first and breadth-first traversal. An intermediate strategy is to specialize the prerequisite relation into *hard* prerequisites, which are always covered before the goal topic, and *soft* prerequisites, taught only when the student displays a deficiency.

Control and Reasoning About Examples

Another example of reasoning about tutoring primitives is shown by the activities of ExGen (Suthers & Rissland, 1988; Woolf, Suthers, &

Murray, in press). ExGen takes requests from various components of the tutor and produces an example, question, or description of the concept being taught. For example, the two configurations in Figure 6.3 and the two "universes" in Figure 6.4 can be produced by ExGen. A "seed" example base contains prototypical presentations of each type. ExGen's modification routine expands this into a much larger virtual space of presentations as needed. Its purpose is to give the tutor flexibility in its presentation of tutoring primitives (e.g., presentation of an example with accompanying questions and tasks), without needing to represent all possible presentations explicitly.

ExGen is driven by *example generation specialists,* or knowledge sources, each of which examines the current discourse and student model and produces requests (weighted constraints) to be given to ExGen. Example generation specialists may be thought of as tutoring rules, encoding such general prescriptives as "when starting a new topic, give a start-up example," or "ask questions requiring a qualitative response before those involving quantities."

Requests input to ExGen are expressed as weighted constraints called *requests* (see Figure 6.6). The constraints are written in a language that describes logical combinations of the desired attributes of the example, and the weights on them represent the relative importance of each of these attributes. Attributes include boom angle or boom length for the statics tutor and universe size and density for the thermodynamics tutor. The returned example generally meets as many of the constraints as possible in the priority indicated by the weights.

The tutoring strategy impacts on this layer of presentation selection by ordering the relative importance of the recommendations produced by each of the example generation specialists. Within a strategy, each specialist has a weight multiplied by the weight of the requests produced by the specialists. Altering the behavior of the presentation control is simply a matter of changing the weights on the specialists by selecting a new strategy.

For instance, one specialist requests that presentations describing the

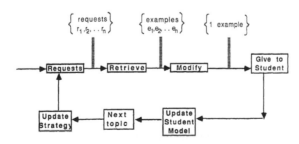

FIGURE 6.6 Reasoning about examples.

current KU be given and another requests that the student be questioned. These competing requests are ordered by the current tutoring strategy. We are also examining strategies for temporal ordering of the presentation of examples, such as Bridging Analogies (Brown, Clement, & Murray, 1986; Murray, Schultz, Brown, & Clement, 1990) and Incremental Generalization.

Acquiring Tutoring Primitives Knowledge

Knowledge acquisition of tutoring primitives knowledge or acquiring and encoding the questions, examples, analogies, and explanations used in a particular domain is still a difficult problem. We need to know not only the primitives used by the expert, but also the reasoning used to decide how and when to present each primitive. We achieve knowledge acquisition for tutoring primitives through a graphical editor built into TUPITS, which is used by the instructional designer to encode and modify both primitives and the reasons why one primitive might be used over another. The graphical editor allows a teacher to generate and modify primitives without working in a programming language. The system currently presents a user with a sheaf of cards listing a series of primitives. Users choose a card and bring the primitive into an edit window, from which they build new primitives.

TOOLS FOR REPRESENTING
DISCOURSE KNOWLEDGE

Our tutors are beginning to represent and reason about alternative responses to the student. Choices are concerned with how much information to give and what motivational comments to make. For instance, the machine must decide whether or not to:

- talk *about* the student's response;
- provide *motivational* feedback about the student's learning process;
- say *whether* an approach is appropriate, *what* a correct response would be, and *why* the student's response is correct or incorrect;
- provide hints, leading questions, or countersuggestions.

Motivational feedback may include asking questions about the student's interest in continuing or providing encouragement, congratulations, challenges, and other statements with affective or prelocutionary content. Control is modulated by the active tutoring strategy, which in turn places constraints on what feedback or follow-up response to generate. The strategy may also specify that system action be predicated on whether the student's response was correct, or whether any response was given.

Reasoning About Discourse Level

As a start to this process we have defined several high-level response strategies and tactics (see Figure 6.7). For example, we have designated an informative response tactic as one in which the machine will elaborate, give reasons, and congratulate the student. For each concept represented in the machine, some of these primitive responses are available and the machine will generate the requested tactic. However, we also advise the system about strategies such as Socratic tutoring, being brief, and being verbose. Here we indicate a priority ordering; thus to be Socratic, the machine must place highest priority on the tactic called coy and secondary rating on the tactic to be informative. If there is a conflict between the checks and the crosses in the model shown in Figure 6.7, that notation with the highest priority will win.

Managing Discourse

We realize that a more flexible and responsive discourse management technique is critical to a tutoring or consultant system. By discourse management, we mean the system's ability to maintain interactive dis-

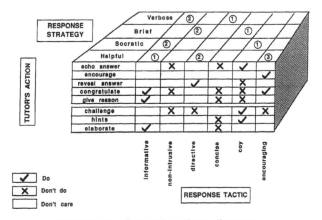

FIGURE 6.7 Reasoning about discourse.

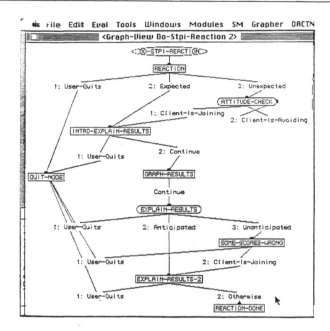

FIGURE 6.8 *Discourse ACtion Transition Network: DACTN.*

course with the user and to custom-tailor its responses beyond the
generalized discourse levels already suggested. Ideally, the system should
tailor its response to the idiosyncracies of a particular user. Machine
discourse and response need not be in natural language to be effective
(Servan-Schreiber, 1983).

For example, the system should ensure that an intervention relates
directly to an individual's personal history, learning style, and on-line
experience with the system. It should dynamically reason about a user's
actions, the curriculum, and the discourse history. In doing this tutors
should make users feel that their unique situation has been responded to
appropriately and sensitively. In this way the system simulates one-on-one
human tutoring behavior. The mechanism we use to do this is called a
Discourse ACtion Transition Network (DACTN)[4] which represents and
controls human–machine dialog. Figure 6.8 shows a DACTN for responding to a user about an inventory test of questions that she took in the
system described in the next section. This graphic is taken directly off the
screen of that system.

Sometimes the intervention steps designated by a DACTN are based

---

[4]Rhymes with ACT-IN.

on a taxonomy of frequently observed discourse sequences that provide default responses for the tutor (Woolf & Murray, 1987). The discourse manager reasons about local context when making discourse decisions. Here local context is an aggregate of the client profile and response history.

The DACTN represents the space of possible discourse situations: *Arcs* track the state of the conversation and are defined as predicate sets whereas *nodes* provide actions for the tutor. The discourse manager first accesses the situation indicated by the arcs, resolving any conflicts between multiply satisfied predicate sets, and then initiates the action indicated by the node at the termination of the satisfied arc.

Arcs represent discourse situations defined by sets of predicates over the client profile and the state of the system. For instance, the value of the arc "CLIENT-IS-AVOIDING" (top-half of Figure 6.8) is determined by inferring over the current state of the profile and recent client responses. Placing actions at the nodes rather than on the arcs, as was done with Augmented Transition Networks (ATN) (Woods, 1970), allows nodes to represent abstract actions that can be expanded into concrete substeps when and if the node is reached during execution of the DACTN. For example, the node "EXPLAIN RESULTS" (middle of Figure 6.8) expands into yet another complete DACTN to be executed if this node is evaluated in the course of the intervention.

Each user response causes the user model, or in this case the personality profile, to be updated, which in turn affects the interpretation and resolutions of subsequent interactions. DACTNs allow discourse control decisions to be based on a dynamic interpretation of the situation. In this way the mechanism remains domain-independent and flexible enough to allow dynamic rebuilding—decision points and machine actions can be modified through a graphics editor, as explained in a later section. DACTNs have been implemented in two domains, one of which is described in the next section.

Example Discourse Knowledge

Time, Energy, and Vision (TEV) is a consultant tutor that presents interventions directed at improving an individual's personal time perspective. The goal is to move individuals toward awareness of how they handle time and deal with such items as commitment, interruptions, and obligations. The system uses two phases that model the human-to-human consultation process: (a) initial client assessment, and (b) intervention/ evaluation (see Figure 6.9) (Slovin & Woolf, 1988).

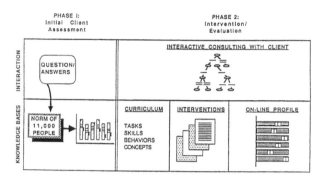

FIGURE 6.9   Two phases of the consultant.

Phase 1: Initial Client Assessment

During the first phase, TEV gathers information about the individual's attitudes, knowledge, and skills using an assessment instrument that, in a noncomputerized version, has been normed on 11,000 individuals. The client is presented with a series of statements that focus on attitudes, knowledge, and skills related to time perspective. (the Stanford Time Perspectives Inventory, described in Gonzalez & Zimbardo, 1985). For each statement, the client is given a choice of five ratings ranging from very characteristic to very uncharacteristic and is asked to indicate "How characteristic is this of you?" Example statements include the following:

- Thinking about the future is pleasant to me.
- If things don't get done on time, I don't worry about them.
- I do things impulsively, making decisions on the spur of the moment.
- I try to live one day at a time.

Responses are evaluated according to the established interpretation of the instrument and then used in two ways. First they are shown to the client in a graph displaying the client's rating among his age-group peers (see Figure 6.10). Then an explanation of the results is provided[5] along with an opportunity for the client to react (see Figure 6.11). The evaluation and the client's response are used as the initial database to form an internal client profile. The profile is used to help determine the future direction of the consultation process and to generate expectations about client re-

---

[5]The dialogue is not generated through natural language processing, rather through menu input and canned text output. This might be a limitation of the system. However, prior work in the area of computer-based therapy (Servan-Schreiber, 1987) shows that clinically significant therapy can be achieved in spite of this limitation.

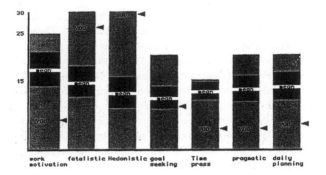

FIGURE 6.10 Evaluation of a client who displays a present-oriented time perspective.

Tutor: Your scores indicate that you have a basically present-oriented time perspective. Do you agree?

Person A: No, I think I also consider the future in my life.

Tutor: Well, let's look more closely at your scores, and see where you think they are wrong.

Person A: OK.

Tutor: Your score on the hedonism scale indicates that you may be extremely similar to people who are primarily interested in having a good time, taking risks, and who often act impulsively. Does that sound like you?

Person A: Mostly, but it sounds a little extreme.

Tutor: OK, let's look now at the fatalism scale; it indicates that you may be very similar to people who live one day at a time in order to avoid planning for a future they believe is determined by fate. Is that what you do?

Person A: Yes, I guess so.

Tutor: Let's look at one more scale, goal-seeking. Your score here shows that you may not be similar to people who plan for the future and get satisfaction from setting and achieving their goals. Do you agree?

Person A: It is true that I don't do much goal setting

Tutor: It was mainly your scores on these scales that led me to view you as basically a present-oriented person. Since you disagree with the hedonism score slightly, why don't we say slightly present-oriented?

Person A: Yes, that sounds more like me.

FIGURE 6.11 Dialogue about the evaluation of Figure 6.10.

sponses. It becomes the primary determining knowledge base for designing the consultation and is constantly updated to provide a moment-to-moment view of the client.

Phase 2: Intervention/Evaluation

The second phase uses the profile described to consult with the client. Here the goal is to create an ongoing dialogue that leads the client to form and hold a more balanced time perspective. A second goal is to improve the client's repertoire of useful time-management behaviors. These goals are achieved through dialogue, specifically through the use of interventions, or exercises and presentations designed to facilitate awareness of time perspectives. Interventions also provide learning tasks and help the client practice skills. Example interventions are "Learning to Say No," "Life Goals," and "Time Wasters." Dialogue strategies are derived from a large repertoire of similar activities used in one-on-one and group counseling over the last 15 years by experts in clinical psychology. These strategies and interventions have proven effective in teaching time-management skills for large numbers of people.

TEV's orientation as a consultant tutor has led to a view of interventions as dialogues. Each intervention is seen as a distinct segment of an ongoing dialogue between TEV and the client that is extended by presentation of the next intervention. The consultation experience for clients is uniquely defined by the composite of high-level interventions and low-level discourse actions resulting from their responses to the system.

Representing Discourse Knowledge

One characteristic aspect of the computational model of didactics described here is the *plan of action* or lesson plan that enacts didactic operations. The *local context* in which a particular plan of action is triggered (Wenger, 1988) was described in an earlier section. In TEV, the system represents knowledge of discourse as alternative plans. Alternative curriculum activities are stored as predefined plans and alternative discourse moves are stored as different plan contingencies in these prestored plans (see Figure 6.12). The consultant has limited planning ability to manage these plans and plan contingencies. Pedagogical activities and discourse knowledge, articulated by a clinical psychologist, generate a lesson plan in response to client input during the lesson.

The plan of action is a unit of decision in the didactic process that manages knowledge about the curriculum, the available teaching resources, and the client's needs. The curriculum consists of a prioritized overlay of skills, behaviors, and concepts that the client should be able to understand, demonstrate, and integrate into her life. (For example, one of the skills the machine presents is to keep a "to-do" list or to have clients keep a record of how they spent time in the previous week.) The plan of action is controlled by the Tev's Intervention Selection Mechanism (TISM), which models an expert's ability to select appropriate interventions for a specific student. For each instructional objective, several pedagogical approaches (DACTNs) are indicated as being able to achieve the chosen

MULTIPLE DISCOURSE CONTROL LEVELS

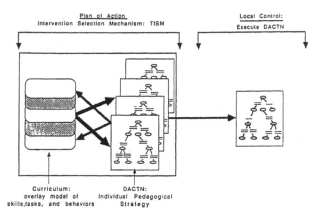

FIGURE 6.12   Levels of control in TEV.

objective (see Figure 6.12). Alternatively, for each pedagogical approach, or single DACTN, several curriculum objectives might be achieved. Our experts have developed a library of resources to teach alternative curriculum items, such as identifying time-wasters. During a one-on-one consulting session, TISM chooses among these resources based on an understanding of the needs and learning style of the client.

These resources are represented in the consultant in the form of interventions. The system reasons about the current context before generating the next step in its plan of action. It is constrained by the client assessment, a record of the client's state of knowledge, and system history. The TISM is responsible for establishing a globally coherent instructional objective and for ensuring that curricula items follow each other in a way that matches the client's needs.

Acquiring Discourse Knowledge

Knowledge acquisition for discourse knowledge involves first identifying and then encoding the reasons why an instructor makes decisions about responding to the student and how the teacher decides when such interventions will take place. We facilitate the knowledge acquisition process by use of a graphical editor in which the instructor selects interventions and modifies the dialogue on-line. This editor facilitates piecewise development and evaluation of the system, thus providing an opportunity for a wide circle of people, including psychologists, teachers, curriculum developers, and instructional scientists, to participate in the process of developing the system. The DACTN in Figure 6.8 is a specific instance of this graphics editor.

Psychologists or teachers add a new question or statement directly on the screen. They add arcs and nodes by simply buttoning the mouse on the graphical element to be changed. Graphical inputs are directly translated into LISP code by the system. The user is led through a series of prompts designed to elicit possible interventions and client responses. There are two pieces of information associated with each response: a classification of the response, which is based on the current user profile, and the profile updates related to the choice of this response. Using a small set of classifications, that is, EXPECTED, INDICATES-CONFUSION, AVOIDANCE, and so forth, the expert indicates his understanding of the meaning of each user response. These classifications may depend on the current user profile or other indications of context. The profile modifications may include updates based both on the classification of the response and those specific to this question and response.

Because DACTNs provide a structured framework for representing dialogues, the visual dialogue editor allows an expert to work on knowledge acquisition without having to work with knowledge engineers. In this way, we continue to elicit new interventions from our experts even as development and evaluation of TEV proceeds. By adding interventions to the library and by linking them to the curriculum, we expand TEV's repertoire without reworking the entire system.

The dialogue editor enables the domain expert to directly manipulate a graph of the dialogue where each question, statement, or action is represented in an editable node, and each arc (also editable) represents a discourse situation that could result from the client's response. As each question is added, the graph is updated so the expert always has a view of the current state of the intervention. The underlying DACTN is created dynamically so that at any point in the editing it can be executed against default profiles, allowing the expert to check the appropriateness of the machine's responses.

SUMMARY AND FUTURE OPPORTUNITIES

Current Work

Thus far we have described existing tools for representing, acquiring, and reasoning about tutoring knowledge. Tutoring knowledge has been described both in terms of content (i.e., topics, questions, and examples) and in terms of context (i.e., tutoring strategies and discourse interventions). Current tools provide a generic framework that allows development of multiple tutors. Several application systems have been described, namely those in statics, thermodynamics, and time management, along with a few tools, namely TUPITS, DACTNs, and ExGen. The tools and applications provide a test-bed for exploring new issues and new tutoring functionality. Ultimately, we expect to build systems that can reason about the choice of tutoring strategy based on a clear representation of a student's cognitive knowledge. No extant system yet has this capability.

Technology for Teaching and Learning: Some Predictions

We can make several predictions about technology for teaching and learning in the future based on extrapolation from the kind of work described earlier and from other work in progress around the world. In these predictions, we look both at short-term objectives and at long-term opportunities. Short-term objectives involve 1–5 years work, or the equivalent of one or two doctoral theses, and the participation of several researchers; these objectives can be divided into technological and educational objectives. Long-term opportunities reflect changing educational norms based on continued use of intelligent teaching environments. Achievement of these goals would require 5–10 years of research effort, leadership from visionaries, and long-term commitment of resources and energies, possibly including the work of approximately four to six doctoral students.

Short-Term Technological Objectives. Short-term technological objectives include:

- Wide expansion of tutoring systems into new training and teaching areas as computer prices go down and memory size and processing time goes up.
- Improvement of representing and reasoning capabilities of AI systems, made possible by advances in AI, discourse methods, and cognitive science technologies.
- Establishment of a real interaction between communities of instructional designers and builders of tutoring systems.
- Establishment of criteria for determining the suitability of a domain for construction of a new tutor. Such criteria might include type of topics (e.g., concepts, definitions, or procedures), difficulty of teaching these topics, number of repetitious training sessions needed (e.g., military training), and

ability of a host institution to incorporate the tutoring system within existing curricula.

- Distribution of tutoring systems tools, including knowledge bases and control structures, to different sites for experimentation with new applications and new student populations.

Short-Term Educational Objectives. Short-term educational objectives are different from the short-term technological goals. Whereas the latter dealt with advances in content (specifically information technologies), educational goals focus on the context and address issues around bringing information technology into education. These goals include:

- Support of distributed educational agents that will move training and literacy away from formalized classrooms. Distributed agents include the family, industry, broadcast media (electronic networks, television, video), and the community. Intelligent tutoring systems contribute to this process by enabling people and machines to communicate unconstrained by place or time and free of conventional temporal or physical restrictions.
- Support of students in becoming autonomous scholars. Tutoring systems should facilitate access to foreign knowledge bases, on-line encyclopedias, graphics, real-time, long-distance results (e.g., stock market closings), and other scholars and other knowledge bases.
- Establishment of human–machine partnership. Humans and machines already participate in limited joint problem-solving activities by utilizing abilities in which each excels: Humans are best at intuitive thinking, reasoning from incomplete or uncertain knowledge, and using analogies from disparate fields to draw conclusions; machines are best at memory retention, computation, pattern matching, planning, and organizing tools.
- Establishment of world-wide multimedia communication. A variety of media (including television, movies, audiovisuals, and programming) are now accessible through computers. Electronic networks should facilitate rapid access to these media and AI will provide intelligent agents to search databases and retrieve information wanted and needed by individual users.
- Construction of megascale knowledge bases in which all recorded encyclopedic knowledge is available from a keyboard.

Many additional technical and educational opportunities exist in the short term. In terms of AI technology we have not effectively included student models, qualitative reasoning, machine learning, hypertext (Yankelovich, Meyrowitz, & van Dam, 1987), or multimedia (e.g., AI systems that include videodisc, speech, or film) into our tutors. Additionally, one standard deviation learning improvement for intelligent tutors as compared with lecture-style teaching is not good enough. Given the resources put into development of these systems, they should produce two standard deviation improvement over lecture-style teaching just as does one-on-one human tutoring.

Other problems awaiting solutions arise from educational and societal issues such as:

- Limited number of powerful AI-based computers available to education and industrial training sites. Increased memory size and reduced prices on general-purpose machines should eliminate this problem.
- A generation of entrenched and unusable computers in the classroom.
- Public school resistance.
- The difficulty of integrating intelligent tutors into existing curriculum and educational systems.

Long-Term Opportunities.   Much work is required to take advantage of long-range technological and educational opportunities, and it is possible that the available hardware and software technology does not allow for full realization of these opportunities at the present time. Yet the following description of the long-term view of education provides a feeling for the vision that many researchers hold. We envision a tutoring system that includes:

- AI mechanisms that model the thinking processes of domain experts, tutors, and students.
- Intelligent environments that supply students with world-class laboratories within which they build and test their own reality.
- The ability to provide students with (a) the *ah-ha* experience, in which the machine recognizes the student's intention; (b) the *over-the-shoulder* experience, in which the machine aids and advises the student; and (c) the *out-of-the-world* experience, in which the machine provides an environment rich enough for discovery.

To fully use advanced information technology in education, we would need the following:

- Stores of knowledge easily accessible for joint human–machine problem solving.
- Widely available encyclopedias of information and knowledge bases that contain the sum of human knowledge.
- Computational agents that enable networking of human and machine problem solvers.

How can we solve the myriad of problems that will emerge en route to these multiple goals? How do we handle the research opportunities and fully exploit the potential of advanced technology in education? An explicit and preformed agenda is not necessarily the only answer; often research breakthroughs emerge from practice, experimentation, and risk-taking. Researchers must be willing to commit resources, to make mistakes, and to continue to experiment. This chapter describes research that amounts to a single data point in the space of possible solutions. The work as described may survive, and it may be used only as a stepping stone, allowing others to push on ahead with new experiments. Study and repeated research efforts will enable the future of this field to unfold.

ACKNOWLEDGMENTS

This work was supported in part by a grant from the National Science Foundation, Materials Development Research, No. 8751362. It was also supported in part by the Air Force Systems Command, Rome Air Development Center, Griffiss AFB, New York, 13441 and the Air Force Office of Scientific Research, Bolling AFB, DC 20332 under contract No. F30602-85-0008. This contract supports the Northeast Artificial Intelligence Consortium (NAIC). Partial support was also received from URI University Research Initiative Contract No. N00014-86-K-0764.

REFERENCES

Atkins, T. (1982). *The second law.* San Francisco: W. H. Freeman.

Brown, D., Clement, J., & Murray, T. (1986). Tutoring specifications for a computer program which uses analogies to teach mechanics. *Cognitive Processes Research Group Working Paper,* Department of Physics, University of Massachusetts, Amherst, MA.

Duckworth, E., Kelley, J., & Wilson, S. (1987, November). AI goes to school. *Academic Computing,* pp. 6–10, 38–43, 62–63.

Gonzalez, A., & Zimbardo, P. (1985, March). Time in perspective. *Psychology Today,* 21–26.

McCalla, G., Greer, J., & the Scent Team (1988). Intelligent advising in problem solving domains: The scent-3 architecture. *Proceedings of the International Conference on Intelligent Tutoring Systems* (pp. 124–133). University of Montreal, Canada.

MacMillian, S., Emme, D., & Bekowitz, M. (1988). Instructional planners: lessons learned. In J. Psotka, L. D. Massey, & S. Mutter (Eds.), *Intelligent tutoring systems: Lessons learned* (pp. 229–257). Hillsdale, NJ: Lawrence Erlbaum Associates.

Murray, W. (1988). *Control for intelligent tutoring systems: A comparison of blackboard architectures and discourse management networks* (Tech. Rep. No. R-6267). FMC Corporate Technology Center.

Murray, T., Schultz, K., Brown, D., & Clement, J. (1990). An analogy-based computer tutor for remediating physics misconception. *Interactive Learning Environments, 1*(2), 79–101.

Reichman, R. (1985). *Making computers talk like you and me.* Cambridge, MA: MIT Press.

Servan-Schreiber, D. (1983). Artificial intelligence in psychiatry. *Journal of Nervous and Mental Disease, 174,* 191-202.

Servan-Schreiber, D. (1987). From intelligent tutoring to computerized psychotherapy *Proceedings of the Sixth National Conference on Artificial Intelligence* (pp. 66-71). (AAAI-87). Los Altos, CA: Morgan Kaufmann.

Slovin, T., & Woolf, B. P. (1988). A consultant tutor for personal development. *Proceedings of the International Conference on Intelligent Tutoring Systems* (pp. 162-169). University of Montreal.

Suthers, D., & Rissland, E. (1988). *Exgen: A constraint satisfying example generator* (Tech. Rep. No. 88-71). Amherst, MA: University of Massachusetts, Computer and Information Science Department.

Wenger, E. (1988). *Artificial intelligence and tutoring systems.* Los Altos, CA: Morgan Kaufmann.

Woods, W. (1970). Transition network grammars for natural language analysis. *Communications of the ACM, 13*(10), 591-606.

Woolf, B., & Cunningham, P. (1987). Multiple knowledge sources in intelligent tutoring systems. *IEEE Expert, 2,* 41-54.

Woolf, B., Suthers, D., & Murray, T. (in press). *Discourse control for tutoring: Case studies in example generation* (Tech. Rep.). Amherst, MA: University of Massachusetts, Computer and Information Science Department.

Woolf, B., & Murray, T. (1987). A framework for representing tutorial discourse. *International joint conference in artificial intelligence.* Los Altos, CA: Morgan Kaufmann.

Yankelovich, N., Meyrowitz, N., & van Dam, A. (1987). Reading and writing the electronic book. *IEEE Computer, 20*(9), 15-30.

Generating Coherent Explanations to Answer Students' Questions

Liane Acker
James Lester
Art Souther
Bruce Porter
University of Texas at Austin

There are two ways that an intelligent tutoring system (ITS) can present domain knowledge to a student: reciting "canned text" and generating explanations directly from the domain knowledge. Generating explanations offers several advantages. First, systems that generate explanations do not have to anticipate every question; thus, they may be able to provide explanations even for unexpected questions. In addition, the exact form of the explanation can be shaped to fit the current situation and student. Moreover, as the domain knowledge changes, generated explanations are always consistent with the knowledge; in contrast, canned explanations must be altered. Finally, the tutor can directly use generated explanations in tasks like evaluation and diagnosis. For example, it might evaluate the quality of a student explanation or diagnose the basis for a faulty conclusion.

Current ITSs demonstrate a limited solution to the problem of generating explanations. Their success results from limitations placed on the form and extent of domain knowledge. These limitations include dedicating the ITS to a single task (Clancey, 1987; Hollan, Hutchins, & Weitzman, 1984), representing the domain knowledge with a relatively small number of rules or axioms (Brown, Burton, & de Kleer, 1982; VanLehn & Brown, 1980; White & Frederiksen, 1987), covering only a small portion of the domain (Brown, Burton, & Zdybel, 1973), and explicitly partitioning the knowledge base according to the tasks for which the knowledge will be used (Brown, Burton, & de Kleer, 1982; White & Frederiksen, 1987).

There is an important class of tutors, however, for which these limitations are unacceptable. The domain of these tutors is the knowledge conveyed in introductory college courses. For most subjects, this *fundamental knowledge* broadly surveys the domain, contains multiple, highly integrated viewpoints, and is not reducible to a small number of principles or axioms. Such a complex knowledge base poses a serious problem for explanation generation: To answer a question, a generator must select only the knowledge needed for a coherent explanation.

This chapter presents an *explanation-generation method* that addresses this problem in the context of answering questions using an extensive knowledge base. This method uses *view types* to select knowledge for answering questions.[1] Extensions of the method for generating elaborate explanations and teaching plans are also discussed.

REPRESENTING FUNDAMENTAL KNOWLEDGE

To investigate the problem of answering questions using fundamental knowledge, we have constructed a knowledge base in the domain of botany, with emphasis on plant anatomy, physiology, and development.[2] We have chosen this domain because it lies between well-characterized and ill-characterized domains. Plants as living organisms provide a rich source of relatively complex relationships, but they do not pose the representational difficulties of animal (and especially human) behavior.

Like most domains, botany is concerned with objects (i.e., plant anatomy) and the processes that change them (i.e., plant physiology and development). It also incorporates both commonsense and expert knowledge. For example, the commonsense notion that living things require nutrients supports the expert knowledge that plant embryos consume endosperm, a food source in seeds.

The Botany Knowledge Base is designed to be multifunctional. Unlike conventional expert systems (e.g., MYCIN), it is not committed to any particular task or problem-solving method. Rather, it encodes general knowledge that can support diverse tasks and methods. For example, the knowledge base could be used by programs that diagnose ailments, tutor students, organize reference materials, and so on.

The backbone of the knowledge base is a hierarchy of botanical objects and processes (Figures 7.1 and 7.2). Each of these concepts is represented with a node, and relations between concepts are represented

---

[1]Once selected, this knowledge constitutes a core from which an ITS's natural language generator may fashion an explanation. However, natural language generation is outside the scope of our current project.

[2]A complete description of the knowledge base may be found in Porter (1988).

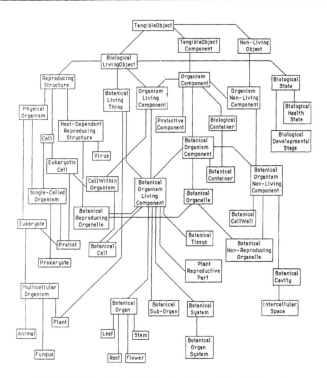

FIGURE 7.1 The top level of the object hierarchy.

with arcs. The hierarchy permits information about general concepts to be passed to more specific concepts by a process called *inheritance*. For example, *biological growth* is a *biological production event;* therefore, it involves the intake of assimilable raw materials and the output of more complex organic substances.

Relations in the Botany Knowledge Base are also organized hierarchically (Figure 7.3). For example, *actor* is a relation between an event and an object involved in the event, and *producer* is a specialization of *actor* in which the event is a production event. This organization permits information associated with a relation to be inherited, such as methods for computing a relation's value.

The fundamental knowledge of each concept in the Botany Knowledge Base is elaborate. For example, Figure 7.4 is the representation of the concept *photosynthesis*. Representing this process requires encoding information from multiple viewpoints, such as "photosynthesis viewed as photochemical energy transduction" and "photosynthesis as a producer of glucose." This complexity is unavoidable, but poses problems for question

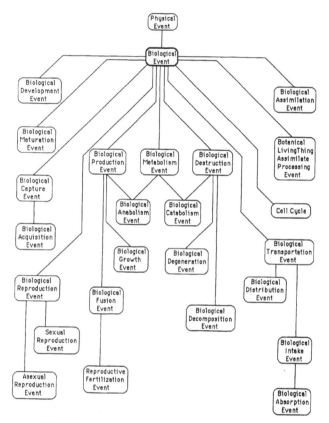

FIGURE 7.2 The top level of the event hierarchy.

answering. Specifically, how can an ITS locate and organize the knowledge
that answers students' questions?

The complex network of relationships in the Botany Knowledge Base
provides many possible paths for explanation generation. Most of these
paths are incoherent because of incompleteness, circularity, and endless
meandering. Each of these problems is illustrated with the following
descriptions of photosynthesis, derived from Figure 7.4:

- Photosynthesis has carbon dioxide as a raw material.
- Photosynthesis consists of two subprocesses: the light reactions, which are
  located in the thylakoid in the chloroplast (the location of photosynthesis).
- Photosynthesis consists of the photosynthetic light reactions subprocess,
  which has the raw material ADP, which is the raw material for photophosphorylation, whose input energy form is electron excitation energy, which is

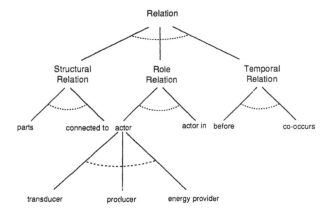

FIGURE 7.3 A fragment of the relational hierarchy.

held by the excited chlorophyll electron, which is part of chlorophyll in the excited state . . .

Clearly, methods are required to restrict pathways through the knowledge base, while simultaneously providing sufficient information for explanation. As described in the following sections, our research develops methods for generating coherent explanations of domain knowledge.

RELATED WORK ON QUESTION ANSWERING

A review of past question-answering systems reveals a correlation between the number of different kinds of knowledge a system uses and the range of its question-answering capabilities. Different kinds of domain knowledge, such as taxonomic, partonomic, strategic, casual, and temporal, are required for answering different questions. Question-answering systems do not use this breadth of knowledge, so their question-answering capabilities are limited.

Rule-based expert systems are the most limited. These systems typically include only the knowledge needed to perform a particular task. In addition, they do not distinguish the different kinds of domain knowledge; rather, the different kinds of knowledge are implicit in the rules and the rule interpreter. As a result, such expert systems have limited ranges of question-answering ability. For example, MYCIN (Shortliffe, 1976) answers the questions, "What blood infection accounts for the patient's symptoms?" and "What is the most appropriate drug for treating

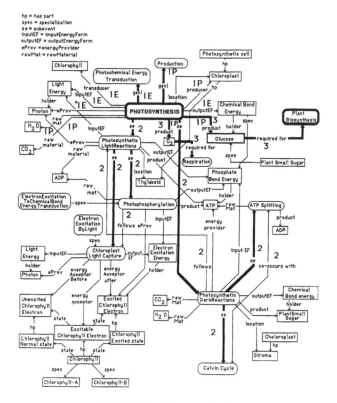

FIGURE 7.4   Photosynthesis.

this patient?" Its explanation of an answer is the inference path constructed during case diagnosis. However, MYCIN cannot define the medical terms it uses, explain the causality underlying its problem-solving rules, or elaborate its explanation.

Systems with more kinds of domain knowledge have greater question-answering capability. This is directly demonstrated by NEOMYCIN, an extension of MYCIN (Clancey, 1983). NEOMYCIN represents its domain knowledge explicitly and includes hierarchies of domain concepts and generalized versions of MYCIN's rules. As a result, NEOMYCIN can answer a larger variety of questions. For example, NEOMYCIN can explain the strategy and causal relationships underlying rules. Another system, XPLAIN (Swartout, 1983), generates expert systems that include the same kinds of knowledge that NEOMYCIN added to MYCIN. Like NEOMYCIN, the systems XPLAIN produces can answer questions not only about what they are doing, but also about why they are doing it.

Although NEOMYCIN and XPLAIN represent a significant advance in question answering over conventional expert systems, their capabilities fall far short of the requirements of an ITS designed to teach fundamental knowledge. Such an ITS requires the ability to answer many more types of questions. Past ITSs provide a patchwork of support for such a broad question-answering facility. Each system achieves its range of question-answering ability by using a particular kind of domain knowledge.

Burton and Brown's SOPHIE tutor (Brown, Burton, & Bell, 1975) extends the kinds of domain knowledge that NEOMYCIN uses by including a simulation model of electronic circuits. The additional knowledge implicit in this model enables the system to answer not only problem-solving questions such as those answered by NEOMYCIN, but hypothetical questions as well. Although this significantly increases the range of its question-answering abilities, SOPHIE's procedural representation precludes using the model to answer other types of questions. For example, SOPHIE cannot provide definitions or descriptions of domain concepts and cannot answer general questions about how the objects and events in the domain affect one another.

Burton and Brown's METEOROLOGY tutor (Brown, Burton, & Zdybel, 1973) explicitly represents knowledge of the processes underlying its simulation model. As a result, the tutor can answer not only hypothetical questions but also questions about the causal relationships between processes. Its extended knowledge base of process concepts greatly increases the range of its question-answering abilities. However, because its knowledge of nonprocess concepts is limited, the tutor relies on canned text to define and describe most concepts.

Carbonell's SCHOLAR (Carbonell, 1970), one of the earliest ITSs to address question answering, describes domain concepts using a semantic network representation of its domain, geography. SCHOLAR can also answer questions about the attributes of domain concepts and can compare attributes. It can do this because of its sophisticated knowledge base of geographic regions and their interrelationships. However, whereas METEOROLOGY's question-answering range is limited by its lack of nonprocess knowledge, SCHOLAR's range is limited by its lack of process knowledge, temporal knowledge, and causal knowledge.

McKeown's TEXT system (McKeown, 1985b) answers the same kinds of questions addressed by SCHOLAR but uses more principled techniques. SCHOLAR relies on distances between network nodes and numeric tags to determine the relevance of a particular piece of knowledge to answering a question; TEXT uses knowledge base access procedures (*rhetorical predicates*) based on detailed analyses of text structure. TEXT's knowledge base enables it to generate sophisticated responses to requests for concept descriptions and comparisons. However, like the other systems, its range of question-answering capabilities is restricted by the kinds of knowledge in its knowledge base.

We have seen that a correlation exists between the different kinds of knowledge a system uses and the range of its question-answering capabilities. Although systems that use restricted knowledge bases succeed, an ITS designed to teach fundamental knowledge in a field like botany must use many kinds of knowledge to answer a broad range of questions.

To answer many types of questions from a large, complex knowledge base, a system must determine the intent of a student's question and generate a response using relevant portions of the knowledge base. As described in the next section, our solution to the first task uses a predefined set of question types. A later section discusses the focus of our current research: the use of *view types* for selecting relevant knowledge to answer the student's question.

QUESTION TYPES

A question type is a template for a class of questions that share the same conceptual representation and are answered using the same answer-generation strategy. Understanding a student's question results in classifying it according to particular question type. It is important to classify questions on the basis of conceptual representation, rather than syntactic form, because the same question can be phrased in many ways and a particular phrasing can have different meanings in different contexts (Lehnert, 1977). One way to facilitate classifying students' questions is to restrict the allowable syntax for each question type. Another advantage of using such a restricted interface is that the capabilities of the system are made clear to the student: Any question that is not "askable" is not answerable.

In her question-answering system QUALM, Lehnert presented 13 conceptual categories of questions about narrative texts (Lehnert, 1986). Hughes (1986) organized these question types into a hierarchy and added definition and comparison questions. We have extended this set to accommodate questions about the physical structure of objects, the roles of objects in processes, examples of concepts, and hypothetical situations.

Furthermore, we have restructured Hughes's question-type hierarchy so the system can refine questions. (In Hughes's hierarchy, only question types at the lowest level of the hierarchy are answerable.) When the student asks a type of question that has subtypes, the system has the option of refining the question into a more specific question (or into a combination of more specific questions) covered by one of the subtypes. To make this refinement, the system might rely on a set of defaults or, in a more sophisticated system, on the student model, the dialogue history, and the knowledge base. In this way, the system can apply very specific and direct question-answering strategies even to a very general question. The following is a summary of the hierarchy of question types we have developed:

- How is X defined?
  - What kind of thing is X?
  - What are some examples of X?
  - Describe the spatial/temporal structure of X.
    * Describe the spatial/temporal substructure of X.
    * Of what is X a spatial/temporal component?
  - What are the properties of X?
  - In what events is Object X an actor?
    * Where does X come from?
  - What events/objects does X affect (and how)?
    * What events does X cause?
    * What events does X prevent?
    * What events does X enable?
    * What events does X modulate?
  - What events/objects affect X (and how)?
    * What conditions are sufficient/necessary for X?
    * What would be the effect on X if Condition C were true/false?
    * What processes/conditions/quantities influence Quantity Q of X?
- Compare/contrast X with Y.
  - How is X different from the prototypical Y?
  - How are the values for characteristic C of X like/different from the values for characteristic C of Y?
  - How is the spatial/temporal structure of X like/different from the structure of Y?
  - How is the role of Object X in Process P like/different from the role of Object Y in P?
  - How is the effect of X on Z like/different from the effect of Y on Z?
  - How is the effect of Z on X like/different from the effect of Z on Y?
- What are the values for Characteristic C of X?
- Why does X have the Value V for Characteristic C?
- Why doesn't X have the Value V for Characteristic C?
- How is X related to Y?
- How does Object X perform Process P?
- What concept has the following properties and relations?
- What would be implied if Condition C were true/false?

Three points should be noted regarding this hierarchy. First, it is not always possible to rephrase a question of a particular type so that it becomes one of its subtypes. Second, the hierarchy is not strict; some question types share subtypes. Third, the hierarchy is not exhaustive; more question types will undoubtedly be added as research progresses.

DETERMINING THE CONTENT
OF A QUESTION RESPONSE

There are two steps to answering a question: determining the content of the response, and transforming the response from an internal representation into natural language (*realization*). Much research has been done on realization, as evidenced by some excellent natural language generation components, such as Penman (Mann, 1983) and MUMBLE (McDonald & Pustejevsky, 1985). Our current research focuses on the first task, content determination.

Explanations answering students' questions must be coherent. Studies of discourse coherence have focused primarily on one aspect of coherence, *cohesion*. Cohesion is the effects of organization and realization on overall coherence (de Beaugrande, 1980; Grimes, 1975; Halliday & Hasan, 1976; Hobbs, 1983; Joshi & Weinstein, 1981). However, little attention has been paid to the question, "To insure coherence, how should the content of individual portions of an explanation be selected?" Halliday and Hasan (1976) termed this aspect of coherence *semantic unity*.

Selecting the content of an answer so that it is a semantic unit is a difficult problem. This is particularly true when generating explanations from a complex representation of fundamental knowledge. Our solution exploits the fact that implicit in such a representation are numerous *viewpoints* of each concept. For example, the representation of pollen in the Botany Knowledge Base includes knowledge of pollen as an actor in plant reproduction, as well as knowledge of pollen as an object composed of other parts and substances. A viewpoint is a semantic unit, thus selecting knowledge by viewpoints insures coherence.

Other researchers have proposed using viewpoints to select knowledge for explanations (McKeown, 1985a; Swartout, 1983). However, their approach explicitly encodes viewpoints in the representation of domain knowledge. Viewpoints in Swartout's XPLAIN are annotations that indicate when to include a piece of knowledge in an explanation. McKeown explicitly represents each viewpoint as a separate classification hierarchy. However, explicitly representing all possible viewpoints is not practical for a large-scale knowledge base of fundamental knowledge.

The alternative is to dynamically generate viewpoints. To do this, we must determine what characterizes a viewpoint so that those portions of the knowledge base that constitute viewpoints can be selected automatically. The TEXT system generates viewpoints by using schemata of rhetorical predicates. These schemata represent patterns of discourse structure. Each rhetorical predicate represents a means for describing information and has an associated technique for extracting relevant propositions from the knowledge base. Suthers (1988) designed a *view retriever,* which partitions the knowledge base according to a domain model and then uses rhetorical predicates similar to those used by McKeown. Our solution extends the techniques McKeown and Suthers developed: it accommodates the many different kinds of knowledge contained in a fundamental knowledge base.

View Types

We propose that a small number of *view types* is sufficient to characterize all viewpoints within physical domains. The view types that we have identified so far are:

- class-dependent (explaining a concept in terms of a class hierarchy)
- structural (explaining the physical or temporal structure of an object or process)
- functional (explaining the role of an object in a process)
- modulatory (explaining how one object or process affects another)
- attributional (specifying the properties of a concept)
- comparative (comparing or contrasting two concepts)

A view type defines the relations and properties of a concept that are relevant when considering the concept from a viewpoint belonging to that view type. It specifies *necessary relations,* which must be included, and *permissible relations,* which may be included but are not required.

The *class-dependent* view type emphasizes how a concept fits into a class hierarchy. There are two subtypes: the *categorical* view type and the *enumerative* view type. The categorical view type emphasizes the properties and relations a concept inherits from one of its generalizations. For example, "flower as reproductive organ" is a categorical viewpoint. This viewpoint considers the flower in terms of how it is like the prototypical reproductive organ, including knowledge of reproductive parts and processes. This view type corresponds to the notion of perspective proposed by Bobrow and Winograd (1977) except that the concept generalization does not have to be an immediate generalization.

The enumerative view type describes a concept in terms of its instances or specializations. This corresponds to describing a concept by

giving examples. For instance, an enumerative viewpoint of plant reproduction includes knowledge of sexual and asexual plant reproduction.

The *structural* view type emphasizes an object's subparts or superparts
(termed *substructural* and *superstructural* view types, respectively). An example of a substructural viewpoint is "seed as consisting of the endosperm
and the embryo, both contained by the seed coat." This viewpoint
considers the subparts of the seed. An example of a superstructural
viewpoint is "endosperm as a part of the seed contained in the seed coat."
This viewpoint considers the superparts of the endosperm. As illustrated
by these examples, a structural viewpoint includes those relations that
specify how the parts are interconnected.

In addition to describing the *physical* structures of objects, the
structural view type also describes the *temporal* structures of entities and
processes. The temporal substructure of an entity is the stages it goes
through during its existence. The substructure of a process is its subevents.
For example, a temporal substructural viewpoint is "Photosynthesis as the
light reactions followed by the dark reactions." Similarly, temporal superstructural viewpoints also belong to the structural view type.

The *functional* view type emphasizes the role of an object in a process.
By definition, it includes some kind of *actor in* relationship, such as *producer,
agent,* or *raw material.* For example, the viewpoint "chloroplast as the
producer in plant photosynthesis" employs the functional view type.
Although this example illustrates a direct relationship between an object
and a process, sometimes the relationship is indirect. A part or specialization of the object may be the actor, rather than the object itself. For
instance, one function of a seed is to protect the plant embryo, though
strictly speaking it is the seed coat, a part of the seed, that protects the
embryo. The *part of* relation is defined as permissible for the functional
view type.

The *modulatory* view type emphasizes how one object or process
affects (or is affected by) another object or process. A modulatory
viewpoint necessarily includes at least one modulatory relation, such as
causes, enables, prevents, requires, required for, facilitates, or *inhibits.* An example
of a modulatory viewpoint is "sunlight as a requirement for plant growth"
or "embryo growth as a cause of seed coat rupture." Permissible relations
also may be included, as with the functional view type.

The simplest view type is the *attributional* view type, which emphasizes
a concept's properties, such as *color* and *weight.* Properties have values that
fall along a range or spectrum.

Finally, the *comparative* view type uses a subordinate view type to
compare two concepts. For example, two concepts can be compared
according to their structure, their function, or their effects on other
concepts. Examples include comparisons between concepts within the same

category, as in "the similarities and differences between photosynthesis and chemosynthesis as energy transfer processes," and comparisons of the functional role of two objects, as in "the differences between 'chlorophyll a' and 'chlorophyll b' in photosynthesis."

View types are abstractions of viewpoints. To isolate a particular viewpoint from the knowledge base, the system selects an appropriate view type and specifies a concept of interest and a reference concept. A *concept of interest* is the main topic of a viewpoint. A *reference concept* is the term to which the concept of interest should be related. (No reference concept is required for the enumerative and attributional view types.)

For example,

- View Type: Functional,
- Concept of Interest: Pollen,
- Reference Concept: Plant Reproduction,

specifies the viewpoint "the functional role of pollen in plant reproduction." Thus a view type, when applied to a concept of interest and a reference concept, specifies a particular viewpoint.

A question-answering system can use view types to generate coherent answers to a student's question in the following way. The question determines the concept of interest. The system selects a view type and reference concept using the student model, dialogue history, teaching plan, domain knowledge, and domain-independent knowledge about view types. For each valid pairing of a question type and a view type, the system has a strategy for selecting knowledge that coherently answers the question using the concept of interest and the reference concept to guide access to the knowledge base. The following sections describe these strategies for two of our question types.

Strategies for the Definition Question Type

A definition question can be answered using a single view type or a combination of view types. The six view types we have developed, either singly or in combination, were adequate to characterize over 50 definitions from a botany textbook.

For each of our six view types we have developed a corresponding *definition-generation strategy,* a procedure for selecting the portion of the knowledge base relevant to defining a concept from that particular point of view. Each strategy selects domain knowledge about the concept of interest and its relationship to the selected reference concept. This knowledge constitutes the basis for a coherent definition according to a particular viewpoint. We illustrate these strategies using the questions, "What is photosynthesis?" and "What is chlorophyll?"

Categorical Definitions. The definition-generation strategy for the categorical view type is to select knowledge explaining how the concept of interest (*photosynthesis*) is a specialization of the reference concept. For the categorical view type, the reference concept can be any generalization of the concept of interest. Two possible choices in this case are *production* and *photochemical energy transduction*. (See Figure 7.4.)

A system using this strategy first collects all relations and properties that the concept of interest inherits from the reference concept. The relations inherited to *photosynthesis* from *production* include *producer, products,* and *raw materials* (see Figure 7.4, paths marked 1P). Then the system selects all values specific to the concept of interest that appear on these inherited relations. For example, *photosynthesis* has the value *chloroplast* on relation *producer.* Similarly, the values for the relations *products* and *raw materials* are selected ((*oxygen, glucose*) and (*water, carbon dioxide*), respectively). Thus, the resulting definition is:

> Photosynthesis is a kind of production that has a chloroplast as the producer, water and carbon dioxide as the raw materials, and oxygen and glucose as the products.

If *photochemical energy transduction* is the reference concept instead (see Figure 7.4, paths marked 1E), the result is:

> Photosynthesis is a kind of photochemical energy transduction that has chlorophyll as the transducer, a photon as the energy provider, light energy as the input energy form, and chemical bond energy as the output energy form.

This example illustrates how a question can be answered in a variety of ways using the same view type, simply by selecting different reference concepts.

Enumerative Definitions. The definition-generation strategy for the enumerative view type is to collect the *instances* or the *specializations* of a concept in the knowledge base. For example, an enumerative definition of chlorophyll is:

> There are two types of chlorophyll: chlorophyll-A and chlorophyll-B.

If an unmanageable number is found, then the system presents only a subset of the examples to the student.

Structural Definitions.   The definition-generation strategy for the structural view type is to select the substructural or superstructural relationships of an event or object. A substructural definition reports the values on the *parts* or *stages* relations of objects, or the *subevents* relations of events. This definition also includes relations that describe the interconnection of parts or the ordering of subevents or stages. For example, a substructural definition of photosynthesis is:

> Photosynthesis is an event consisting of two subevents: the light reactions followed by the dark reactions. The light reactions consist of chloroplast light capture followed by photophosphorylation. The dark reactions consist of the Calvin cycle and ATP splitting, which occur simultaneously.

(Figure 7.4, paths labeled 2). A superstructural definition is constructed in a similar manner and contains information about how the object or event is a component of an encompassing object or event. The strategy is to report the values on all relations that indicate what the object or event is part of, connected to, or contained in.

Functional Definitions.   The definition-generation strategy for the functional view type is to select relations from the knowledge base that explain the role of an object in a process. This involves searching the knowledge base for a path from the concept of interest to the reference concept that consists of one *actor in* relation and any number of permissible relations. Unlike spreading activation, this strategy effectively constrains the search by restricting the kinds of relations that may be traversed. For example, to answer the question "What is chlorophyll?" (with *chlorophyll* as the concept of interest), a possible reference concept is *photosynthesis*. The strategy is to look for some kind of *actor in* relation directly linking *chlorophyll* to *photosynthesis*. If no relation is found, as in this example, the strategy is to determine if *chlorophyll* has an *actor in* relation to some process that can be linked to *photosynthesis* through a series of *generalization* and *superevent* relations. Failing this, the strategy is to find a path from one of the specializations or parts of *chlorophyll* to *photosynthesis*. This succeeds, and results in:

> A part of chlorophyll is an excitable chlorophyll electron, which is the energy acceptor in chloroplast light capture. Chloroplast light capture is a subevent of the photosynthetic light reactions, which is a subevent of photosynthesis.

Modulatory Definitions.   The definition-generation strategy for the modulatory view type selects knowledge that explains how the concept of interest affects or is affected by the reference concept. This strategy involves searching for a path from the concept of interest to the reference concept consisting only of modulatory and permissible relations. For example, suppose the reference concept is *plant biosynthesis*. The search begins at *photosynthesis,* but because no modulatory relations emanate from the concept *photosynthesis,* a permissible relation must be chosen. One of the permissible relations is *products,* with values *oxygen* and *glucose. Oxygen* has a modulatory relation (*required for*) to *respiration,* and *glucose* has the same relation to *plant biosynthesis* (See Figure 7.4, paths labeled 3). The resulting explanation is:

> Photosynthesis has product glucose, which is required for plant biosynthesis.

Attributional Definitions. The definition-generation strategy for the attributional view type involves collecting all property relations on the concept of interest, such as *color* and *weight.* Next, the values found on the relations are selected. As with the enumerative view type, this strategy is not used alone; rather, it is combined with other view types to add detail to a definition.

Strategies for the Comparison Question Type

A definition question also can be answered from the comparative view type. Answering a definition question with the comparative view type is equivalent to recasting the question "What is X?" as the question "How is X similar to and different from Y?", where Y is chosen by the system. In other words, selecting the comparative view type for a definition question is equivalent to refining the question from the definition type to the comparison type.

For a comparison of two concepts to be coherent, the comparison must be made according to one or more viewpoints (McCoy, 1985). Thus, to answer a comparison question, the system must be provided with the two terms to be compared (X and Y) and must select or be given a view type and a reference concept. The system must also know whether to provide similarities, differences, or both.

Comparing two concepts is a three-step process:

1. Define Concept X with the chosen view type and reference concept (using one of the definition-generation strategies described earlier).
2. Define Concept Y with the same view type and reference concept.
3. Give the similarities and/or differences in these two definitions.

The strategy for the comparison in step 3 depends on the view type selected. As an example, we turn to a discussion of these techniques for the categorical view type.

When the view type of the comparison is categorical, the system looks for the similarities or differences in two categorical definitions. Categorical definitions consist of a set of relations that originate at the reference concept. To make the comparison, the strategy is to pair the relations from these two sets. This is done by determining which relations match, either exactly or abstractly. Two relations match abstractly if one is a more general version of the other or if they share a common generalization. For example, the relations *actor* and *producer* match abstractly because *producer* is a specialization of *actor*. (See Figure 7.3.) The pairing process attempts to find a set of matches that minimizes the distance between paired relations in the relation hierarchy. Once the pairing of relations is complete, the system can make the comparison.

First, consider a similarity-based comparison. This entails giving the values and constraints on the paired relations that X and Y have in common. A more detailed presentation of similarities would also include the similarities of the nonidentical values. We illustrate a similarity-based, categorical comparison by comparing *photophosphorylation* and *respiration,* with *production* as the reference concept. The two categorical definitions to be compared are:

- Photophosphorylation is a production process that has a photosynthetic cell as the producer, ADP as its raw material, and ATP as its product.
- Respiration is a production process that has a biological cell as its producer, glucose, ADP, and oxygen as raw materials, and water, carbon dioxide, and ATP as products.

The first step in making the comparison is pairing the relations included in the first definition (*producer, raw materials,* and *products*) with the relations included in the second definition (also *producer, raw materials,* and *products*). Relation pairing in this example is trivial because the relations match exactly.

After the relations are matched, the values are matched. The only value that appears in both definitions on the relation *raw materials* is ADP, and the only value that appears in both definitions on the *products* relation is ATP. These two similarities are included in the result, along with the reference concept (*production*). The result of the similarity-based comparison is:

Photophosphorylation is like respiration in that both are production processes that have ADP as a raw material and ATP as a product.

No common value is found on the *producer* relation, but a more extensive presentation of similarities would include a comparison of the values *photosynthetic cell* and *biological cell*.

We now turn to a discussion of difference-based, categorical comparison: Two types of differences may be presented:

- differences in values between X and Y on paired relations
- relations that occur on one concept but not the other

As an example of a difference-based, categorical comparison, consider again *photophosphorylation* and *respiration*, but with *energy transduction* as the reference concept. The two categorical definitions to be compared are:

- Photophosphorylation is an energy transduction process that has an excited chlorophyll electron as the energy provider, electron excitation energy as the input energy form, and phosphate bond energy as the output energy form.
- Respiration is an energy transduction process that has glucose as the energy provider, carbon bond energy as the input energy form, and phosphate bond energy as the output energy form.

Again, relation pairing in this example is trivial because the relations in the definitions (*energy provider, input energy form,* and *output energy form*) exactly match. The only kind of differences in this example is the first kind (differing values on paired relations). The resulting categorical, difference-based comparison would be:

> Photophosphorylation differs from respiration in that the input energy form of photophosphorylation is electron excitation energy, while for respiration it is carbon bond energy. Also, the energy provider for photophosphorylation is an excited chlorophyll electron, while for respiration the energy provider is glucose.

A special case of categorical comparison is one in which a concept is contrasted with one of its generalizations. This kind of comparison describes how a concept differs from some norm. The strategy is to select all information about the concept of interest that overrides information inherited from the generalization. For example, *photosynthetic cell* can be contrasted with the typical *botanical cell*. The result would be:

> The photosynthetic cell is a type of botanical cell that has a chloroplast part in addition to the normal parts of a botanical cell. The color of a photosynthetic cell is green.

DISCUSSION

Because view types are high-level organizers of knowledge, they can be used to generate coherent explanations from an extensive knowledge base. Each view type provides a category of semantic relations that can be coherently combined. For example, a functional explanation of an object uses relations that describe its role in processes.

However, in addition to coherence, numerous other factors determine the adequacy of a tutor's explanations. We are improving the question answerer by addressing two of these factors. The first involves emphasizing the concepts that are most important to the topic. For example, although an explanation of the concept *flower* could include both its relation to *plant reproduction* and *plant development,* the explanation should emphasize the former. The question answerer can emphasize important concepts if the knowledge base includes this type of information.

The second factor involves sensitivity to the context in which an explanation is generated. The context includes the student's background and interests, and the previous dialogue between the student and the question answerer. A good explanation is tailored to the student, and it refers to previous explanations while avoiding redundancy. The question answerer can be sensitive to context by modeling the student and recording the dialogue history.

While these additions provide a question answerer with sensitivity to context over time, they do not provide mechanisms for coherent responses extending over more global bodies of text. Improvements over this dimension may be accomplished by extending the reach of view types and developing a facility for generating larger expositions of domain knowledge.

Using View Types to Generate Connected Text

View types can be extended to the global level in two ways. First, they can be extended to the organization of larger segments of text through view type chaining; second, they can provide an overall zeitgeist or viewpoint for the particular domain.

View Type Chains. An investigation of connected text in scientific textbooks has revealed that certain sections are best characterized by the chaining of two or more simple view types. Useful chains include categorical-structural, structural-functional, structural-modulatory, and enumerative-structural-functional. The last chain produces a *particular instance* of a structural-functional relationship, for instance, the way that the parts of *my* car engine interact to allow *its* engine to run.

Our current efforts are directed at understanding which of these view type chains are useful in the generation of connected text. It is clear that one member of a chain acts to constrain the information that another member of the chain provides. Thus, in the structural-modulatory case, only those parts of an object that enable subprocesses of the process of interest are retained for presentation; the other parts are discarded.

We are working on a grammar that can more formally characterize the view types and their interactions. This *view type grammar* is being designed for use in both a parsing mode, to interpret connected text, and in a production mode, to generate text from a knowledge base. In addition to defining the coherent and relevant content within the knowledge base for a particular response, this grammar may provide a rough grammatical order for presenting this content.

View Types as Global Zeitgeists. View types can be used to characterize the prevailing orientation in many scientific fields. In many physical domains "structure as an enabler of function" is the prominent notion. This can be represented by a subtype of the structural-modulatory view type chain that emphasizes enablement. When applied to a specific field, this chain generates a prevailing viewpoint. For example, in biology, the organism can be thought of as the global-level concept of interest, and the "living process" that the organism engages in as the reference concept. Application of the structural-modulatory view type produces the viewpoint of "organism structures as enablers of the various processes that collectively constitute living."

Within an overall field are subfields that either preserve this viewpoint, emphasize one aspect of the view type chain over another, or emphasize a very different view type. Subfields of biology include physiology, anatomy, and taxonomy. Physiology concentrates on the functions of organisms and usually discusses the parts of the organism only in relation to their function; functions are considered even if the parts carrying out these functions are unknown. On the other hand, anatomy emphasizes structures, often mentioning the function that is enabled when it is known but not being obligated to do so. An example of a subfield that does not preserve the prevailing viewpoint is taxonomy, which is concerned with the classification of organisms and naturally takes the categorical viewpoint.

Local viewpoints should support global-level themes. To this end, we believe that the global view type can help guide the choice of view types at the local level. We are investigating the possibility of prioritizing the view types in terms of their ability to support the global view type in a field. For example, if the global view type is structural-modulatory, a paragraph on the *structure* of some organism part like the heart can set up a later discussion of how the parts of the heart *enable* the various subprocesses that constitute its *function*.

Although the extension of view types can provide larger bodies of coherent content for presentation, it is not sufficient for generating presentations in a successful ITS. An ITS requires domain-specific plans for generating presentations, and it must have methods for flexibly interpreting these plans in light of information it receives from a student model and a dialogue history. In the following section, we discuss research on representing presentation plans and interpreting these plans in a context-sensitive fashion.

Representing and Interpreting Presentation Plans

A primary goal of teaching is to communicate a body of knowledge to the student. Consequently an ITS should be able to generate a presentation of a large body of domain knowledge. Just as a college instructor can construct an hour-long lecture on a topic in his field of expertise, an ITS should be able to construct an extensive exposition of a topic within its domain. Unlike the professor whose lecture is a monologue, however, an ITS should engage in an interactive dialogue with the student. An ITS must be able to customize its presentations to the needs of the current student and dialogue because students' backgrounds are idiosyncratic and mixed-initiative tutoring sessions proceed in an unpredictable fashion.

To address these problems, we are developing a representation of presentation plans that would allow an ITS to incrementally generate an exposition of a large body of domain knowledge. We are also developing techniques for interpreting these plans in a manner that is appropriate for the variable contexts of mixed-initiative tutoring sessions.

To generate a presentation, an ITS should have access to meta-knowledge about how to organize expositions of the domain knowledge. This *presentation knowledge* should include information about what subtopics are important for a topic, what subtopics are related to the topic but are less central, and what prerequisite relations exist between the sub-topics. Moreover, because the ITS should be sufficiently flexible to accommodate the needs of different users and different dialogues, the presentation knowledge should allow the ITS to generate many different presentations of the same topic.

The presentation knowledge is represented by a Stratified Prerequisite Identification Network (SPIN). Figure 7.5 depicts a small fragment of a SPIN for *angiosperm reproduction*. A SPIN is a data structure that is

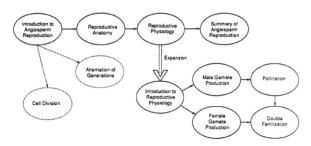

FIGURE 7.5 SPIN for angiosperm reproduction.

partitioned into layers, where each layer consists of a set of directed acyclic graphs. In each graph, the nodes represent topics, and the arcs represent prerequisite relations. There is an arc from node p to node q if topic p must be covered before topic q. Hence, in the example in Figure 7.5, *male gamete production* must be discussed before *pollination*.

A node in a SPIN may have an *expansion,* which is a graph at a lower layer. An expansion represents the fact that a topic may have a number of subtopics. For example, subtopics of *reproductive physiology* include *male gamete production, pollination,* and *double fertilization.*

Each node is marked as *required* or *optional.* This encodes the fact that some topics must be covered in a presentation whereas other topics may or may not be discussed (depending on the needs and interests of the student). For example, *reproductive anatomy* must be discussed, and *alternation of generations* is optional.

To generate a presentation on a particular topic, a planner can traverse the SPIN associated with that topic by choosing a node for which all of the predecessors have been processed. In many cases only a partial order has been imposed on the nodes in a graph, thus the planner has considerable flexibility. If the node has an expansion, then the procedure is applied recursively to that expansion; otherwise, the system dynamically generates a presentation for the node. This process is described later. The traversal terminates when all of the required nodes in the highest level have been processed.

It is important to note that each SPIN node without an expansion consists of specifications for generating a paragraph-length exposition of the topic: it does not contain a piece of canned text. The expositions are generated cooperatively by the planner and the question answerer, with the planner playing the role of the "question asker." The planner issues requests to the question answerer to generate explanations, which the planner then organizes. The specifications in the SPIN nodes are sufficiently unconstrained that many interpretations are possible, depending on the content of the student model and the dialogue history. The interpretation process includes making decisions about whether the system should generate definitions of relevant concepts and how much detail the discussion should include.

To illustrate using Figure 7.5, when the planner encounters the *double fertilization* node in its traversal of the SPIN, it first examines the student model and the dialogue history to determine if the student is already knowledgeable about this topic or if the topic has already been discussed as a result of a question the student asked. If a discussion of the topic is warranted, the planner consults a library of presentation strategies and applies the appropriate strategy to the specifications in the SPIN node.

Next, the planner examines the dialogue history to determine which concepts in the "first-pass" exposition are new to the student and hence need to be defined. To generate a definition, the planner supplies the question answerer with the term to be defined, a view type, and a reference concept. The planner must also must decide how much detail to include in the exposition. In our example, the SPIN specifications suggest that the level of detail should at least include a discussion of the two subprocesses of double fertilization — egg fertilization and endosperm fertilization.

If the students' questions during the presentation indicate he or she is unfamiliar with concepts that are prerequisites for the concepts being discussed, then the planner generates a presentation on those topics. For example, if the student asks why an egg is haploid (i.e., why it has only one of each kind of chromosome), the planner explains the basic model of gamete production in which cells divide, thereby halving the number of chromosomes.

SPINs offer one way of representing domain-specific presentation knowledge. However, constructing a SPIN is extremely time-consuming. To counter this problem, we are developing heuristics that will simplify SPIN construction for future projects. Despite being labor-intensive, SPINs offer a means of representing plans that can be used to generate customized, coherent presentations of large bodies of knowledge.

CONCLUSIONS

An important task for ITSs is providing coherent explanations in answer to students' questions. There are two basic approaches to providing explanations: presenting "canned text" and generating explanations directly from the knowledge base. Unlike using "canned text," generating explanations allows for flexible presentations of domain knowledge. Furthermore, for large-scale knowledge bases, it is not feasible to provide "canned text" in anticipation of every possible question that could be asked of the system.

Current ITSs offer a limited solution to the problem of generating explanations because they use restricted forms of domain knowledge. These restrictions include dedicating the ITS to a single task, representing the domain knowledge with a small number of axioms or rules, representing only a small portion of the domain, and explicitly partitioning the knowledge base according to the tasks for which the knowledge will be used. However, these restrictions are unacceptable for ITSs designed to teach fundamental knowledge.

Selecting coherent and relevant knowledge for a given application and circumstance emerges as a major problem because fundamental knowledge is highly complex. We have proposed a selection method that uses domain-independent view types to isolate viewpoints, which are coherent portions of the knowledge base. A small number of view types appears to be sufficient for characterizing all viewpoints within physical domains. These view types are the functional, modulatory, structural, class-dependent, attributional, and comparative view types. A viewpoint is specified by selecting a view type, concept of interest, and reference concept. Strategies derived from the view types are used to generate explanations according to a particular viewpoint.

View types and their associated strategies can be used by a question-answering system to generate coherent explanations in the following way. A question asked by the student would determine the concept of interest. The system would then select a view type using information in the student's question and knowledge about the applicability of the view types to the particular question type. Next, it would select a reference concept appropriate for the view type. Then it would use the strategy associated with the view type to retrieve from the knowledge base the network of nodes and arcs that forms the basis of a coherent answer to the student's question.

We have applied view types to the generation of explanations for the definition and comparison question types. In future work we plan to develop strategies to address the other question types in our question type hierarchy.

Although view types provide a way to select coherent knowledge for an explanation, other factors also influence the quality of an explanation. Our current research addresses some of these factors. One project is combining view types to characterize a field's zeitgeist and to generate elaborate explanations. Another project is planning the presentation of an entire subject and customizing explanations to individual students.

We expect our research on generating explanations from large-scale knowledge bases to contribute technology for electronic retrieval and manipulation of knowledge. Major advances in computer hardware technology, such as CD-ROMs and videodiscs, permit archiving vast libraries. Computer software for accessing these archives is essential, but is currently in the early stages of research. However, the preliminary results foreshadow a significant advance in teaching technology from static, immutable textbooks to interactive, adaptive tutoring systems.

ACKNOWLEDGMENTS

We appreciate the work of Ken Murray, Karen Pittman, and Tom Jones on the Botany Knowledge Base Project.

Support for this research was provided by the Air Force Human Resources Laboratory and NASA through RICIS grant ET.14. Additional support was provided by the National Science Foundation under grant IRI-8620052 and donations from Apple, Texas Instruments, and the Cray Foundation.

REFERENCES

Bobrow, D., & Winograd, T. (1977). An overview of KRL, a knowledge representation language. *Cognitive Science, 1*, 3–46.

Brown, J. S., Burton, R. R., & Bell, A. G. (1975). SOPHIE: A step towards a reactive learning environment. *International Journal of Man–Machine Studies, 7*, 675–696.

Brown, J. S., Burton, R. R., & de Kleer, J. (1982). Pedagogical, natural language, and knowledge engineering techniques in SOPHIE I, II, and III. In D. Sleeman & J. S. Brown (Eds.), *Intelligent tutoring systems* (pp. 227–282). London: Academic Press.

Brown, J. S., Burton, R. R., & Zdybel, F. (1973). A model-driven question-answering system for mixed-initiative computer-assisted instruction. *IEEE Transactions on Systems, Man, and Cybernetics, 3*(3), 248–257.

Carbonell, J. R. (1970). AI in CAI: An artificial intelligence approach to computer-aided instruction. *IEEE Transactions on Man–Machine Systems, 11*(4), 190–202.

Clancey, W. (1983). The epistemology of a rule-based expert system — A framework for explanation. *Artificial Intelligence, 20*, 215–251.

Clancey, W. (1987). *Knowledge-based tutoring: The GUIDON program.* Cambridge, MA: MIT Press.

de Beaugrande, R. (1980). *Text discourse and process.* Norwood, NJ: Ablex.

Grimes, J. (1975). *The thread of discourse.* The Hague: Mouton.

Halliday, M., & Hasan, R. (1976). *Cohesion in English.* London: Longman.

Hobbs, J. R. (1983). Why is discourse coherent? In F. Neubauer (Ed.), *Coherence in natural-language texts* (pp. 29–70). Hamburg: H. Buske.

Hollan, J., Hutchins, E., & Weitzman, L. (1984). STEAMER: An interactive inspectable simulation-based training system. *AI Magazine, 5*(2), 15–27.

Hughes, S. (1986). Question classification in rule-based systems. *Expert Systems,* 123–131.

Joshi A. K., & Weinstein S. (1981). Control of inference: The role of some aspects of discourse structure — Centering. *Proceedings of the Seventh International Joint Conference on Artificial Intelligence* (pp. 385–387).

Lehnert, W. (1977). The process of question answering. *Cognitive Science, 1,* 47–73.

Lehnert, W. (1986). A conceptual theory of question answering. In B. Grosz, K. Jones, & B. Webber (Eds.), *Reading in natural language processing.* (pp. 651–657). Los Altos, CA: Morgan Kaufman.

Mann, W. (1983). An overview of the PENMAN text generation system. *Proceedings of the National Conference on Artificial Intelligence* (pp. 261–265).

McCoy, K. (1985). The role of perspective in responding to property misconceptions. *Proceedings of the Ninth International Joint Conference on Artificial Intelligence* (pp. 791–793).

McDonald, D., & Pustejevsky, J. (1985). Description directed natural language generation. *Proceedings of the Ninth International Joint Conference on Artificial Intelligence* (pp. 799–805).

McKeown, K. (1985a). *Tailoring explanations for the user* (Tech. Rep. No. CUCS-172-85) New York: Columbia University.

McKeown, K. (1985b). *Text generation. Using discourse strategies and focus constraints to generate natural language text.* New York: Cambridge University Press.

Porter, B., Lester, J., Murray, K., Pittman, K., Souther, A., Acker, L., & Jones, T. (1988). *AI research in the context of a multifunctional knowledge base project* (Tech. Rep. No. AI88-88). Austin: University of Texas, AI Laboratory.

Shortliffe, E. H. (1976). *Computer-based medical consultations: MYCIN.* New York: American Elsevier.

Suthers, D. (1988). Providing multiple views for explanation. *Proceedings of the AAAI-88 Workshop on Explanation,* (pp. 12–15).

Swartout, W. (1983). XPLAIN: A system for creating and explaining expert consulting programs. *Artificial Intelligence, 21,* 285–325.

VanLehn, K., & Brown, J. (1980). Planning nets: a representation for formalizing analogies and semantic models of procedural skills. In R. Snow, P. Frederico, & W. Montague (Eds.), *Aptitude, learning, and instruction: Cognitive process analyses* (Vol. 2 pp. 95–138). Hillsdale, NJ: Lawrence Erlbaum Associates.

White, B., & Frederiksen, J. (1987). Qualitative models and intelligent learning environments. In R. Lawler & M. Yazdani (Eds.), *Artificial Intelligence and education* (pp. 281–306). Norwood, NJ: Ablex.

From Training to Teaching:
Techniques for Case-Based ITS

Christopher K. Riesbeck
Roger C. Schank
Northwestern University

This chapter focuses on the teaching of knowledge-intensive domains, such as biology, history, and weather forecasting, in contrast to other chapters in this volume that discuss teaching high-performance skills (e.g., Fink, chap. 9; Regian, chap. 10) or basic concepts (e.g., Bonar, chap. 3; Acker and colleagues, chap. 7; Woolf, chap. 6).

It has become a truism in artificial intelligence (AI) that knowledge is crucial. Clever algorithms, fancy data structures, and elegant formalisms will not save an AI program that does not know what it is doing. Success in AI depends on both quantity of knowledge (how much the program knows) and quality (how accurate is the knowledge, how accessible is it, and so on).

Consider what distinguishes a good encyclopedia from a bad one. It is not the "data structures" involved; both have labeled articles and a master index. Rather, it is the quality of the articles and the appropriateness of the index terms that matters. Similarly, an AI program—or a person—needs the right knowledge and the right indexes to be intelligent. It follows that a major task in education is to teach both knowledge and the indexes that make that knowledge accessible.

But that raises the classic AI question, "How should knowledge be represented?", and the classic educational question, "How should knowledge be communicated?" In much of what is called *knowledge-based AI*, the representation question is answered with *rules*. Rules have the form "if situation then conclusion," Problems are solved and situations are understood by chaining rules together.

There are a number of problems with this approach. Coming up with a reasonable set of rules is a very difficult, if not impossible, task for many domains. Even in domains with rules, such as mathematics, the computational complexity of combining them to form inference chains may be too great to be feasible.

Furthermore, rules have their limits as a way of communicating knowledge. Although detailed formulas and general principles are rulelike, neither are sufficient for describing a domain. Real domains, such as weather forecasting, have so many detailed formulas and so many exceptions to the general principles that a student would be overwhelmed by any tutoring system that tried to present them all.

There is an alternative to rules, however, and that is to represent domain knowledge in the form of many example cases that embody, either explicitly or implicitly, the relevant formulas and principles. Problems are solved by adapting previous solutions for similar problems. Situations are understood by adapting previous interpretations for similar situations.

Case-based reasoning has a number of potential advantages for solving AI problems, but this chapter focuses on the impact this technology can have on intelligent tutoring systems (ITSs).

CASE-BASED TEACHING

It is well understood in many complex domains that the best teaching method is case-based. Law and business schools teach cases rather than rules. Recent research in AI suggests that there is a valid psychological reason for this, and we are now designing AI teaching methods that use cases to teach. We believe that many, if not most, skills can be taught in a case-based fashion.

Most training involves teaching trainees to know what to do and when to do it. Trainees are successful to the extent that they do what they are told to do when they are supposed to. The trick is that trainees must abstract information from the situations they have been told about and apply it to situations for which they were not specifically trained.

To learn to deal with specific cases, one must learn the prototypical cases, the standards that serve as the basis from which one learns how to deal with a new situation. A computer system that is a real-life simulation can create a situation, posed as a problem to the trainee, and ask for a response. A good teacher forces conjectures on the part of the trainee and simulates real-world situations. A trainee would be expected to respond with the right answer, or, failing that, would be presented with a situation where that question has been asked before and where a good answer was given in response. The trainee would then be encouraged to try a variation of the previous good answer. Learning by copying is an important part of learning; learning to move from copying to creative adaptation is another. And learning to know what cases to try to adapt, that is, learning what makes cases relevant, may be the most important part of all. Thus, in our approach, a trainee is developing a battery of situations — cases — and appropriate ways to respond in those situations.

A recent book, *Thinking in Time,* by Neustadt and May (1986), describes how decision making occurs in government and how the authors actually go about teaching decision makers to improve their ability in this area. A great deal of what is said in the book indicates that government decision makers, like everybody else, reason by reminding. They need to make decisions, so they recall similar situations and try to reason from them.

Two situations in the book are noteworthy in this context. The first is the Bay of Pigs invasion and the second is the *Mayaguez* incident. Decision makers in both cases recalled and argued from past cases in history. In the Bay of Pigs case, the prototype was an incident in Latin America 10 years earlier that caused a little-known invasion by the United States that seemed to work. In the *Mayaguez* incident, the prior case was the *Pueblo* incident from a few years before.

In both of these remindings, we have a situation where decision makers had an incident brought to mind that had occurred a few years before, that is, within the memory of decision makers, and that was *superficially* similar. I emphasize the word *superficial* because, as the authors point out, that is all that was in common. The *Pueblo* and the *Mayaguez* were both ships with Spanish names flying U.S. flags captured in Asia, but one was a military ship and the other was a commercial ship. One was captured by an enemy government, whereas the other was not. In fact, these incidents had very little in common with the exception that when President Ford heard about the *Mayaguez* he decided not to do what had been done with the *Pueblo* and almost created a great deal of difficulty for the people he was trying to save.

But although reminding is the right and natural thing to do, it does not mean much if you do not have much to be reminded of. There is a real problem with the corporate memory of the government and of the world in general. Education means having enough cases available so that when a decision needs to be made, one or more very close matches from history come to mind. The more relevant evidence available, the more likely an intelligent decision is to result.

Thus, it becomes clear that a system of selecting and presenting cases to a decision maker can be an important means of enhancing good decisions. For a student, interacting with a system that can present past history when needed allows for the possibility of learning what one needs to know when one wants to know it. Teaching students about Vietnam may put them to sleep. But charge them with having to make a decision about Nicaragua and they may, all of a sudden, become quite interested in Vietnam. If students suggest invasion, a suitable historical precedent is retrieved and described. If they mention economic support, a different story would be recalled. If they mention ignoring the situation, yet another story surfaces, and so on.

Case-based teachers, then, would be well-indexed libraries of prior situations. The trick in creating them is properly indexing them. Good teachers try to present facts and alternative interpretations as neutrally as possible. This is quite difficult for people, but, for obvious reasons, much easier for machines.

Most of all, such systems would allow students to do hypothetical reasoning in complex domains while becoming active learners about subjects they themselves decide to explore. This is what education can and ought to be about. Because learning is really the accumulation of cases, learning and creativity involves the adaptation of imperfectly fitting cases to new situations.

CASE-BASED REASONING

The most common model of cognition in AI is *rule-based reasoning*. It distinguishes two kinds of knowledge: *facts* and *procedures*. Facts are represented using propositions, frames, and/or semantic networks. Procedures are represented with if-then inference rules. To explain a situation or solve a problem, a rule-based reasoner applies various combinations of rules to various facts until a chain of reasoning, that is, a proof, is found. The proof may be wrong, because the rules and facts are dubious and the combination rules heuristic, but a rule-based reasoner remains a very thoughtful creature. Usually, however, a rule-based reasoner is also a very forgetful creature. Proofs are forgotten, so that when the same or similar situation arises again, the same problem-solving behavior must be reenacted.

We have argued elsewhere, however, that everyday intelligence is just not that thoughtful and certainly not that forgetful (Riesbeck & Schank, 1989). People quickly relate events and problems to prior experience. When personal knowledge is stretched too far, as when the man in the street is asked to evaluate complex political events, absurd responses can result. But in familiar situations, sophisticated answers come quickly and robustly, as when average people go to a restaurant or shop for groceries, experienced car mechanics see a familiar situation, or chefs encounter a tricky situation they have dealt with before.

We call reasoning from experience *case-based reasoning* (CBR) (Schank, 1982; Kolodner, 1988; Kolodner & Riesbeck, 1986). CBR is important in domains such as politics or cooking, because it is very difficult, if not impossible, to formalize them with rules. In these domains, reasoning from examples is the only serious option. CBR is also important in domains that have too many rules, as in weather forecasting or economics, or too many ways in which the rules can be applied, as in mathematics, programming, or game playing. In these domains, cases suggest approximate answers, thereby limiting how many rule combinations must be explored.

At the heart of CBR are two processes: *indexing* or labeling, and *adaptation*. When new experiences come into the system, they need to be labeled for future retrieval. When retrieved to deal with a new situation, cases needed to be adapted to fit the current circumstances.

Cases need two kinds of indexes: *concrete* and *abstract*. Concrete indexes refer to objects and actions usually directly mentioned in the case. Abstract indexes refer to more general characterizations of the case. For example, a chef might index a recipe by concrete indexes such as ingredients and basic type (stew, stir fry, casserole, etc.), as well as by more general characterizations, such as how easy it is to prepare, what kind of people like it, what kind of cooking problems it solves, and so on.

The *indexing problem*, as it is usually called in CBR research, is the problem of determining the appropriate abstract and concrete indexes for cases. How we index incoming cases (instances of going to a restaurant, proofs by contradiction, monetarist arguments, and so on) determines what cases we will compare the inputs against. A very general index will cause a case to be retrieved even when it shares no specific details with the current situation. *Romeo and Juliet* is useful for understanding *West Side Story*, even though the details differ greatly.

Figure 8.1 shows the reasoning and learning components of a typical CBR system. An input describing a problem or situation is analyzed and used to retrieve one or more similar cases in the case library. The solution that was used in the most similar case is then adapted to solve the input problem. If it works, the new solution is added to the case library. This is *success-driven learning*. Ideally, a CBR system should never repeat the same problem-solving process. If the new solution fails, then two things happen. First, the failure is analyzed and the solution repaired. If the repaired solution works, it is added to the case library. Second, new indexes for labeling cases are created, based on the failure analysis, so that similar inputs in the future will retrieve the repaired solution, not the one that led to the failure. This is called *failure-driven learning*. Ideally, a CBR system

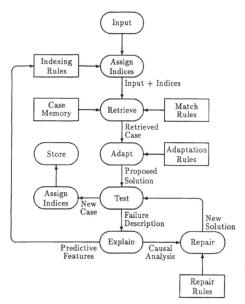

FIGURE 8.1 CBR flow chart.

should never repeat its mistakes. More details of CBR, along with examples of various CBR systems can be found in Kolodner and Riesbeck (1986) and Riesbeck and Schank (1989).

CBR relates to ITS research in two ways. First, CBR is a *model* of cognition and learning that suggests the goal of an ITS system should be to teach the cases as well as how to index them. Rules can be useful, even crucial, but they do not become intuitive and useful until there is a rich case base showing when the rules apply and when they do not.

Moreover, CBR is a *technology* for building ITS, a technology that stresses the construction, indexing, and use of large libraries of related, sometimes redundant, examples, rather than the development of inference engines and highly tuned sets of rules.

In the following sections, we describe three complementary technologies for building case-based ITSs:

- CBR itself, in particular the indexing of cases with labels that allow cases to be used in a variety of circumstances;
- direct memory access parsing, to enable natural language access to cases; and
- reactive tutorial plans that take into account the contents of the case base, current pedagogical goals, and the state of the student.

INDEXING CASES

If we simply indexed cases with words and phrases:

- synonyms would have to be included for each index word;
- cases would have to be reindexed when the language of the student population changed;
- common uses of words might not agree with the case library's, for example, *bug* and *insect* are synonyms to the average person, but not to a case library about entomology;
- ambiguous words would retrieve unrelated cases, for example, *bug* would index cases in entomology and computer programming; and
- the student would not know why a case was retrieved, for example, *beef* and *inflation* might both retrieve a description of Argentina, but for different reasons.

We need to separate lexical connections from conceptual ones. Linking words and phrases to concepts should be taken care of by the interface, as discussed in the language understanding section. Furthermore, we need to indicate how an index concept relates to a case. Thus, we might index a case as "a kind of . . . ," "an instance of . . . ," "a part of . . . ," "the cause of . . . ," and so on, where each ". . . " is filled in by some concept. Beyond these simple semantic relationships are others such as "is analogous to . . . ," "is often accompanied by . . . ," "is a prototypical instance of . . . ," "is an exception to . . . ," "is summarized by . . . ," and so on.

Consider an ITS in the domain of programming, and how powerful it could be if it knew that:

- Computer programs are analogous to cooking recipes.
- The bubble sort is a classic instance of a computer program.
- PROLOG is an exception to the procedural view of programming languages.

Even in simple semantic networks, these kinds of indexes can be useful: robins and sparrows are prototypical birds, the penguin and ostrich are exceptional, one goal of flocking behavior can be summarized by "safety in numbers," and so on.

Getting these indexes means analyzing domain experts, tutors, and students to find the concepts each uses to organize experience. The concepts students use need to be tied to the concepts domain experts use. Some of what a student knows can be characterized as instances or examples of specific domain concepts, for example, BASIC (a student concept) is an instance of a *procedural language* (a domain expert concept). Other student concepts can be characterized as abstractions of more specific domain concepts, for example, *monkey* (student concept) is really a subclass (domain expert concept) that excludes chimpanzees.

CONNECTING LANGUAGE TO KNOWLEDGE

Teaching knowledge-intensive domains such as biology or history commonly involves natural language. There are texts, summaries, questions, answers, problem specifications, and so on. Even in weather forecasting, where problem situations are specified with maps and numeric annotations, there are the briefings where forecasters summarize their analysis and prognosis, and instructors critique the briefing. Certainly, our normal picture of a tutor–student interaction involves natural language dialogue.

Natural language understanding remains one of the hardest problems in AI. There are no systems that can understand a significant corpus of text; that is, there are no systems that can produce meaning representations usable by a reasoning system or an ITS. The difficulties are particularly noticeable in dialogues, where grammatical rules become the most context-dependent. The classic example of this is the sentence, "George thinks vanilla." It looks nongrammatical and nonsensical in isolation, but is in fact perfectly fine after the question, "What flavor ice cream does Mary like?"

Our approach has been to radically rethink what language understanding is all about. The standard model of language understanding is the *meaning construction model:* Text is understood by putting pieces of meaning together. To understand "George thinks vanilla," fit together the pieces: *a person named George, the action of thinking,* and *a flavor called vanilla.* The meaning construction model fails in this situation, because *vanilla* can not be an object or style of thinking. To fix this, the system assumes that vanilla is an elliptical reference, and searches memory for what it might be referring to. The system "changes modes," so to speak, going from construction to memory search.

In our view, language understanding is always memory search. Texts are always references to existing knowledge structures, and the goal of the language understander is to chase down those references. The Direct Memory Access Parser (DMAP) (Riesbeck & Martin, 1986; Riesbeck & Schank, 1989) is an implementation of an understander based on memory search. When DMAP sees words and phrases, it searches for the concepts those words could refer to. When DMAP sees a sequence of concepts, it searches for larger memory structures that such a sequence could refer to, and so on.

Unlike most systems, DMAP does not have a lexicon of word senses. Instead, attached to each concept or case are patterns or sequences of words and concepts that might be used to refer to that concept or case. By intersecting references as the text is read, DMAP determines which memory structures account for the text as a whole. (DMAP uses a marker passing algorithm, described in detail in Riesbeck & Martin, 1986, and Riesbeck & Schank, 1989.) Figure 8.2 shows the reference sequence that recognizes "George thinks . . . ," which is attached to the *believe* memory structure.

DMAP has memory structures representing dialogue structures, such as questions and answers, with reference sequences attached to different kinds of questions, for example, "What *object* does *actor action?*" and answers, for example, "*object.*" One kind of answer is a version of the believe memory structure, where the *object* of the believing is the answer to the question. The question, "What flavor ice cream does Mary like?", followed by the statement of belief, "George thinks vanilla," satisfies the reference sequence for a particular question-and-answer memory structure.

We believe that the memory search approach is ideal for ITS for several reasons:

- Language entry is simpler, that is, attaching sequences to memory structures; getting the right memory structures remains hard, but an intelligent system needs them, whether or not language is involved.
- The reference model of language seems particularly appropriate to the highly referential nature of dialogues.
- Special cases are easy to capture, for example, questions about certain topics or the use of particular phrases.
- Only modest extension is required to use reference sequences in reverse to describe concepts and cases in natural language; choosing what to say when remains a hard problem, but putting it into words is not.

TUTORIAL PLANS

A third problem in teaching knowledge-intensive domains is covering the curriculum. The more students discover things on their own, the better, but an ITS should take advantage of any situation where important topics can be introduced. For example, consider the following dialogue that took

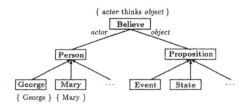

FIGURE 8.2 DMAP reference sequences.

place between a human biology professor and a student, where the student was asked to design an animal.

Student: I want to design a cow-like thing. But I want my cow to have six legs.

Professor: I'll let you if you want. But I'll tell you that there aren't any.

Student: Why aren't there?

Professor: That never happened because cows evolved from animals that only had four legs. Not that it's impossible, but that it never happened. That's an interesting point: Several things we could get to are possible, but they just never happened. That's the way history went.

Student: I'm going to give it six legs.

Professor: Go ahead. What are the legs for?

Student: I want it to run fast.

Professor: Why do you think six legs will make it go fast?

Student: You tell me.

Professor: I don't think you can reason whether it will or not because there are six-legged things around. Some of them are very fast for their size, like ants. Insects in general really truck out.

The types of the answers the professor gave depended on exactly what he knew and what he thought was interesting to teach. For example, when the student mentioned a six-legged cow, the professor knew that no such thing existed, that no analogous creature existed, such as any six-legged mammal, and that the reason was more evolutionary than functional. If the professor knew about six-legged cows in Borneo, he could have mentioned them. If he knew about six-legged cats, he could have mentioned them. If he knew that mammals cannot function with six legs, he could explain why. In this case, the professor talked about evolution because (a) it could be related to why cows do not have six legs, and (b) evolution is an important concept in biology.

Although the student asked the questions and proposed the variations, the content and options made available in the dialogue were controlled by the professor, who opportunistically inserted examples, generalizations, questions, and so on, as he felt appropriate. This is called a *mixed-initiative dialogue* (Carbonell, 1970). However, there is a problem with achieving mixed-initiative dialogues because it is hard to specify in advance a set of tutorial scripts or plans that can apply in all circumstances. Whether or not it is appropriate to answer a student's question with another question, or an example, or a hint, depends on the content of the question, the expertise of the student, the history of the dialogue, and so on.

Until recently, plans in AI were very rigid. For example, a plan for getting milk might be "get in car; drive to store; buy milk; drive home." There was a sharp division between *planning time* when the plan was constructed, and *execution time* when the plan was executed (Charniak & McDermott, 1985). Such a model of planning cannot work in the real world, where too many things are unknown to be able to specify all actions completely. Where is my car exactly? On which side of the garage? Does it have enough gas? Has construction finished on Main Street? Has the price of milk changed? Do I have enough money in my wallet?

Firby (1989) redefined plans to consist of sets of *reactive action packages* (RAPs) rather than sequences of actions. Each RAP is a little program responsible for achieving some small goals, such as "get in car." A RAP tests to see if its goal is already achieved. If not, the RAP selects an appropriate method to execute to achieve that goal, based on the current situation. The method might be a primitive action or another RAP. Thus, my "get in car" RAP would have a test "be in car," and methods for achieving that goal, such as "look to see where car is; go to that location; get inside car." "Get inside car" would itself be a RAP that would unlock the car if necessary, open the door, and so on. A RAP monitor keeps the RAPs in a queue and selects for execution those RAPs with important goals or impending deadlines. It is important that many low-level planning decisions are deferred until execution time, allowing the system to deal with unexpected obstacles and take advantage of unexpected opportunities.

This execution-time context-sensitivity is the key feature we want to exploit with our tutorial RAPs. The goals will be pedagogical: concepts to be covered, skills to be confirmed, difficulties to be resolved, and so on. The methods will be dialogue techniques: give a hint, give an analogy, ask a leading question, tell a story, review a previous case, and so on. The tests will look not at the real world, but at memory: past elements of the dialogue, prior experience with the student, examples with a given set of features, and so on. For example, a tutorial RAP might look for examples of nonsocial insects in memory. We see our tutorial RAPs as being much like the DACTNs described by Woolf (chap. 6, this volume), with two differences. First, we are most interested in RAPs that make opportunistic use of domain knowledge found in memory, and, second, we want to encode our tutorial RAPs as memory structures.

A CASE STUDY

It is easy to say that an ITS should have such and such properties. Building such a system is another matter. Calls for mixed-initiative dialogues, for example, are almost as old as the field of computer-based education. The problem is getting from where we are to where we want to be. Just as it is hard for students to learn in isolation from real-world contexts, so it is hard for ITS designers to construct solutions separate from some real system. But it is easy for an ITS design to become an all-or-none affair. Either domain knowledge and linguistic abilities are there, or nothing works.

Our approach is to build a tutoring system in phases, where the early phases build the knowledge base and the later phases add the intelligent interaction. A key constraint is that every phase should be a useful product in its own right, and that each phase is more attractive to the student than the previous phase.

As an example, consider the design in the next section for a case-based tutoring system in the domain of weather forecasting. This is a very preliminary design, inspired by conversations with personnel at the Weather Training Division at Chanute Air Force Base. The proposals and claims, however, are those of the authors alone.

Weather Forecaster Training

The Weather Training Division at Chanute Air Force Base in Rantoul, Illinois, trains weather forecasters for all of the armed services. The intensive 22-week course covers everything from basic principles of weather and climate to detailed techniques for analysis and forecasting. The students are high school graduates, normally with several years of service, but with no significant experience in forecasting.

The course is a mixture of class and lab work, where lab work means applying techniques taught in the classes to real weather data. At several points in the course, there is a major evaluation period, where each student analyzes a set of data and/or forecasts and presents a briefing to the instructors, who then critique both the analyses and the briefing style.

The students have a lot to learn and a lot to do. An analysis and/or forecast can take 6 or more hours to work up. Not surprisingly, the students have trouble managing all the data and rules. Many of the instructors' critiques of student briefings focused on failures of the students to tie together factors from several sources, for example, to connect the motion of a particular system to an upper air jet stream. Often the students would have a correct analysis, but miss many corroborating details.

A Sequence of Tools

As noted by Pirolli (chap. 5, this volume), a key issue is the integration of educational tools into the existing educational system. Introducing a new tool into a crowded educational curriculum is made much harder if it takes time from the class day, has to be forced on the students, or requires additional training for the instructors. Therefore, we considered introducing case-based ITS into the weather school incrementally, via the following sequence of tools for the student:

- a "dumb" *homework helper* with forms and tools to make it easy to do forecasts on-line faster and more neatly than by hand;
- a "dumb" *case browser,* callable from the homework helper, for scanning a *case library* of weather situations and forecasts;
- a "smart" *case retriever,* callable from the homework helper, capable of retrieving weather situations similar to the current exercise; and finally
- a *case advisor,* callable from the homework helper, that can give hints, advice, stories, cautions, and so on, relevant to the current exercise.

Each succeeding application improves the previous one in an obvious way, but each application is a useful tool in its own right. Figure 8.3 shows the basic set of modules.

The homework helper is the critical "foot in the door." To make the homework helper attractive to students, it should have

- exercise data already on-line;
- drawing and calculation tools that make doing analyses and forecasts faster or more accurate than doing them by hand; and
- the ability to print answers that can be handed in.

An obvious part of such a tool would be a contour chart drawing tool for drawing isobars. The contour tool screen would show a map with numerical data points, just like the paper charts the students currently use. The student would point and click at points in sequence to draw a line, just like following the dots. The tool would automatically generate smooth curves. For the student, the result would be a faster way to generate cleaner charts.

In addition, it becomes easier to check the charts for correctness. Currently, the students check their charts by laying a correct chart on top

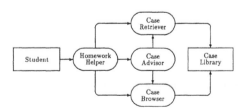

FIGURE 8.3 Forecast tutoring system.

of theirs, and then laying on top of that a colored template with several holes that indicates key locations to compare. This is necessary because trying to match the entire chart would be too tedious. Students then have to decide if their lines are close enough. With the tool, the possibility exists for evaluating the charts automatically, not comparing the lines, but the data points selected for each line.

The case browser module would let the student or instructor specify weather features and retrieve weather cases with those features. The instructors could use this facility to find examples or exercises, and the students could use it to find situations similar to the problem they are working on.

For reasons discussed earlier, we would like to use natural language as much as possible for browser requests. Weather situations are very complex entities, however, and are not easily describable in one sentence. Therefore, we will probably design a "fill in the blanks" request form to help break the request down into well-defined parts. The blanks would then be completed in English.

The case retriever module introduces true CBR to the tutoring system. The retriever will find cases similar to the current exercise, using indexes encoded by domain experts. It will list both the cases retrieved and the index features that connect them to the current case. This list of features is important pedagogically because it captures how experts view weather situations.

The case advisor is the intelligent tutoring module, and the most complex and ambitious component of the system. Students call on the advisor (using natural language) when they reach an impasse during a problem-solving session. Using predefined tutorial RAPs that opportunistically select different kinds of responses depending on what is in memory, the advisor may answer Socratically with a question of its own, give a hint, draw an analogy, refer to the cases returned by the retriever, or browse for cases with particular features.

LONG-TERM GOALS AND VISION

In our vision, the ideal case-based tutor is a raconteur, a teller of stories, a fountain of examples and exceptions. It communicates in the natural language of the student, pushes the student to make conjectures and ask questions, and presents cases not as solutions to problems, but as examples of what has been done before. Ideally, the tutor is fun to interact with because of the stories and cases it tells, not because it has flashy sound and graphics, arcade game interludes, scoring and competitive ranking, or whatever. Students learn because they are the dominant actors in the conversation, led into exploring new concepts and ideas that answer questions students have raised for themselves, based on hints and allusions dropped by tutors in conversation.

On the other hand, our ideal tutor is not a test giver or a question answerer. Tests serve two purposes: as a stick to force the student to learn, and as a means of evaluating what the student has learned. The kinds of objective tests that are usually administered, especially on computers, with their blanks to fill in and multiple choices to select, do a terrible job on both goals. They do not force students to learn, because many students just "'study for the test," learning little, and retaining less. Nor do they evaluate what the student has learned, because such tests only measure simple question-answering skills, and fail to give any indication of a student's creativity (in fact they stifle it) or ability to apply what has been learned in real situations.

Our ideal tutor is not a question answerer, because, in our view, learning results when the student both asks the questions and answers them. The role of the tutor is to either (a) help students who are having difficulty organizing their attack on the problem, by asking a few leading questions, making a simple analogy, or showing an example of a similar situation; or (b) push students with the glib answer into exploring alternatives, by presenting counterexamples, unusual situations, and so on. Except for minor clarifications and pointers, we believe the tutor should never terminate discussion and exploration with "the answer."

In doing this, of course, we need to avoid frustrating the student with evasive noninformative interactions. Part of the solution is to put the student in charge of the problem solving or exploration, and make the tutor more of a Doctor Watson to the student's Sherlock Holmes. That is, the tutor should prompt the student to think things through, carry the tools the student needs, bring up issues that should be examined, and so on, but should not be viewed (by the student or the designers of the tutoring system) as the "brains of the outfit."

Our proposed weather tutor is certainly a long way from our ideal, but it does point in the right direction. It puts the student into a well-motivated context (making forecasts) with real examples to work on. As a homework helper, it does not have a lesson plan that says when a student has to learn something. Instead, it waits until the student wants to know something. As a knowledge resource to be called on when needed, it neither interferes with nor redirects a student's natural flow of problem solving. As a library of cases rather than solutions, it does not tell the student what to do, only what has been done. The role of the homework helper is clearly that of assistant, not holder of answers.

SUMMARY

This chapter described two aspects to the design of knowledgeable ITSs. First, it described the CBR model of what learning a knowledge-rich domain involves. It also proposed the use of CBR for implementing the knowledge base of tutoring systems. Second, it described how a tutor should teach this knowledge, emphasizing guided exploration in a problem-solving context. A student would ask the tutor for help in solving a problem, and the tutor would help, albeit indirectly, with leading questions, hints, case histories, and so on. This dialogue would be guided by tutorial RAPs that are sensitive not just to the history of the dialogue but also to what knowledge is in the tutor's case base and what pedagogical goals are active. The natural language understanding and generation would be handled by a knowledge-based technique called DMAP.

Finally, the chapter outlined an approach to the design of a homework helper for trainees in weather forecasting. The development of the helper is organized into short- and long-term goals. In the short term, we are looking to build useful tools, including on-line calculation and graphic tools for doing analysis and forecast exercises, a case library of weather situations, a "dumb" case browser, and a "smart" case retriever. As a long-term goal, we would build a case advisor, with RAP-like memory structures for its tutorial plans, the weather case library as its source of examples, exercises, analogies, and so on, and DMAP-based natural language understanding and generation.

ACKNOWLEDGMENTS

The research described in this chapter is funded by the Air Force Office of Scientific Research contracts AFOSR-87-0295. We are also very appreciative of the efforts of Lieutenant Colonel Hugh Burns and Major Jim Parlett at the Air Force Human Resources Laboratory, and Colonel Dan White and Major George Whicker at the Weather Training Division at Chanute Air Force Base, Illinois.

REFERENCES

J. R. Carbonell. (1970). AI in CAI: An artificial intelligence approach to computer-assisted instruction. *IEEE Transactions on Man–Machine Systems, 11*(4), 190–202.

Charniak, E., & McDermott, D. (1985). *Introduction to artificial intelligence.* Reading, MA: Addison-Wesley.

Firby, R. J. (1989). *Adaptive execution in complex dynamic worlds.* Unpublished doctoral dissertation, Yale University, New Haven, CT.

Fletcher, J. D. (1985). Intelligent instructional systems in training. In S. J. Andriole (Ed.)., *Applications in artificial intelligence* (pp. 427–451). Princeton, NJ: Petrocelli Books.

Kolodner, J. L. (Ed.). (1988). *Proceedings of the first case-based reasoning workshop.* Los Altos, CA: Morgan Kaufmann.

Kolodner, J. L., & Riesbeck, C. K. (1986). *Experience, memory and reasoning.* Hillsdale, NJ: Lawrence Erlbaum Associates.

Neustadt, R. E., & May, E. R. (1986). *Thinking in time: The uses of history for decision-makers.* New York: The Free Press.

Shapiro (Ed.). *Encyclopedia of artificial intelligence* (pp. 696–701). New York: Wiley.

Riesbeck, C. K., & Martin, C. E. (1986). Direct memory access parsing. In J. L. Kolodner & C. K. Riesbeck (Eds.)., *Experience, memory and reasoning* (pp. 209–226). Hillsdale, NJ: Lawrence Erlbaum Associates.

Riesbeck, C. K., & Schank, R. C. (1989). *Inside case-based reasoning.* Hillsdale, NJ: Lawrence Erlbaum Associates.

Schank, R. C. (1982). *Dynamic memory: A theory of learning in computers and people.* New York: Cambridge University Press.

The Role of Domain Knowledge in the Design of an Intelligent Tutoring System

Pamela K. Fink
Southwest Research Institute

The design and development of intelligent tutoring systems (ITSs) is a highly interdisciplinary endeavor. Top-level design issues such as characterization of the knowledge to be taught and the appropriate approach or approaches to teaching such knowledge require an understanding of psychology, education, computer science, and human factors, as well as the subject matter domain, to name a few.

A standard accepted architecture for an ITS was presented in chapter 1, Figure 1.1 of this book. The major modules include a domain expert, an instructional expert, a student model, an intelligent interface, and possibly a domain simulation. Though earlier ITS efforts tried to keep these major modules separate, experience has shown that the knowledge contained in these modules is highly interrelated, and to perform each of the functions that an ITS must perform requires knowledge available in more than one module at a time. For example, teaching knowledge tends to be embodied in the student model and intelligent interface, as well as in the instructional expert (as illustrated in Burns & Parlett, Figure 1.3 in this volume) and domain expertise resides in the simulation facility and user interface, as well as the domain expert, (as illustrated in Burns & Parlett, Figure 1.4, this volume).

From a software engineering perspective, each of the major modules is a fairly complicated computer program in its own right, and their inherent interrelationships further complicate ITS development. Also, the kind of knowledge that must be embodied can be quite complex. From a psychology perspective, issues in education and learning remain open research topics and what constitutes effective teaching is not always fully understood. But, this kind of knowledge must be used as the foundation of the instructional expert for any effective ITS, and essentially constitutes the design and implementation of an expert system for teaching the particular domain. In addition, domain expertise of the appropriate kind and level for teaching must be implemented into the domain module to be used by the instructional portion of the system for training. This constitutes the design and implementation of a specialized expert system that contains the knowledge and problem-solving skills that must be taught to the student. Thus, the development of an ITS is equivalent to the development of several very different expert systems that all must somehow work together, requiring extensive efforts on the part of experts from all of the fields concerned.

Unfortunately, as with any effort requiring individuals with various areas of expertise, it is difficult to bring them together to work on a single effort. Usually each group representing an area of expertise has its own perspective on the problem and tends to work on a piece of the problem that reflects that particular perspective. This is not to say that experts in the various fields working on ITS do not talk to one another, because they do. They are often quite aware of the work going on from the other viewpoints. However, because they tend not to come together to work on a single problem for any significant period of time, extensive cross-fertilization is difficult.

This chapter attempts to characterize two major viewpoints on the ITS problem represented by two distinct research communities—the psychology/education/human factors group and the computer science/artificial intelligence (AI)/software engineering group. These two perspectives are then examined, highlighting issues in how domain knowledge is viewed in an ITS and how it can affect the design of such a system. Finally, two exemplary training domains are discussed—one is considered knowledge-intensive whereas the other is considered high-performance—along with descriptions of ITSs for those domains. These designs are compared and contrasted to illustrate the effect that the training domain has on the overall architecture of an ITS both as a result of the domain itself and as a result of how that domain should be taught.

TWO PERSPECTIVES
ON INTELLIGENT TUTORING SYSTEMS

The fields of psychology/education/human factors and computer science/AI/software engineering represent two major viewpoints involved in issues of computer-based training and ITSs. An ITS environment has two major components — a human being in the form of the student and a computer system in the form of an intelligent tutor. The psychology perspective is oriented most toward the human learner whereas the computer science perspective is directed at the computer side of the endeavor. Individuals working on ITSs who come from these two areas have different perspectives and questions they want answered from their research. Both groups want to develop useful, working ITSs that truly improve on current available training techniques and that will help to fill the growing training requirements. However, as in the field of AI itself, where cognitive psychology meets computer science, the expectations and goals of the two groups are quite distinct.

Cognitive psychologists look at the field of ITSs as a way of performing experiments to test out theories on human cognition and learning. They want an ITS that can be used with experimental subjects and that is fundamentally sound from a learning theory standpoint. Articles written from the psychology viewpoint take learning/teaching knowledge as the given and tend to emphasize the need for a full-time committed expert in the subject matter material. They draw on work in the area of learning theory that addresses issues in desired learning outcomes and the preconditions for learning situations that will generate these outcomes (see Bloom, 1956; Gagné, 1977). Questions arise concerning how active or passive the tutoring system should be. Some of these decisions are a matter of teaching style, whereas others depend on the type of knowledge being taught and the desired learning outcome. A major area of research interest is whether and how instructional design considerations can be implemented into an ITS in a domain-independent manner (see O'Neil, Slawson, & Baker, 1988; Woolf, 1988). The development of an ITS is a means to that end. Work is even underway to implement an expert system for the development of an ITS that helps an individual design a computer-based training system that follows the Instructional System Design Theory (Merrill, 1987).

Computer scientists, on the other hand, want to develop computational techniques that appear to generate intelligent behavior. These techniques do not necessarily have to mimic the underlying processes that drive how humans might perform, just the surface behavior. A good theory, they hope, will result in well-structured, robust, easily modifiable and maintainable code. Articles written from the computer science standpoint tend to take the availability of a subject matter expert as a given and to emphasize the need to have available psychologists knowledgeable in teaching and learning to support the effort. Work centers on the apparent structure of the knowledge and how it will be used in the targeted problem-solving tasks. Questions arise concerning how such knowledge is similar or different from the knowledge in other domains and other problem-solving tasks. A major area of research interest is the issue of how to represent domain knowledge in such a way that it can be used for many different types of problem-solving tasks and the various viewpoints that a particular problem-solving task will emplace on the basic, fundamental domain knowledge (see Fink, 1985; Porter, Acker, Lester, & Souther, 1988). The development of an ITS is thus an end in itself because it invokes major issues in representing various kinds of knowledge.

Again, this is not to say that either group works to the exclusion of the other. Rather, when design decisions and trade-offs must be made during the development of a system, they are usually made from one perspective or the other, depending on the goals of the project and the researchers. Generally, one could say that the instructional issues tend to be more the province of the psychologically oriented group, whereas the domain issues tend to generate more interest within the computationally oriented group. However, as is obvious from the discussion and the illustrations in the figures in chapter 1 of this volume, these two perspectives overlap in the development of an ITS, and design decisions in one will affect design decisions in the other. The ultimate ITS will require that such decisions be made jointly, with the best expertise available from both psychology/education/human factors and from computer science/AI/software engineering.

The interrelated nature of the instructional and subject matter issues in an ITS sometimes makes it difficult to determine which design decision drives another. For example, the selection of a teaching method and student model type will dictate decisions concerning the implementation of the domain expert. However, these selections should be made based on a consideration of the type of domain being trained and the performance and skill levels to be achieved by the student.

From one perspective, however, the design and implementation of the domain knowledge in an ITS can, in some ways, be considered the focusing factor for the design and implementation of the rest of the ITS. The type of knowledge and/or skill that must be trained, or the desired learning outcome, will drive the appropriate instructional methods to be employed. It will also provide input to the kind of user interface that is appropriate, such as text or graphics, and first- or second-person. Finally, the representation of the expertise will dictate the structure of the student model and how it is compared with the expert model to determine how the student is doing. Obviously, there are many other issues that must be taken into consideration in designing and implementing these major components of an ITS. But, the subject matter domain is one of the primary forces that can tie together all of the modules of an ITS.

ASPECTS OF DOMAIN KNOWLEDGE

The term *domain knowledge* has been used in several ways by the various groups involved with ITSs. It can mean anything from the subject matter area to the desired performance outcome. In the area of AI, domain knowledge tends to refer to the subject matter material. Here, it is used to refer specifically to the subject matter material that is to be imparted to the student as it relates to the task to be trained. Thus, domain knowledge can span the range of formal and informal fields of knowledge and skill that might need to be assimilated by a student, including diagnosis and repair of devices and systems, legal reasoning, cooking, typing, public speaking, operation of equipment, mission planning, and so forth.

Within the field of AI, the knowledge in a domain is classically broken down into two types: *declarative* and *procedural* (see Charniak & McDermott, 1985; Nilsson, 1980; Rich, 1983; and Winston, 1984). Declarative knowledge involves issues in representation and refers to the facts, figures, objects, and interrelationships between objects in a domain, whereas the procedural knowledge involves issues in search and how such techniques are used to solve a particular problem. As is true with any artificial division, the dividing line is fuzzy and certain issues could be placed on either side. However, the breakdown does provide for a distinction between some very different kinds of knowledge and the field of AI has developed a variety of computational techniques for representing and using these types of knowledge. Fundamental theoretical work in AI centers on developing computational techniques to handle these two types of knowledge. This has resulted in the notions of knowledge representation and search. From an AI perspective, the domain knowledge is an entity that has content and structure, as well as procedures for accessing and utilizing this content and structure.

A similar breakdown of knowledge into declarative and procedural is acknowledged in the area of psychology as well (see Anderson, 1982; Kyllonen & Shute, 1988; Sleeman & Brown, 1982; Van Lehn, 1988). The approach to learning, teaching, and testing declarative versus procedural knowledge is very different, regardless of the subject matter being taught. Declarative knowledge can be defined operationally by stating that it is the knowledge that can be elicited through recognition, clustering, and sorting type tests, whereas procedural knowledge can be defined as the knowledge that is demonstrated when a task is performed requiring the sequencing and/or selection of an appropriate rule or rules. This kind of distinction, along with the complexity of the knowledge (i.e., how much information and how fast it must be utilized in problem solving) and the appropriate learning strategies for each has been used in the development of a taxonomy of learning skills (Kyllonen & Shute, 1988).

KNOWLEDGE REPRESENTATION

Knowledge representation is one of the major areas of research in AI today. It could be defined as the organization and codification of knowledge, and the placement of the result into a computer program in some kind of computer usable form. What kind of knowledge is organized and codified has changed through the years, depending on the current philosophy for building an intelligent system. Earlier work, during the 1960s, emphasized the representation of general problem-solving knowledge. The goal was to keep knowledge about a specific problem area to a minimum and to use powerful universal problem-solving techniques that would be capable of solving any type of problem (Newell & Simon, 1963). Later work, during the 1970s and 1980s, emphasized the representation of more specific, domain-oriented knowledge (see Buchanan & Feigenbaum, 1978; Duda, Gaschnig, & Hart, 1979; Shortliffe, 1976). Here the object is to fill a computer program with as much knowledge about a particular problem area as possible and to use weaker, but more specific, techniques to solve a specific set of problems. The first paradigm resulted in the development of general purpose problem solvers whereas the latter has resulted in expert systems.

The current design principle for intelligent systems, namely "in the knowledge lies the power" (Feigenbaum, circa 1980), meaning that the amount of power or intelligence displayed by a computer system is directly related to the amount of specific, domain-oriented knowledge embodied in it, has led to an increase in the importance of knowledge representation to the field of AI over the last 15 years. The current practical success of the area of AI known as expert systems is a direct result of this pragmatic approach to building intelligent systems. This technology fosters the belief that intelligent behavior can result from the appropriate application of specific knowledge in a given situation, so much work has centered around how to get such specific knowledge into a computer program and apply it at the appropriate time during a problem-solving task. Today, the approach is still very problem- and domain-oriented, which is quite different from the earlier work in general purpose problem solvers. Experience has shown that reasonably intelligent behavior can be obtained by a computer program if the system has all of the specific, detailed knowledge for what to do in all of the situations that it may face. The result has been the development of a multitude of intelligent systems, usually referred to as expert systems, but better described as "idiot savants." Such systems can be developed to have nearly expert capabilities in the particular problem-solving area for which they have been well-prepared with knowledge, but they break down quickly as the problem moves out of that specific area.

Over the years, the research in knowledge representation has resulted in the development of various techniques for representing knowledge, including production rules, frames, semantic networks, and scripts. Each of these techniques is best-suited for representing a particular kind of knowledge. For example, production rules work well for more dynamically oriented knowledge based on heuristics and condition–action pairs. For more static knowledge, frames work well for representing hierarchies of objects with their attributes and values whereas semantic networks handle the representation of relationships well. Combinations of these techniques, such as rules that manipulate frames or semantic networks that connect sets of frames into relationships, is also possible. All of these techniques are good for representing the kinds of knowledge used more or less consciously during a problem-solving task. They can represent classes of objects in the world (i.e., frames) or chains of reasoning in a particular situation (i.e., production rules).

From a computer science/AI/software engineering perspective, these knowledge representation techniques may or may not have a psychological foundation. The primary goal is to find an internal representation of the knowledge that is computationally sound and that allows for well-designed and general software development as well as the desired behavior. However, there are psychologically oriented arguments for the use of many of the techniques, such as Minsky (1975) for frames, Schank and Abelson (1977) for scripts, and Anderson (1987) for production rules. Some techniques are founded on the basis that the structures can explain certain aspects of human behavior such as the expectation that supports visual understanding or social motivations, or the actual dynamics of skill transition. The emphasis here is on explaining the input and output capabilities of a human when undergoing some form of learning. Given an input in the form of some training sequence, these structures explain the acquisition and/or modification of the input that can then be used to verify the learning through a testing sequence.

From a computational perspective, knowledge representation is an important issue in an ITS because it is by this means that the system obtains a knowledge of the domain to be tutored, as well as a knowledge of what the student does and does not know with respect to that knowledge. These portions of an ITS are often referred to as the domain expert and student model, respectively. In addition, an ITS uses the knowledge from these two modules, along with some form of teaching knowledge, to determine how to proceed during a training session. Thus, representation of knowledge of various sorts is essential to the development of an ITS. The remainder of this chapter focuses on issues in representing domain knowledge and the effect that the domain knowledge has on the rest of the design of an ITS.

REPRESENTING DOMAIN KNOWLEDGE
IN AN INTELLIGENT TUTORING SYSTEM

As indicated in the previous sections, work in AI in the area of knowledge representation has gone through several phases. The first phase emphasized the procedural aspects and the development of general types of problem solvers. A second phase emphasized the more static aspects and the development of special purpose problem solvers. These later systems resulted in the generation of a specific viewpoint on the domain knowledge oriented toward how it is used to solve the particular problems of interest.

Though some work in AI is again underway to represent generic domain knowledge independent of the task to be performed (Porter et al., 1988), most representations center on the development of an appropriate task-oriented viewpoint of the knowledge. This same philosophy is reflected in the definition of the term representation given by Waterman in his book *A Guide to Expert Systems* (1986), which he defines as "the process of formulating or viewing a problem so it will be easy to solve" (p. 11). Thus, the selection of one or more of the various techniques for representing the knowledge in a given situation depends on the task to be performed, as well as the inherent structure and nature of the domain.

The task to be performed, namely the goal of a training system, provides a viewpoint on the generic, primary, or basic knowledge about the domain. A more fundamental, generic, non-problem-oriented representation of knowledge in a domain can serve as a foundation for the generation of a variety of viewpoints of that knowledge for different problem-solving tasks. For example, in the domain of automobiles, the task of diagnosing malfunctions generates various viewpoints of the knowledge about cars, mechanics, and electronics. This is illustrated in Figure 9.1, where such viewpoints might include a functional representation that allows a mental simulation of how the automobile works and an experientially based representation that provides quick condition–action, pattern-matching capabilities, as well as many other viewpoints. This notion of viewpoint can act as a filter or organizer that can remove or enforce particular structures on the original generic knowledge that results in simplifying the specific problem-solving task. For example, the filter that would generate the quick condition–action, pattern-matching capabilities in a particular diagnostic problem-solving domain would involve something like the notion of "compilation" (Chandrasekaran & Mittal, 1983), where "shortcut" rules are generated that link signs and symptoms to hypotheses about what might be wrong rather than requiring some extensive chain of reasoning to determine the association based on structure and function. Work has also been done on how a variety of such viewpoints can be used simultaneously

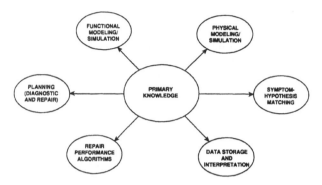

FIGURE 9.1 A variety of viewpoints on the fundamental knowledge used in performing diagnosis and repair.

in diagnostic problem solving (see Fink, 1985; Fink & Lusth, 1987). Figure 9.2 illustrates this notion of a task-oriented viewpoint that creates a projection onto the more generic, task-independent version of the knowledge.

One would hope that work in ITSs could benefit from all of the research and experience that has accumulated through AI work in knowledge representation and expert systems. At first it seems reasonable to assume that an expert system for a particular task should be useful as the expert module in an ITS. Unfortunately, for various reasons this is not always the case, because an expert system developed without tutoring in mind most likely will not embody the knowledge to be trained in an appropriate format for training. An expert system may be able to solve a problem but not necessarily in the way that one would wish to train people to do it. Some work has been done in the area of representing and using knowledge in a way similar to human experts for certain training tasks such as diagnosis (Clancey & Letsinger, 1981; Smith, Fink, & Lusth, 1985) but much work still remains.

Furthermore, the knowledge representation techniques used in ex-

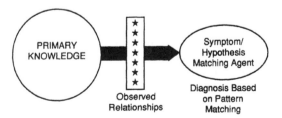

FIGURE 9.2 Creating a knowledge projection by using experience to enforce structure on the primary knowledge of a given system.

pert systems are not always well suited for representing the "knowledge" required for training certain types of tasks, such as those involved with the performance of a certain skill. These kinds of domains require a viewpoint on the knowledge that includes physical skills, so one would not tend to build an expert system to perform the task in the first place. These skills require both a knowledge of the capability indicated by accuracy, as well as the ability to perform the task quickly and accurately while doing something else (referred to as an *automated skill;* see Regian & Shute, 1988). Representing the accuracy of the task involves the more traditional approaches in knowledge representation, whereas representing the knowledge that indicates speed and automaticity issues is a somewhat novel viewpoint. To perform a particular skill initially does require a certain amount of knowledge and some conscious thought when using that knowledge. However, as an individual solves more and more problems and gets better and better at a given task, this knowledge somehow becomes easier to use. An experienced expert, especially in a performance-based task, is much quicker at finding and using the appropriate knowledge to solve a particular problem. Through experience, the more general, novice-type knowledge gets reshaped into more specific, expert-type knowledge while not losing its original, more fundamental usability. This transition from novice to expert in a human during learning is an important issue for knowledge representation in an ITS. It is of particular importance in the training of performance skills where the original knowledge is no longer used, at least not consciously, to perform a given task. Such domains are referred to as *high performance* domains (Regian & Shute, 1988).

Most of the intelligent tutoring research to date has focused on tasks from knowledge-rich domains. For example, Anderson's LISP Tutor (Anderson, Farell, & Sauers, 1984), Brown and Burton's SOPHIE system for electronic diagnosis (Brown, Burton, & deKleer, 1982), Carbonell and Collins's SCHOLAR system for South American geography (Carbonell, 1970), and Woolf and McDonald's MENO-TUTOR for diagnosing nonsyntactic bugs in computer programs (Woolf & McDonald, 1985) all deal with domains that emphasize the conscious use of knowledge. Such tutoring systems attempt to impart certain static and/or procedural knowledge that the student is then tested on as much for the knowledge content as for the problem-solving skill.

Tasks that are primarily performance-based have not attracted much intelligent tutoring research attention to date from either the psychology or computer science sides of the field. Tutoring systems in these domains must be capable of imparting not only a certain amount of knowledge but also of drilling the student in the use of this knowledge to the point where the student no longer needs to concentrate on the actual problem-solving task. At this point, the task is "automatized," and the individual is free to concentrate on other, more cognitively demanding issues while still performing the trained task. Testing to determine if individuals have a particular piece of knowledge is quite different from testing to determine if they have automatized a particular skill based on that knowledge. How such knowledge and skills should be trained also varies greatly from the approaches used in more traditional ITS domains.

TUTORING/TRAINING COGNITIVE
VERSUS PHYSICAL SKILLS

The type of knowledge to be learned is determined by the subject matter domain and the desired problem-solving outcomes. The taxonomy of learning skills developed by Kyllonen and Shute (1988) provides a useful way of illustrating how radically different two learning domains can be in terms of content and required skill level. For example, diagnosis and repair is a knowledge-intensive task. In the technical/nontechnical versus fast/ slow processing speed plane used by Kyllonen and Shute, it is a highly technical discipline where slow, quality decisions can be required. On the other hand, a learning domain such as console operations tends to be much less technically oriented and requires quick decision making, to the point where it is not apparent that decisions are even being made. This places the domains of diagnosis and repair versus console operations at diagonal ends of this two-dimensional space. Training in diagnosis and repair or troubleshooting proceeds through many processes from acquisition of static knowledge and schema to procedures using generalized rules and mental models. Training in console operations also requires the acquisition of static knowledge and procedures, but rather than structuring these basic building blocks into more complex forms of knowledge, they are then used to automatize the skill to a point where the cognitive knowledge is no longer needed to perform the task. Such diversity in terms of content and training goals results in very different ITS designs, from the viewpoint of pedagogy as well as domain knowledge representation. Two such systems are described in the following sections.

Training the Diagnosis and Repair of Complex Systems

The problem of diagnosis and repair has been studied a great deal over the last 10 to 15 years. From the AI perspective, uncountable numbers of expert systems have been designed and implemented to perform diagnosis in some form from biological to electrical to mechanical systems (see Chandrasekaran & Mittal, 1983; Davis, 1980; DeKleer & Brown, 1982; Fink & Lusth, 1987; Forbus, 1981; Genesereth, 1982; Kuipers, 1984; Patil, Szolovits, & Schwartz, 1981; Shortliff, 1976). The approach has usually been taken from one of two tracks — using high-level, experience-based, condition-action pairs, or using low-level, functionally or physically based models of the device or system. Some have argued for the combination of these approaches to improve diagnostic performance. This area is currently undergoing active research in an effort to generate advanced or next-generation diagnostic expert systems. From the psychology side, the problem of teaching diagnosis has also been studied, resulting in a domain-independent instructional strategy for diagnostic problem solving (O'Neil et al., 1988). It is interesting to note that the instructional strategy described by O'Neil and his colleagues requires physical, functional, and heuristic knowledge about the device or system to be diagnosed, which are all areas of active research in knowledge representation in AI. As a result of all this study, the problem of diagnosis and repair is probably one of the better understood problem-solving strategies, and it is considered a fairly knowledge-intensive task.

An expert system that combines two knowledge representation paradigms by utilizing both functionally and experientially based knowledge of the device or system to be diagnosed has been under development for research purposes for several years. The system is called the Integrated Diagnostic Model (IDM) (Fink & Lusth, 1987). Its development has been based on the philosophy that a human expert utilizes many different forms of knowledge when performing diagnosis, as is illustrated in Figure 9.1, and that an expert system producing similar performance must have access to the same kind of knowledge. The experience-based portion of the system contains the heuristic knowledge concerning the diagnosis and repair of the device in question. However, rather than use the standard approach of production rules to capture knowledge, the IDM is implemented using semantic networks. In this way, the actual diagnostic process of collecting symptoms, making hypotheses, verifying the hypotheses through further data collection, and recommending a repair can be modeled. The model-based portion of the system uses object-oriented programming techniques to provide qualitative simulation capabilities. A ball-and-string display of the device is also provided so that the user can see the functional connectivity relationship(s) between components. As a result of this design, the IDM can provide expertise in the diagnosis and repair of an electrical or mechanical device at two different levels. The experiential portion can provide the rules-of-thumb used in solving the various problems, whereas the functional portion can provide how the device works.

A simple tutoring system was developed using the IDM as the

domain expert (Smith et al., 1985). It was designed to allow a student the opportunity for free-play with the device as well as to provide direction through problem-solving exercises. Various components can be set to various states, either by the student or the system, and simulations run that show what happens to the system as a whole. The system can also request students to indicate what they think will happen under such conditions.

Tutoring at the Experiential Level.   The experiential portion of the IDM can provide the knowledge needed for teaching the diagnosis and repair of a device at a high level. Using the student model, the tutoring executor can select an initial node from the hypotheses level of the knowledge base as a problem for the student to solve.

The problem selected by the tutoring executor can then be presented to the student in either of two ways, depending on the information in which the student is currently being trained. First, the system can provide students with a hypothesis and require them to provide a set of observations and tests to be performed to verify the hypothesis. Students can also be required to suggest how the problem should be solved. Second, The problem can be presented by giving students a set of observations that will in some way help to verify the chosen hypothesis. Students are then required to determine the chosen hypothesis and its subsequent solution by asking questions and obtaining test results.

Thus, for example, in teaching the diagnosis of problems of an automotive electrical system at the experiential level, the tutoring system could give the student a symptom, such as "the battery will not stay charged," and require the student to go through the process of observations and tests to determine if the battery is bad, if there is a loose connection, if the generator is not working properly, and so forth. The tutoring system could also give the student a hypothesis, such as "the generator is not working properly" and require the student to provide tests to determine the symptoms that such a state would produce.

Tutoring at the Functional Level.   The functional portion of the IDM can provide the knowledge needed for teaching diagnosis and repair of a device from basic principles about the physical and functional properties of the device. Four useful types of student–teacher interactions can be generated from the functional model. They concern system structure, system behavior, fault propagation, and failure analysis.

In the system structure mode, the student can learn about the functional connectivity of system components. The first step is to let the student review the organization of the system. Review can begin in a top-down manner, showing the relationships between higher level entities first. When these are learned, the entities can then be shown in more and more detail. Thus, to tutor about the automotive electrical system structure from the functional model, the student could be quizzed with questions like "What fuse controls the turn signals," or "How many wires lead into the emergency light relay." The answer is readily available to the tutoring system by checking the functional model. Figure 9.3 shows a partial diagram of the functional representation of an automobile electrical system as it appears in the IDM.

A second type of interaction teaches the student the dynamic behavior of the system. The tutoring executor presents a list of settings of the devices incorporated into the overall network. The student is then asked to describe the state of the system based on these settings. To check the student's replies, the model can be adjusted and simulations performed. So, for example, the dynamic behavior of the automotive electrical system can be taught by questions such as "How do the tail lights behave when the left turn signal and the emergency lights are on at the same time?", or "Under what circumstances does the emergency light relay make a connection between the wire from fuse 1 and the wire to the parking lights?" Students can input their responses through the use of a mouse to set parameters on the graphic representation indicating the appropriate state of the device.

A third teaching mode concerns fault propagation. Here, the tutoring executor asks what results if a particular node is malfunctioning. The fault is introduced into the model and, as with system behavior, a simulation is run on the modified model. The results of the simulation are

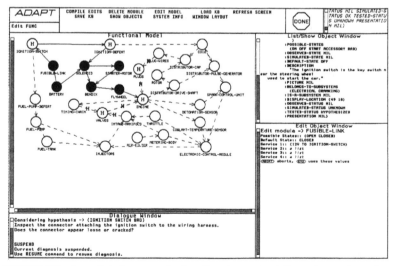

FIGURE 9.3 A partial diagram of a functional representation of an automotive electrical system in the IDM.

then compared against the student's answer. In order to teach fault propagation in the automotive electrical system, a fault must be injected into the system. One such question is "What happens if fuse 1 blows?" The student is left to propagate the effect of the fault throughout the system, using the mouse and graphics interface.

A final type of interaction concerns failure analysis, which teaches the student to diagnose problems. In this mode, the tutoring executor gives the student a list of symptoms. The student's task is to determine the possible causes of the problem. Again, the student's answers are checked by the ITS using the fault-then-simulate method. To teach failure analysis in the automotive electrical system example, the student is presented a symptom such as "the turn signal lights are not working." By using deductive reasoning based on earlier interactions with the system, the student should be able to isolate the probable cause.

Conclusions. Diagnosis and repair is a knowledge-intensive task and therefore requires that an ITS for training such problem-solving skills contain a variety of knowledge. It appears that the IDM system design could serve as an excellent basis for the domain expert in an ITS that implements an instructional strategy such as that presented in O'Neil and colleagues (1988) because it allows teaching the two major types of skills required in diagnostic problem solving—experiential and functional. This mixture allows the curriculum designer to pick the most appropriate representation for each skill as it is addressed. For example, much of the overall description of the device or system and how it functions could be generated automatically from the functional knowledge base. Appropriate diagnostic problem-solving task strategies can be taught directly using the experientially based portion of the system. Drill and practice are readily available through the graphic interface that allows the student to interact directly with a functional representation of the system.

Apprenticeship Training for a High Performance Domain

With the proliferation of technologically advanced, complex devices in today's society, a need has arisen for individuals who are proficient in the use and maintenance of such devices. Such skills require a very pragmatic, application-oriented view of the appropriate knowledge. That is, they require a viewpoint on the generic knowledge oriented toward the task to be performed, as illustrated in Figure 9.2. Current educational and training methods tend to emphasize the traditional approach of teaching knowledge in its more general theoretical form, with little if any discussion of its relationship to how it might be applied in real-world situations or tasks. That is, they teach knowledge such as what appears at the center of Figure 9.1. This has tended to create a gap between the educational environment where the knowledge is acquired and the real world where it is applied (Gott, 1988).

Training Knowledge Versus Skill.   The knowledge that is required by high performance tasks is of a form that allows the individual to perform them "without thinking about it." This is a somewhat novel viewpoint on the knowledge that results in freeing up cognitive processing for the performance of more knowledge-intensive tasks. For example, a good doctor or nurse will be capable of talking to the patient or thinking about the diagnosis while taking a patient's blood pressure or drawing a patient's blood. At the point where cognitive processing is no longer required for performing the task, the skill is said to be *automatized* (Regian & Shute, 1988). A skill that has been automatized has the advantage of longer retention and better performance under stress—very useful characteristics in many situations (Schneider & Shiffrin, 1977).

To address the problem of training high performance skills, a five-step training methodology was developed that reflects the five stages of knowledge/skill that must be acquired by the student of such a domain (Fink & Sines, 1989). The types of learning strategies recommended at each phase of the training were selected from the list that appears in Kyllonen and Shute (1988, Table 1, p. 15). The five phases are as follows:

1. Static Overview Knowledge (part of the "modeling" phase of apprenticeship learning). The static overview knowledge taught in phase one consists of the general, enabling knowledge concerned with the skill to be performed. It provides the "big picture" view of the objects in the domain that are important to performing the task and their relationships to one another. A system overview should be organized from the viewpoint that is desirable for performing the particular task and not necessarily include everything there is to know about the equipment. Representation of such knowledge is fairly straightforward since frames and semantic networks work well for structured, static knowledge. If training is oriented towards the operation of a particular piece of equipment, then the system would have a knowledge of all of the important pieces and components, their names, their descriptions, their functions within the system as a whole, etc. An appropriate learning strategy for this particular kind of knowledge is simply rote memorization. The student needs to assimilate all of the facts and relationships with little need for further exploration and no need for modification. He/she needs to be capable of identifying components based on appearance, location, and any other attributes salient to the task to be trained. An ITS can simply present the information and then test it in a static format such as multiple choice, fill-in-the-blank, or identification. The student is assumed to know the material when he/she can answer all of the test questions correctly.

2. General Procedure-Oriented Knowledge (another part of the "modeling" phase of apprenticeship learning). The teaching of the initial, general procedural information, like the overview knowledge, involves fairly static knowledge. Each step can be presented in the order in which it should occur, along with the reasons and motivations for performing that particular step at that particular point in time. Though the knowledge is about a procedure, it is static in nature. A directed graph format is appropriate in such a situation because it is capable of representing the sequential nature of the knowledge. The nodes of the graph correspond to frames that represent the steps of the procedure while the arcs indicate the legal transitions between steps. An appropriate learning strategy for this knowledge is again rote memorization with possibly some learning from instruction. Though what is presented could be learned exactly as presented, a student may choose to internalize the procedure in a slightly different way than it is actually presented by the tutoring system, especially at the beginning of training when all conditions and exceptions that govern the sequence of steps in the procedure are not apparent. Testing can again use such techniques as multiple choice, fill-in-the-blanks, and identification to ensure that the student has assimilated enough of the general knowledge to move on to the next step. The student is assumed to know the material when he/she can answer all of the test questions correctly.

3. Guided-Example Exercises (the "coaching" phase of apprenticeship learning). The third phase of the training process, guided example, begins to move into actual skill acquisition. In this phase the student is presented with some specific examples of procedures to be performed and is guided, or coached, through them. The goal of this phase is to provide the student with enough experience in actually performing the procedure to acquire the ability to do it fairly accurately. However, the ability to prompt the student and coach him/her through the performance of a task during this phase of training requires a considerable amount of knowledge. First, the system must itself know the procedure and how to perform correctly on the specific exercise. This knowledge is provided by the directed graph representation of the procedure developed for phase two of the training. Second, it must not only be able to identify when a student is performing the task incorrectly but also be able to infer why the student has made the error so that it can provide appropriate feedback. This can be quite difficult since the only source of information that the system has available from which it can deduce what the student does and does not know is the student's input to the system during the exercise, how long it took for the student to respond, and the student's performance on previous exercises. Further details of how errors are detected, identified, and remediated in this phase of training is discussed in Fink & Sines (1989). The type of learning strategy applied here is drill and practice. The student

can refine and tune his/her knowledge through applying it in a variety of situations through the assignment of exercises to be performed. Testing in this phase involves determining if the student can perform a given exercise with enough accuracy and reasonable speed to indicate that he/she has actually learned the procedure and knows what to do at each step.

4. Unguided-Example Exercises (the "fading" and "reflecting" phases of apprenticeship learning). The fourth phase of the training process, unguided example, requires the student to perform example exercises without guidance or support from the tutoring system. Feedback is only provided when the student indicates that he/she has completed a given exercise. Then the system can provide an assessment of the student's performance in terms of accuracy and speed. The goal of this phase is to provide the student with enough experience in performing the procedure straight through without interruption to acquire the needed speed while maintaining accuracy. The knowledge required to evaluate student performance in this phase is not as extensive as that required during the guided example phase because the system is no longer trying to catch the errors, interpret them, and provide appropriate feedback to the student as the errors occur. The system still needs to know how to perform the procedure and to identify when errors have occurred, but this identification occurs too late to help guide the student back onto the right track. Accuracy is assumed in this phase and speed of performance is the focus. It is at this phase that the problem of how to represent skill rather than cognitive knowledge becomes an issue. Accuracy in many cases will have to be absolutely correct, but the acceptable speed may vary a lot, depending on the actual domain as well as the student. Thus, representation of skill must be a sliding scale that evaluates both accuracy and speed with respect to the domain of application as well as the perceived potential capabilities of the student. The type of learning strategy applied in this phase is again drill and practice. The student can refine and tune his/her skill through repeatedly applying his/her knowledge to perform the requested procedure. Testing in this phase involves determining if the student can perform a given exercise with increased speed while maintaining accuracy, indicating that he/she has acquired a certain level of proficiency in performing the task.

5. Automated-Example Exercises (an addition to the "reflecting" phase of apprenticeship learning). The fifth and final phase of training provides the student with exercises that will help him/her to automate task performance, meaning that the student will become capable of performing another task that requires cognitive processing while maintaining speed and accuracy in the primary task. Here the student is presented the same kind of exercise as in the previous two phases of training but in addition

must also perform a secondary task, such as hitting a particular function key on the computer keyboard based on the pattern of tones heard. The goal is to bring the student to the point where he/she no longer has to think about how to perform the primary procedure being trained. The student knows the procedure so well that cognitive effort is no longer required to perform it. Representation of skill level in this phase of training is currently just an expansion of the notions already used in the previous stages of training such as accuracy and speed measurements. In this phase, however, these measurements must be used for judging student performance in both tasks at the same time. The type of learning strategy applied in this phase is again drill and practice. The student can refine and tune his/her skill through practice in a variety of situations. Testing in this phase involves determining if the student can maintain accuracy and speed on a given exercise in the primary task while performing a secondary task also to some criteria, indicating that he/she has acquired a certain level of automaticity in performing the procedure.

This five-phase process was developed from the computer science/AI/software engineering perspective of the problem, where concern for useful knowledge representation and utilization paradigms are of primary concern. However, this approach is very similar to the apprenticeship model of learning presented in Collins, Brown, and Newman (1987), where the perspective is psychologically oriented. The static and general procedural overviews constitute the *modeling* phase, the guided-examples stage is equivalent to the *coaching* phase, and the unguided-example stage performs the same function as the *fading* phase. Though not directly equivalent, the automated example stage could be considered the high performance domain version of the more knowledge-intensive *reflecting* phase.

This five-step training process moves the student gradually through the various phases of skill development. How long a student might spend at any given level of training is, of course, unknown. To some degree it will depend on the difficulty of the domain as well as the individual student's capabilities. In the last three phases of training, where skill acquisition is taking place, no set number of trials, level of accuracy, or rate of performance improvement is predetermined. These can be varied based on student aptitude and the domain complexity. When to move on to the next level of training versus when to remain at the same level or even backup and remediate, can be determined based on the individual student's performance and progress. Some students may never perform as well on the task as other students. Thus, the system must be capable of recognizing when a student has "peaked" on a particular training phase. The goal is to determine how skillful students are based on actual performance, not on how many times they have done the procedure. This requires a decision on how accurate is accurate enough and how fast is fast enough at each level of training to indicate that the student has acquired a proficiency at that level and is ready to move on to the next level of training. These are issues where AI-based techniques can be used to provide the training system with the needed knowledge to make these decisions on a case-by-case basis, thus moving toward a more adaptive, individually responsive ITS.

Training Console Operations.   An ITS for a high performance domain is currently under development that follows this idea of apprenticeship training. The area of application is the operation of consoles in the Mission Control Center at Johnson Space Center. An example of such a console, namely the front-room propulsion console, is presented in Figure 9.4. These consoles vary somewhat from one system control function to another, but they generally consist of:

1. one or more video displays;
2. numerous sets of indicator lights, referred to as display decoder drive event lights (DDD lights); and
3. various manual entry devices consisting of numeric thumbwheels and push button indicators including the voice keyset, the manual select keyboard (MSK), the summary message enable keyboard (SMEK), and the display request keyboard (DRK).

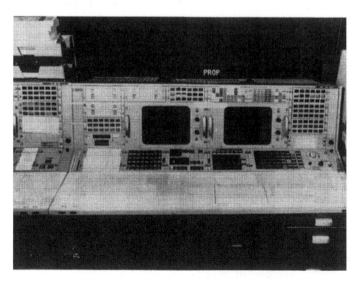

FIGURE 9.4 Mission control center console.

In addition, there may be one or more other panels for displaying various times associated with the mission. These consoles may also be attached to one or more strip chart recorders for recording sets of analog signals.

In order to become proficient at operating such consoles, flight controllers must learn how to perform the following tasks, among others:

1. format the various DDD light panels using the MSK;
2. select, display, and read a variety of video display formats using the MSK, SMEK, and DRK; and
3. select and listen to various voice loops using the voice keyset.

They must learn to operate these consoles in an automatic manner because such operations are only a means for achieving another goal, namely ensuring the safe and correct operation of a particular system, such as propulsion, during a space shuttle mission. Should a situation arise where data must be accessed, analyzed, and interpreted, the flight controller must be capable of quickly and effectively accessing the needed data from various video displays and DDD lights without specific thought as to how to manipulate the various keyboards. The controller is too busy trying to diagnose the situation to be concerned with how to get the data. Thus, console operations can be classified as a high performance domain.

Initial work on the ITS for console operations has centered on training the operation of the manual select keyboard (MSK). This is the keyboard used during initialization of the console for the ascent, orbit, and descent phases of a space shuttle mission. Initialization requires the formatting of all DDD light panels, the selection of several video displays to get information concerning general system status, and the selection of various voice loops to listen in on appropriate monologues and dialogues. Eventually the tutoring system could be expanded to include training on all of the various components of a console, as well as a general console overview. Figure 9.5 provides a hierarchical, graphic representation of the

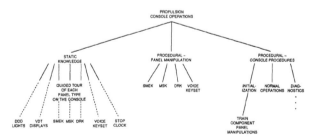

FIGURE 9.5 An illustration of the knowledge needed to operate a mission control console.

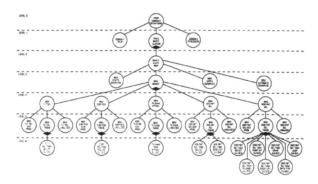

FIGURE 9.6 The five-phase training curriculum for the manual select keyboard (MSK).

knowledge needed to effectively operate a Mission Control Console. Figure 9.6 provides a detail of the five-phase training curriculum for the MSK.

The display for the tutoring system is organized into three major windows, as illustrated in Figure 9.7. Across the top third of the screen is a complete graphic representation of the entire console. This provides the student with an overall layout and organization of the console. The lower left half of the display provides an area where one of the panels from the console can be expanded to provide further detail. The figure shows the MSK panel. The lower right half of the screen provides the text interface

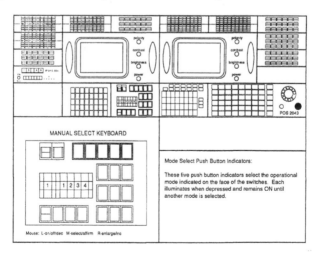

FIGURE 9.7 A graphic representation of the user interface to the ITS for console operations.

where the tutor can present information, assign exercises, and accept student responses to specific verbal questions.

The graphic display of the console is mouse-sensitive. Under certain conditions it allows the student to select panels by clicking over them with the mouse to have them expanded in the lower left window of the display. When a panel is expanded and displayed in the lower left window, it too is mouse-sensitive. A student can manipulate it by clicking the mouse over its components, thus incrementing or decrementing a thumbwheel counter, changing the setting of a lever switch, turning a push button indicator on or off, or just getting a display of the text written on the object. In this way, a large portion of the console functionality is simulated graphically and the student can gain experience in performing console operations through these simulated manipulations. The simulation provides high cognitive fidelity, but lower physical fidelity.

Training on the use of the MSK proceeds through the five phases previously described. The first phase of training on the MSK provides an overview of the MSK layout and structure. The MSK panel is expanded in the lower left window on the screen and the system steps through each of its functional components, highlighting them on the graphics display and describing them with text in the lower right window. This particular phase is illustrated in Figure 9.7, where the mode select push button indicators are highlighted in the graphics on the left and their description appears in the text on the right. Students can move forward and backward at their own pace through this portion of the tutorial. At the end, students must pass an identification test where they are asked to click over the various components of the console to indicate their response to the tutoring system's questions in order to proceed on to the next phase of the training. Based on the score, students are either allowed to move on or required to review the material.

Manipulation of the MSK can take place in one of five modes selected with the push button indicators in the upper right corner of the MSK panel. The procedure for manipulating the MSK varies depending on the mode selected, so the student's training consists of five general procedures to be mastered. Because all of the objects on the MSK panel remain the same for each procedure, the first static overview phase applies to all procedures. However, at the procedural overview phase, the training tree branches allow the student to concentrate on learning one of the procedures at a time. A task selection node called *MSK modes* is used to select the mode of operation and Phases 2, 3, and 4 of training are then subsumed under each independent task (see Figure 9.6).

As a result, in the second phase of training, an overview of the procedural process for manipulating the MSK in one single mode, for example display request mode, is given. This is done in a manner similar to the MSK overview. Components are highlighted in the appropriate order and explanations about each step of the procedure are provided. For example, to request a particular video display to appear in the right monitor of the console, the push button indicator with DISPLAY RE-QUEST written on it must be pushed, the number of the display entered on the right four lever switches, and the RIGHT MONITOR ENTER push button indicator pressed in the lower right corner of the MSK. A number of other steps must be performed as well, but these are the key steps. The order of all steps does not matter, with the exception of pressing the monitor enter push button indicator, which must be done last. Thus, the procedure could be represented where five actions comprise an unordered group that constitutes the first step, called *set-up,* and the monitor enter action comprises a second step, called *execute.* Of course, some sequences are more logical than others and the current system enforces a specific order for performing these actions. In order to move on to the next phase of training, the student must identify each step in the correct sequence.

The third phase of the training again concentrates on manipulation of the MSK panel in the same mode as just presented (i.e., DISPLAY REQUEST). The system generates and solves specific examples of the procedure as a demonstration for the student. For two of the modes, AES format select and DDD format select, there are multiple specific tasks to be taught. For example, selecting a format and deselecting a format involve manipulating the same objects in the MSK in the same order, but in slightly different ways. Thus, for these modes the Phase 3 demonstration and practice exercises are repeated for each specific task in sequence (see Figure 9.6). The student performs the assigned exercise by manipulating the mouse over the appropriate components of the MSK in the correct order to perform the requested operation. For example, the system may request that the student cause the video display number 12 to appear on the left display monitor. The system will prompt the student at each step and verify its correctness before moving on to the next step. If an error occurs, rules based on the error that the student has just made and the student's history of errors are used to coach the student to perform the procedure correctly. Satisfactory performance in this phase of training is based mainly on accuracy, but speed is also considered. When a student has consistently performed the assigned exercises with complete accuracy and the speed of performance has more or less plateaued, then the system allows the student to move on to the next phase of training.

In Phase 4 of training the tutoring system no longer guides or coaches the student through the exercises. Instead the system simply presents an exercise, initially concentrating only on a single mode of MSK operation, and the student must manipulate the MSK appropriately with the mouse to achieve the requested action. If Phase 3 was repeated for several specific tasks, then this phase acts as a cumulative testing phase, randomly presenting exercises for all of the tasks the student has learned within this mode of MSK operation. Then, if a student begins making mistakes on a particular type of task, the appropriate task is selected for remediation.

The static procedure, guided example, and unguided example sequence of phases is repeated for each of the five modes of MSK operation. The fourth phase of the training wraps up with a cumulative lesson, called MSK-speed-examples, where tasks from all modes are given in random order for the student to practice. At this point the system watches which modes of MSK operation the student is having trouble with, so if remediation is necessary, it will be in the appropriate mode. Based on consistently performing with complete accuracy and reaching a point where speed is no longer improving significantly but is at an acceptable level, the system then allows the student to move on to the final phase of the training.

The final phase is a repeat of the fourth phase but with an additional task that must be performed simultaneously by the student. While requesting a particular video display or formatting a set of DDD lights, the student must also acknowledge certain patterns of beeps by hitting the appropriate function key. The system assumes that the student has successfully automatized the MSK manipulation process when the accuracy in performing both tasks has reached 100% and the speed of performing the assigned exercise and responding to the beeps has reached an acceptable peak for that particular student.

It is important to note that during the final three phases of training, where skill is being acquired and tested, no predefined number of trials is used to determine whether or not the student should move on. Advancement to the next phase in training depends on the particular student's performance. Although accuracy is required to be 100% correct, ultimate speed can vary based on the student. The system looks for the student's leveling off in order to determine when to move on. The decision to backup and review material is based on how much difficulty the student is having attaining the required accuracy. Remediation can backup selectively based on student errors and even backup all the way to the start of the training program if necessary. In this way the system can be used to refresh the memories of individuals who have been interrupted in their training for a period of time, as well as those who are seeing the material for the first time.

Implementation of this tutoring system has utilized fairly low-level software development tools due to the need for the graphics interface and the constraints placed on the delivery platform. Using graphics primitives, C, and (CLIPS), fairly fundamental AI-based programming paradigms were implemented for representing the expert and student knowledge. In addition, we were able to develop a model of how progress should take place during a training session. A tree structure connecting frames of information provides the basic representation of the expert knowledge, student model, and curriculum. A specialized tree search implements the application of the curriculum based on the student model to generate an appropriate training session. Rules are used at certain points to guide the search appropriately with respect to the current perceived state of the student's skill level.

Conclusions. The training of a high performance skill requires a large amount of drill and practice. Students must repeatedly perform the task in order to become better at it, regardless of the amount of cognitive knowledge they may have concerning the task. An ITS appears to be an ideal means of providing such drill and practice in the initial phases of training. Such a system is capable of providing customized training practice in a high-cognitive-fidelity/low-physical-fidelity environment. Studies are currently underway to determine how effective and efficient such training methods are as opposed to more traditional approaches requiring expensive, high-fidelity three-dimensional simulators or time on the actual equipment.

ISSUES AND FUTURE RESEARCH

As has been illustrated by the two domains and their respective tutoring systems discussed in this chapter, the design of such systems can vary greatly, depending on the type of task to be trained. A knowledge-intensive domain, such as diagnosis and repair, requires complex knowledge bases and allows a more free-form approach to training. A high performance domain, such as console operations, has a much less complex knowledge base that is fairly factually oriented but a much more rigid approach to training. Both systems allow a certain amount of free-play, providing students with an opportunity to explore and investigate at their own direction. However, both systems also provide at least a certain amount of direction and guidance to insure that the student is acquiring the appropriate knowledge in a way that will be useful to performing the task in which they are being trained. We hope this direction and guidance will produce the desired training results in a manner that is more efficient and effective than completely undirected free-play.

Training a domain and a task, whether it is cognitive or high performance–oriented, is a knowledge-intensive task both with respect to the domain as well as how to teach it. Short-term goals for research oriented toward domain knowledge and its role in an ITS include the following:

- Explore the spectrum of potential domains that could be trained using an ITS and attempt to classify them based on a useful taxonomy. This work is currently being performed, to some degree, by individuals working on issues of knowledge representation and utilization as they apply to problem solving. The wide variety of problem-solving tasks of interest to training need to be systematically identified, analyzed, and classified in a way that would allow the attributes relevant to issues of training to become apparent.

- Develop/validate knowledge representation techniques for the various classes of domains and teaching methodologies. A consistent and verified methodology for representing the knowledge required in an ITS would allow a general method and framework for ITS development to evolve.

- Develop prototype ITSs that appear representative of the domain classes experimenting with knowledge representation and training techniques to validate and modify the classifications with respect to training effectiveness. The only way to test a theory is to try to use it in real-world applications. The generation of large numbers of ITSs in a wide variety of fields would allow the theory to be tested, modified, and enhanced based on the experience gained in building real systems. Areas selected for implementation should come from all areas of the training world, from the military, to industry, and even the public school system.

Long-term goals for such research include the following:

- Solidify a taxonomy of domains and their respective teaching and learning strategies. Such a taxonomy, if done correctly, will provide a foundation for developing ITSs. It will allow all individuals involved in ITS development to learn from the work done previously. It should highlight where successes have taken place and where more research is needed.

- Develop ITS components based on the domain classifications that will allow a system developer to utilize them as needed in the development of a complete ITS for a particular domain. This should be the ultimate goal of research in intelligent tutoring. A set of ITS development tools would allow the rapid development of ITSs, thus bringing down the cost of such systems and allowing them to be more accessible to larger groups of people. The key will be in the development of the appropriate set of tools and this will depend on the effectiveness of the training taxonomies developed.

As is implied by both the short- and long-term goals, a major concern in the development of ITSs is the large amount of time currently required to design and implement an ITS; everything must be developed from scratch. The field will benefit greatly from the definition of some workable theories on teaching and learning as they apply to classes of domains and the development of software tools to support the implementation of ITSs that reflect these theories.

REFERENCES

Anderson, J. (1982). Acquisition of cognitive skill. *Psychological Review, 89,* 369-406.

Anderson, J. (1987). Production systems, learning, and tutoring. In D. Klahr, P. Langley, & R. Neches (Eds.), *Production system models of learning and development* (pp. 437-458). Cambridge, MA: MIT Press.

Anderson, J., Farell, R., & Sauers, R. (1984). Learning to program in LISP. *Cognitive Science, 8,* 87-129.

Bloom, B. S. (1956). *Taxonomy of educational objectives: Cognitive domain (Handbook I).* New York: McKay.

Bloom, B. S. (1984, June-July). The two-sigma problem: The search for method of group instruction as effective as one-to-one tutoring. *Educational Research, 13,* 4-16.

Brown, J. S., Burton, R. R., & deKleer, J. (1982). Knowledge engineering and pedagogical techniques in SOPHIE I, II, and III. In D. Sleeman & J. S. Brown (Eds.), *Intelligent tutoring systems* (pp. 227-282). London: Academic Press.

Buchanan, B., & Feigenbaum, E. (1978). Dendral and meta-dendral: Their applications dimension. *Artificial Intelligence, 2*(1, 2), 5-24.

Carbonell, J. R. (1970). AI in CAI: An artificial intelligence approach to computer-aided instruction. *IEEE Transactions on Man–Machine Systems, 11*(4), 190-202.

Chandrasekaran, B., & Mittal, S. (1983). Deep vs. compiled knowledge approaches to diagnostic problem-solving. *International Journal of Man–Machine Studies, 19*(5), 425-436.

Charniak, E., & McDermott, D. (1985). *Introduction to artificial intelligence.* Reading, MA: Addison-Wesley.

Clancey, W. J., & Letsinger, R. (1981). NEOMYCIN: Reconfiguring a rule-based expert system for application to teaching. *Proceedings of the Seventh International Joint Conference on Artificial Intelligence, 2,* 829-836.

Collins, A., Brown, J. S., & Newman, S. E. (1987). Cognitive apprenticeships: Teaching the craft of reading, writing and mathematics. In L. B. Resnick (Ed.), *Cognition and instruction: Issues and agendas.* Hillsdale, NJ: Lawrence Erlbaum Associates.

Davis, R., (1980). Reasoning from first principles in electronic troubleshooting. *International Journal of Man–Machine Studies, 19*(15), 403-423.

DeKleer, J., & Brown, J. S. (1982). Foundations of envisioning. *Proceedings of the National Conference on Artificial Intelligence* (pp. 434-437). Pittsburgh, PA.

Duda, R., Gaschnig, J., & Hart, P. (1979). Model design in the prospector consultant system for mineral exploration. In D. Michie (Ed.), *Expert systems in the microelectronic age.* Edinburg, Scotland: Edinburg University Press.

Feigenbaum, E. (circa 1980). General comment about the AI field.

Fink, P. (1985). Control and integration of diverse knowledge in a diagnostic expert system. *Proceedings of the Ninth International Joint Conference on Artificial Intelligence* (pp. 426-431). Los Angeles, CA.

Fink, P. (1988, April). Issues in representing knowledge for training high performance skills. *Proceedings of the Second Intelligent Tutoring Systems Research Forum* (pp. 23-37). San Antonio, TX.

Fink, P., & Lusth, J. (1987). Expert systems and diagnostic expertise in the mechanical and electrical domains. *IEEE Transactions on Systems, Man, and Cybernetics, 17* (3), 340–349.

Fink, P., & Sines, L. (1989). An intelligent tutor for a high performance domain. *Proceedings of the AIAA Computers in Aerospace VII Conference.* (pp. 572–580). Monterey, CA.

Forbus, K. (1981). Qualitative reasoning of physical processes. *Proceedings of the Seventh International Joint Conference on Artificial Intelligence,* (pp. 326–330). Vancouver, Canada.

Gagne, R. M. (1977). *The conditions of learning* (3rd ed.). New York: Holt, Rinehart & Winston.

Genesereth, M. (1982). Diagnosis using hierarchical design models. *Proceedings of the National Conference on Artificial Intelligence* (pp. 278–283). Pittsburgh, PA.

Gott, S. P. (1988). Apprenticeship instruction for real-world tasks: The coordination of procedures, mental models, and strategies. In E. V. Rothkopf (Ed.), *Review of research in education* (Vol. 15, pp. 97–169). Washington, DC: American Educational Research Association.

Harloe, E. D., & Fink, P. K. (1989). Integrating model-based and experience-based knowledge in a diagnostic expert system. *IJCAI Workshop on Artificial Intelligence Applications to Manufacturing,* Detroit, MI.

Kuipers, B. (1984). Commonsense reasoning about causality: Deriving behavior from structure. *Artificial Intelligence, 24*(1–3), 169–203.

Kyllonen, P. C., & Shute, V. J. (1988). A taxonomy of learning skills. In P. Ackerman, R. Sternberg, & R. Glaser (Eds.), *Learning and individual differences* (pp. 117–163). San Francisco: W. H. Freeman.

Merrill, M. D. (1987). An expert system for instructional design. *IEEE Expert, 2*(2), 25–31.

Minsky, M. (1975). A framework for representing knowledge. In P. Winston (Ed.), *The psychology of computer vision* (pp. 211–277). New York: McGraw-Hill.

Newell, A., & Simon, H. A. (1963). GPS, a program that simulates human thought. In E. Feigenbaum & J. Feldman (Eds)., *Computers and thought.* New York: McGraw-Hill.

Nilsson, N. J. (1980). *Principles of artificial intelligence.* Palo Alto, CA: Tioga.

O'Neil, H. F., Slawson, D. A., & Baker, E. L. (1988, April). Design of a domain-independent problem-solving instructional strategy for intelligent computer-assisted instruction. *Proceedings of the Second Intelligent Tutoring System Research Forum* (pp. 91–101). San Antonio, TX.

Patil, R. Szolovits, P., & Schwartz, W. (1981). Causal understanding of patient illness in medical diagnosis. In *Proceedings of the Seventh International Joint Conference on Artificial Intelligence,* (pp. 893–899). Vancouver, Canada.

Porter, B., Acker, L., Lester, J., & Souther, A. (1988, April). Generating Explanations in an Intelligent Tutor Designed to Teach Fundamental Knowledge. *Proceedings of the Second Intelligent Tutoring Systems Research Forum* (pp. 55–69). San Antonio, TX.

Regian, J. W., & Shute, V. J. (1988). AI in training: The evolution of intelligent tutoring systems. *Proceedings of the Conference on Technology and Training in Education* (pp. 371–379). Biloxi, MS.

Rich, E. (1983). *Artificial intelligence.* New York: McGraw-Hill.

Schank, R. C., & Abelson, R. P. (1977). *Scripts, plans, goals, and understanding.* Hillsdale, NJ: Lawrence Erlbaum Associates.

Schneider, W., & Shiffrin, R. M. (1977). Controlled and automatic human information processing: I. Detection, search, and attention. *Psychological Review, 84,* 1–66.

Shortliffe, E. H. (1976). *Computer-based medical consultations: MYCIN.* New York: Elsevier.

Sleeman, D., & Brown, J. S. (1982). *Intelligence tutoring systems.* London: Academic Press.

Smith, H., Fink, P., & Lusth, J. (1985). Intelligent tutoring using the integrated diagnostic model: An expert system for diagnosis and repair. *Proceedings of Expert Systems in Government* (pp. 128–134). Washington DC.

VanLehn, K. (1988). Student Modelling. In M. C. Polson & J. J. Richardson (Eds).,

Foundations of intelligent tutoring systems (pp. 57–78). Hillsdale, NJ: Lawrence Erlbaum Associates.

Waterman, D. (1986). *A guide to expert systems.* Reading, MA: Addison-Wesley.

Winston, P. H. (1984). *Artificial intelligence* (2nd ed.). Reading, MA: Addison-Wesley.

Woolf, B. (1988, April). Representing, acquiring, and reasoning about tutoring knowledge. *Proceedings of the Second Intelligent Tutoring Systems Research Forum,* San Antonio, TX.

Woolf, B., & McDonald, D. D. (1985). Building a computer tutor: design issues. *AEDS Monitor, 23*(9–10), 10–18.

Representing and Teaching High Performance Tasks Within Intelligent Tutoring Systems

J. Wesley Regian
Air Force Human Resources Laboratory

Intelligent tutoring systems (ITSs) are advanced computer-based training systems that use artificial intelligence (AI) technology to allow highly individualized instructional interactions with students (Soloway & Littman, 1986; Wenger, 1987; Yazdani, 1986). This chapter describes a currently implemented ITS developed at the Air Force Human Resources Laboratory (HRL) that teaches cognitive skills associated with performing an instrument-only landing in a fighter airplane. The ITS was developed not as an actual training device for instrument flight, but as a testbed for the application of AI to training in a class of task domains (and task components) that have been referred to as high performance tasks (Regian & Shute, 1988) and real-time tasks (Ritter & Feurzeig, 1988). In high performance tasks, there is more of a requirement for speeded, reliable, and automatic task performance than is found in the typical knowledge-rich ITS domains (e.g., medical diagnosis, electronic troubleshooting). The Instrument Flight Trainer (INFLITE) trains students to land a simulated aircraft (F-16) using instruments only. During the process, an intelligent coach monitors the student and provides guidance just as an instructor pilot might guide a student pilot. This guidance is presented verbally, using a speech synthesis device to simulate human speech. The system supports a variety of instructional approaches, including the ability to freeze the simulation to give guidance, prebrief students before training sessions, generate guidance in real-time during training sessions, debrief students after training sessions, anticipate student errors in real-time based on prior student performance, and generate part-task drills to achieve performance goals.

INTELLIGENT TUTORING SYSTEMS

Computer-aided instruction (CAI) is a mature technology used to teach students in a wide variety of domains. The introduction of AI technology to the field of CAI has prompted research and development efforts in an area known as intelligent computer-aided instruction (ICAI). In some cases, ICAI has been touted as a revolutionary alternative to traditional CAI. According to Dede and Swigger (1987), "With the advent of powerful, inexpensive school computers, ICAI is emerging as a potential rival to CAI" (p. 1). In contrast to this, one may conceive of computer-based training (CBT) systems as lying along a continuum that runs from CAI to ICAI. Thus, ICAI may be seen as an evolution of CAI rather than as a revolutionary alternative. There is one key difference between the two perspectives because in a revolution the old guard is dismissed and replaced, whereas in an evolution the old guard is a foundation upon which to build. The evolution perspective implies that we are less likely to throw out the strengths and accomplishments of the old guard. This perspective does not imply, however, that there are no important differences among CBT systems.

For my purposes, I discriminate among CBT systems according to the degree to which the instruction they provide is individualized. My choice of this particular dimension is more utilitarian than precise. A great deal of data from the educational literature indicates that carefully individualized instruction is superior to conventional group instruction (Bloom, 1984; Woolf, 1987). Thus, an important way in which CBT systems differ is in the degree to which their behavior is modified by an inferred "model of the student's current understanding of the subject matter" (VanLehn, 1986, p. 49). The CBT system that is less intelligent by this definition, I conceive of as CAI. Similarly, the system that is more intelligent, I conceive of as ICAI. Often, ICAI systems are referred to as intelligent tutoring systems (ITSs) (Sleeman & Brown, 1982). This term is particularly appropriate, as it brings to mind one-on-one tutoring.

With respect to individualization, it is important to note that virtually all traditional CAI systems are individualized in the sense that they are self-paced, and many are further individualized by virtue of branching routines that allow different students to receive different instruction. CAI systems with branching routines are, in fact, more individualized than those without branching routines. Thus, they are more intelligent by the current definition (although in a weak sense). Nevertheless, in branched CAI the instructional developer must explicitly encode the actions generated by all possible branches, and there is a finite number of possible paths through these branches. As one moves further away from the CAI to the

ICAI end of the continuum, one begins to see a very different and more powerful approach to individualization. This more powerful approach is touched on by Wenger (1987, p. 4) when he referred to explicit encoding of knowledge rather than encoding of decisions. An ITS (a term that probably should be reserved for systems very far toward the ICAI end of the continuum) utilizes a diverse set of knowledge bases and inference routines to "compose instructional interactions dynamically, making decisions by reference to the knowledge with which they have been provided" (Wenger, 1987, p. 5). Thus, individualized instruction in an ITS is an emergent property of several interacting components. These are the expert module, the instructional module, the student model, the interface, and often a device simulation or other instructional environment. These components were described in chapter 1 of this volume, and are discussed further later in this chapter.

Knowledge-Rich
Versus High Performance Domains

Traditionally, if the term applies to a technology less than 20 years old, ITSs have focused on knowledge-rich domains such as electronic troubleshooting, physics, economics, and medical diagnosis. Furthermore, they have focused on the higher level problem-solving components of these domains even though knowledge-rich domains almost invariably involve components of expertise, sometimes called *enabling skills,* which can be characterized as high performance components. For example, electronic troubleshooting involves *schematic tracing,* which is supported by the ability to immediately and accurately combine gate inputs to determine the output of a particular gate type as represented on the schematic. Similarly, expert performance in theoretical physics requires total facility with basic math and algebraic skills. Human instructors can recognize deficiencies in basic enabling skills (especially in one-on-one tutoring situations) and apply methods to correct these deficiencies.

As a rule ITSs are not sensitive to deficiencies in basic enabling skills, even though they are not difficult to identify. Moreover, computers are particularly well suited to providing the kind of drill-and-practice exercises that can correct the deficiencies. In generating instruction for knowledge-rich domains, ITSs may be sensitive to the full range of performance determinants for the domain, and have appropriate routines available for remediation.

Furthermore, there is a place for ITS technology even in primarily high performance domains such as air traffic control, air intercept control, typing, Mission Control console operation, and simple equipment operation.

TUTORS FOR HIGH PERFORMANCE TASKS

Any training program should be designed with an awareness of the underlying cognitive operations that support performance in the targeted task or domain. Tasks may depend on greater or lesser contributions from declarative knowledge, procedural knowledge and skill, or performance skill determinants. These categories of cognitive operations may be said to lie along a continuum that runs from more knowledge-based to more performance-based (see, e.g., Kyllonen & Shute, 1989). Although most complex tasks are supported to some degree by all of these categories of operations, many tasks are heavily weighted toward one end of the continuum. Some tasks, for example, are very knowledge-based, such as electronic troubleshooting or medical diagnosis. Other tasks tend to be much more performance-based, such as air intercept control or typing. Although both types of tasks require a certain amount of knowledge to support performance, knowledge-rich tasks require more depth and breadth of knowledge and are less reliant on performance-based skills. The more performance-based tasks, on the other hand, often require key task components to be cognitively automatized to the point where task performance is smooth, fluid, and effortless. Such an assimilation, or *automatization,* of the task has important benefits. For example, automatized task performance allows the individual to perform other functions at the same time and renders task performance highly reliable under stress (Hancock & Pierce, 1984) and highly resistant to skill degradation (Regian & Schneider, 1986).

The Role of Automaticity
in High Performance Skill Training

The automatic versus controlled processing framework (Shiffrin & Schneider, 1977) provides a theoretical approach to training high performance skills. The framework posits two qualitatively different forms of processing that underlie human performance. Automatic processing is fast, parallel, fairly effortless, not limited by short-term memory capacity, not under direct subject control, and is used in performing well-developed skilled behaviors. This mode of processing develops when subjects deal with training stimuli in a consistent manner over many trials. Controlled processing is slow, effortful, capacity-limited, subject-controlled, and is used to deal with novel, inconsistent, or poorly learned information. This mode of processing is expected at the beginning of practice on any novel task, and throughout practice when a subject's response to a stimulus varies from trial to trial. In this framework, high performance skills are trainable because they involve components that can be executed rapidly, reliably, and with little effort, freeing cognitive resources for performing other nonautomatic tasks (see Schneider, 1985).

In designing training procedures for high performance tasks, two important findings from the automatic versus controlled framework should be considered. The first centers on the distinction between consistent practice and varied (or inconsistent) practice. Consistent practice produces substantial improvements in performance as automatic processing develops. For example, Fisk and Schneider (1983) observed a 98% reduction in visual search comparison rates. Varied practice uses only controlled processing and produces little improvement in performance. For example, Shiffrin and Schneider (1977) observed no change in letter search performance over 4 months of training. The second finding centers on the amount of effort required to perform automatic processing tasks. Consistent practice greatly reduces the amount of effort required to perform a task, allowing controlled processing to be allocated to another task. When subjects have already developed automatic processes to perform one task, they can learn to time-share another task with little or no deficit. After 20 hours of consistent practice in two search tasks, subjects were able to perform both tasks simultaneously nearly as well as they could perform each separately (Fisk & Schneider, 1983; Schneider & Fisk, 1982a, 1982b, 1984). In addition, automatic task performance has the advantage of being far more reliable under stress (see Hancock & Pierce, 1984).

The acquisition of skill with practice is assumed to result from the development of automatic processes, which are used to perform consistent task components. Any applied skill of reasonable complexity is likely to involve both consistent and inconsistent components. Thus, an empirically verified componential breakdown of a complex skill is useful for training. Performance on consistent components is likely to change significantly over extensive practice, whereas performance on inconsistent components is likely to asymptote relatively quickly. Automatization of consistent components has the benefit of freeing up processing capacity that may then be applied to inconsistent components. Furthermore, automatization of consistent components may be facilitated during training by allowing trainees to attend fully to the isolated components.

Part-Task Training Again?

Component-based or part-task training is not a new idea. Although the part-task literature is replete with examples of failed training procedures, there are also examples of highly successful procedures (e.g., Frederiksen & White, 1989). Moreover, many procedural training programs informally break down the training into parts that are trained individually and then in aggregate. Flight instructors often teach students a procedure to scan instruments during flight. This instrument drill is practiced in isolation until the student is comfortable with the procedure. Practice is provided on flight simulators, and students are sometimes encouraged to practice on aircraft in the hangar. By the time the student is actually flying an airplane, the instrument drill is supposed to be second nature.

Under the current perspective, the instrument drill is a task component that should be trained to automaticity so that control processing is freed up during flight for aircraft control. Next consider the problem of trying to do calculus without first automatizing basic math and algebra skills. If the algebraic skills are not automatic they will be unreliable when performed concurrently while allocating controlled processing to performance of the calculus task. The student would be more likely to be error-prone, slow, and unable to perform complex problems. For many tasks it is important to automatize key components of the task.

Time-Compressed Training

One of the benefits that falls out of a componential approach to training is the capability of providing a large number of trials for any given component in a relatively short period of time. For example, in an Air Intercept Control training regime for Naval Air Intercept Controllers it is important to be able to visually estimate the angular heading of a radar blip within 5 degrees accuracy. This level of accuracy takes an average of 2,000 training trials to achieve in laboratory tests. Under normal training conditions, this many trials would require about 5.5 weeks of training time. In a time-compressed angle judgment module (Regian & Schneider, 1986), students perform a video-flash-card version of the task. In this form, students experienced 2,000 trials of the critical task in 3 hours and achieved the requisite accuracy.

AI for Drill and Practice?

AI programming techniques are, of course, not required for building simple drill and practice exercises. The intelligence in high performance training would be manifest in decisions regarding exercise selection and sequencing, decision rules for when to move from one exercise to the next, and perhaps in real-time generation of specialized drill and practice routines. For example, in Air Intercept Control, suppose that the student quickly developed facility with identifying radar blip headings that were near the cardinal points (0, 90, 180, 270) but was still error-prone when identifying other heading angles (e.g., 27). An intelligent system would note this fact and generate drill and practice exercises that were heavily weighted with noncardinal practice trials. In most cases, however, tasks are not purely high performance or knowledge-rich, but rather involve both kinds of components. Aircraft piloting, for example, involves both skill and knowledge.

INFLITE

The INFLITE system is an ITS that trains students to land a simulated aircraft (F-16) using instruments only. INFLITE runs on AT-class microcomputers. It is written in the C programming language and uses the CLIPS[1] expert system shell. The system was designed primarily to operate with a joystick, but also supports a keypad interface. For optimal utility, INFLITE requires a peripheral voice synthesis device capable of converting an ASCII character stream into articulated speech. Such devices are commonly available and relatively inexpensive.

The INFLITE Anatomy

A conceptual anatomy of INFLITE is shown in Figure 10.1. The reader may find it useful to compare this anatomy to the generic ITS anatomy shown in chapter 1 of this volume. In the following paragraphs, each of the five components of the generic ITS anatomy are described, followed by specific reference to the INFLITE anatomy.

In an ITS, the *expert module* is a programmed representation of expert knowledge in the target domain being taught. It is almost identical to what is commonly known as an expert system, except in this context it is by necessity very articulate (able to generate some form of rationale for its actions) and is often capable of generating alternative solution paths (rather than a single best path). The expert module brings domain knowledge to the ITS. In some useful sense, the system knows how to perform the task that it is seeking to teach and can demonstrate that knowledge.

---

[1]The C Language Integrated Production System (CLIPS) was developed by the Artificial Intelligence Section (AIS) of the Mission Planning and Analysis Division (MPAD) at NASA/JSC. INFLITE uses version 4.2, which was developed under joint funding from NASA and the U.S. Air Force.

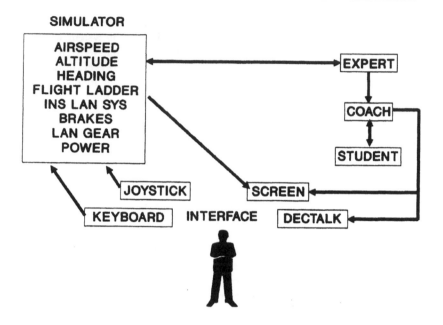

FIGURE 10.1 A conceptual anatomy of INFLITE.

The INFLITE expert module is an expert on performing instrument landings in an F-16 aircraft. The expert is both articulate and capable of real-time generation of alternative solution paths. The expert is, at times, given control of the simulation and allowed to land the aircraft. At these times the expert articulates a rationale for each of its actions so that the student may benefit from this expertise. When the student is in control of the simulation, the expert generates new best solution paths every few seconds as a function of the student's current location and orientation. Thus the student is not penalized for mistakes made early in a flight. Rather, expert guidance is always based on the current situation. Figure 10.2 shows part of a best solution path generated by the expert model for a specific startup configuration. The figure shows actions and when to perform them (in seconds from start time). Each action has an associated rationale that may be articulated directly (as in demo mode) or requested by the coach which is not shown in the figure.

The instructional module is a programmed representation of expert knowledge on pedagogy in the target domain. It is generally not articulate but is usually capable of generating alternative instructional approaches based on the current knowledge level of the current student. Whereas the expert module typically derives from knowledge engineering with an

```
000  START
010  TURN  TO  220
015  POWER  TO  AFT,  THRUST  TO  100%
045  POWER  TO  MIL,  THRUST  TO  75%
055  TURN  TO  180
      .
      .
      .
240  ALTITUDE  TO  100,  THRUST  TO  68%
265  ALTITUDE  TO  0,  AIRBRAKES  ON
280  WHEELBRAKES  ON
```

FIGURE 10.2   An expert module Best Solution Path.

expert practitioner in the target domain, the instructional module may derive from knowledge engineering with an expert instructor in the target domain (which may or may not be the same person as the expert practitioner), with a general training specialist, or both.

The instructional module in INFLITE, referred to as the coach, was designed to be easily redesigned to support empirical research on instructional approaches. Thus, instructional routines (e.g., part-task drills) are compiled and stored independently on disc so that they may be called for in an instructional module *driver file*. This file contains, in a simple and standard format, the top-level curriculum flow (see Figure 10.3) as well as rules for what to present in briefs, when to generate real-time guidance, and so on. The instructional approaches currently supported by INFLITE include the ability to freeze the simulation to give guidance, prebrief students before training sessions, generate guidance in real-time during training sessions, debrief students after training sessions, anticipate student errors in real-time based on prior student performance, and generate part-task drills to achieve performance goals.

The student model constitutes a repository for information about each student that uses the system. At the beginning of an initial tutoring session the student model is merely a place to store specific kinds of information about students in particular formats that will be useful for the instructional module to access. The student model is dynamically updated during tutoring sessions to maintain current information about the student such as what the student knows, what the student does not know, and misconceptions the student may have. The student model brings situational awareness to the ITS. Thus, the system knows who it is teaching to, and can make informed decisions about what to teach next, and how to teach it.

LOG IN ⟶ ‹FIRST TIME?›

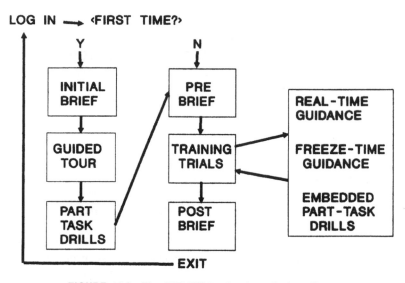

FIGURE 10.3   The INFLITE top-level curriculum flow.

The INFLITE student model includes data on component skills, task skills, and task strategies (see Figure 10.4). Component skills are task components that are taught in isolation during the part-task drills portion of the curriculum flow. In the case of head up display (HUD) skills, scoring algorithms are applied to students' performance during these drills, and they are not allowed to proceed beyond the drills until their score exceeds 0.70. The scores range from 0 to 1. In the case of toggle skills

COMPONENT SKILLS

HUD	AIRSPEED CORRECTION	.73				
	HEADING CORRECTION	.82				
	ALTITUDE CORRECTION	.94				
TOGGLE	POWER	✓				
	THRUST	✓				
	AIRBRAKES	✓				
	LANDING GEAR	✓				
	WHEEL BRAKES	✓				

TASK SKILLS

LEVEL 1		AIRTIME	100				
		GROUNDTIME	11				
LEVEL 2	HUD	AIRCOR		09	-03	08	11
		HEADCOR	12			19	
		ALTCOR				-21	06	00
	TOGGLE	POWER					
		THRUST	08	00	07	07
		AIRBRA	06	-07	06	04
		LANDGE		-06	00	09
		WHEELB				

TASK STRATEGIES

	PRESENTED	APPLIED	CONSISTENCY
STRAT1	1	2	1.00
STRAT2	2	1	0.26
STRAT3	0	1	

FIGURE 10.4   The INFLITE student model.

(knowing which key will toggle a certain indicator), the student need only demonstrate the skill on one occasion. Task skills (the name is somewhat arbitrary) are reflected by latency measures taken during each training trial. With reference to the values shown in Figure 10.4, this student required 100 seconds more airtime and 11 seconds more groundtime than an expert would have required to land and stop the aircraft. Furthermore, the student performed the initial heading correction 12 seconds too late, the first airspeed correction 9 seconds too late, and the second airspeed correction 3 seconds too early. Note that the task skill measures are divided into Level 1 and Level 2 measures. The instructional module can look at Level 1 (gross) indicators to decide what to focus on next (airtime or groundtime) and Level 2 indicators to find the specific source of the student's shortfall.

Task strategies are taught to the students after they have successfully landed the aircraft several times but are no longer making significant reductions in time to land and stop the aircraft. The student model maintains a record of which strategies have been presented and how many times, a record of how many times they have been applied by the student, and a consistency ratio (times applied over opportunities to apply). As an example, Figure 10.5 shows a graph that was created and displayed on the screen along with words that were spoken by the coach in attempting to teach Strategy 1.

The interface provides the methods by which the student interacts with the ITS. The interface may include such output methods as computer-generated graphics and text, recorded video images, or speech synthesizers; and such input devices as a mouse, keyboard, touchscreen, joystick, or voice recognition system. It should be pointed out that the interface should be as simple as possible so that learning to use the ITS does not interfere with learning from the ITS.

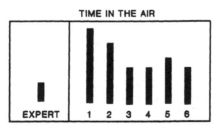

"YOU'RE STILL TAKING TOO LONG TO GET YOUR WHEELS ON THE GROUND. IN FACT, YOU HAVEN'T IMPROVED SINCE YOUR THIRD FLIGHT. NEXT TIME, AFTER YOU REACH YOUR INITIAL HEADING, SPEED UP. DON'T SLOW DOWN AGAIN UNTIL THE TOWER GIVES YOU A NEW HEADING."

FIGURE 10.5 Coach-selected feedback in INFLITE.

The INFLITE interface consists of a joystick, keyboard, screen, and speech synthesis device. The joystick and keyboard are used to control the simulation. The screen and speech synthesis device are used to display the simulation and to output guidance from the coach. The screen display interface to INFLITE is shown in Figure 10.6. The INFLITE interface consists primarily of the HUD, which presents speed, altitude, heading, and flight path ladder indicators, as well as an instrument landing system (ILS) beam indicator when requested. In addition to joystick (or keypad) directional control, the student uses function keys to toggle on-screen panel lights that depict wheel brake, air brake, landing gear, and afterburner status. Finally, the student uses the keypad plus and minus keys to manipulate thrust, which is represented on-screen with a percentage bar.

Many ITSs (e.g., STEAMER, IMTS/Bladefold) use an embedded computer simulation of an electrical or mechanical device to provide an instructional context, or environment. That is, the device simulations are used to teach operation or maintenance of a specific device in the context of an operating model of the device. Other ITSs teach a body of knowledge that is not specific to any particular device, and yet they use other kinds of simulations to provide instructional environments. For example, Smithtown uses a simulation of microeconomics operating in a small town, and the orbital mechanics (OM) tutor uses a simulation of orbital dynamics.

The INFLITE simulator presents an accurate real-time simulation of the interactions among essential flight instruments, balancing processor time among the different functional units in order to avoid disruption of

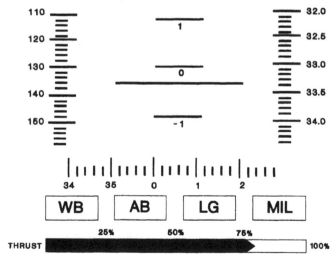

FIGURE 10.6 The INFLITE display interface.

the display. The airspeed, altitude, heading, and attitude of the aircraft interact with one another and with the aircraft controls to simulate the flight characteristics of the F-16. The simulation may be controlled externally by joystick and keyboard input, or internally by the expert module for demonstration purposes.

The INFLITE Curriculum

As stated earlier, INFLITE was designed as an ITS shell that supports a variety of instructional approaches and training techniques. In fact, the system is intended as a testbed to allow systematic research on training for high performance tasks. Therefore, what follows is simply a description of an initial, somewhat representative version of INFLITE.

In the initial familiarization session, the student is given a guided tour of the display interface by an articulate coach. As the coach describes each component of the interface, that component is highlighted on the screen. Next, the student is given a series of practice exercises to engender familiarity with methods of controlling the simulation. When the coach is satisfied that the student is sufficiently acclimated, the student is allowed to begin training trials.

At the beginning of each training trial, the simulation commences with the aircraft in flight, under normal flight conditions and randomly positioned with respect to the target airstrip. The goal of each training trial is to successfully land the aircraft. To do this, the student must follow heading information from flight control, use the joystick to turn the aircraft to successive temporary headings, locate the ILS beam, and follow this beam down to the airstrip.

During each training trial, an intelligent coach monitors the simulation (e.g., airspeed, heading, deviation from ILS beam, etc.) and provides guidance just as an instructor pilot might guide a student pilot. This guidance is presented verbally, using the voice synthesis system to simulate human speech. The student also receives instructions from a ground-based flight controller, again using synthesized speech but with an alternate voice. During early training trials, the coach may choose to freeze the simulation to give guidance. During all trials, student performance information is recorded for later use in prebriefing, interactive comments, and postbriefing by the flight coach. During the postflight debriefs, the coach reviews the student's performance in comparison to performance on earlier flights and highlights specific areas to be worked on in future flights. During early training trials, the coach provides guidance and feedback to the student based on real-time observations, as well as by anticipating problems based on typical novice tendencies. In later training trials the coach additionally anticipates problems based on the current student's performance history. During the preflight briefs, the coach reminds the student of problem areas identified in earlier flights.

The intelligent tutoring is handled by the expert, coach, and student modeling modules built with the CLIPS expert system[2] shell. The expert outlines suggested pilot actions and judges flight conditions. For example, the expert may suggest a change to a heading of 90 degrees to move the aircraft toward the ILS beam center. If the student does indeed choose to move toward the beam, the expert will note the heading chosen and the effect on the alignment of the craft with the ILS beam. The expert reports to the coach any motion toward or away from the landing goal and its subgoals. The student never hears directly from the expert. Instead, the expert provides information to the coach, who decides how best to interact with the student from an instructional perspective.

The coach uses information such as expert performance data, average student performance data, current student performance data, and the history of the current student to make instructional decisions. For example, the coach may choose to intervene with the student by generating a simple warning ("Wes, you've drifted off course again"), by selecting a part-task drill, or by freezing the display and generating a lengthy description of the problem. In the current version of INFLITE, the display is only frozen in early training trials, such as the first time the student

---

[2]For interested programmers, the following is an example of a CLIPS rule definition in INFLITE. The keyword of the definition is "defrule" for "define rule." The name of the rule follows the keyword, then the verbal description. This rule retracts the suggestion that an action be performed to increase the reading on a gauge. The student could have been flying too low relative to his distance to the airport, and has just made the correction himself. The "?request" line triggers the matching of this rule. The subsequent lines (up through the "= >") grab the gauge reading and test for the suggested correction. If the correction has been made, the right hand side of the rule is executed, the suggestion is retracted, and a message is printed to the screen.

```
( defrule EndLowValueCorrection
      "Retract a suggested increase in a gauge
reading"
    ?request < - ( correctionPerformed ?gauge positive
?magnitude )
    ?gaugestatus < - ( gaugecondition ?gauge tooLow
?minValue )
  ( ?gauge ?curValue )
  ( test ( < = ?minValue ?curValue))
  = >
  ( fprintout t crlf "LOW Speed correction
followed . . ." crlf )
  ( retract ?gaugestatus )
  ( retract ?request ))
```

encounters the problem of being aligned with the beam according to the ILS scales but moving away from the beam due to an incorrect heading.

SUMMARY

Intelligent tutoring systems should be sensitive to the full range of performance determinants for their target domain, and should be capable of generating appropriate instructional exercises. Many important tasks, such as aircraft piloting, complex equipment operation, and electronic troubleshooting involve both knowledge-rich and high performance components. At the Human Resources Laboratory, we are investigating ITS architectures that can support the full range of training approaches required for these kinds of tasks.

INFLITE is a prototype example of a potential class of intelligent microprocessor-based training simulators with the goal of filling the gap between classroom instruction and expensive simulation time. Such a class of simulators would be useful during initial training and for refresher training. INFLITE is a high-cognitive-fidelity/low-physical-fidelity simulator targeted to teach key cognitive skills required for high performance tasks after declarative instruction and prior to high-physical-fidelity simulation instruction.

INFLITE will be used as an experimental testbed for purposes of evaluating the relative training effectiveness of various approaches to automated training of high performance skills. For example, variations on the system are being developed with additional flight condition-and-effect simulations, increased student analysis, and increased student–coach interaction initiated by the student pilot. The goals of this work are to extend the range of domains for which ITSs can be applied and to increase the effectiveness of ITSs for knowledge-rich domains. In addition to providing principles for development of tutors in high performance tasks, the principles will apply to intelligent tutoring of high performance task components within knowledge-rich domains.

REFERENCES

Anderson, J. R. (1983). *The architecture of cognition.* Cambridge, MA: Harvard University Press.

Anderson, J. R., Boyle, F., & Reiser, B. (1985). Intelligent tutoring systems. *Science, 228,* 465–462.

Bloom, B. S. (1984). The 2-sigma problem: The search for methods of group instruction as effective as one-to-one tutoring. *Educational Researcher, 13*, 4–16.

Dede, C., & Swigger, K. (1987, April). *The evolution of instructional design principles for intelligent computer-assisted instruction.* Paper presented at American Educational Research Association, Washington DC.

Fisk, A. D., & Schneider, W. (1983). Category and word search; Generalizing search principles to complex processing. *Journal of Experimental Psychology: Learning, Memory, and Cognition, 9*, 177–195.

Frederiksen J. R., & White, B. Y. (1989). An approach to training based upon principled task decomposition. *Acta Psychologica, 71*, 89–146.

Hancock, P. A., & Pierce, J. O. (1984). Toward an attentional theory of performance under stress: Evidence from studies of vigilance in heat and cold. In A. Mital (Ed.), *Trends in ergonomics/human factors I.* New York: North Holland.

Kyllonen, P. C., & Shute, V. J. (1989). A taxonomy of learning skills. In P. Ackerman, R. Sternberg, & R. Glaser (Eds.), *Learning and individual differences* (pp. 117–163). San Francisco: W. H. Freeman.

Littman, D., & Soloway, E. (1986). Evaluating ITSs: The cognitive science perspective.

Newell, A., & Rosenbloom, P. (1981). Mechanisms of skill acquisition and the law of practice. In J. R. Anderson (Ed.), *Cognitive skills and their acquisition* (pp. 1–55). Hillsdale, NJ: Lawrence Erlbaum Associates.

Regian, J. W., & Schneider, W. (1986, July). *Assessment procedures for predicting and optimizing skill acquisition.* Paper presented at ETS conference on diagnostic monitoring, Princeton, NJ.

Regian, J. W., & Shute, V. J. (1988). Artificial intelligence in training: The evolution of intelligent tutoring systems. *Proceedings of the Conference on Technology and Training in Education,* Biloxi, MI.

Ritter, F., & Feurzeig, W. (1988). Teaching real-time tactical thinking. In J. Psotka, L. Massey, & S. Mutter (Eds.), *Intelligent tutoring systems: Lessons learned* (pp. 285–302). Hillsdale, NJ: Lawrence Erlbaum Associates.

Schneider, W. (1985). Toward a model of attention and the development of automaticity. In M. I. Posner & O. S. Marin (Eds.), *Attention and performance XI* (pp. 475–492). Hillsdale, NJ: Lawrence Erlbaum Associates.

Schneider, W. (1982). *Automatic/control processing concepts and their implications for the training of skills* (Tech. Rep. No. HARL-ONR-8101). Champaign, IL: University of Illinois, Human Attention Research Laboratory.

Schneider, W., Dumais, S., & Shiffrin, R. M. (1984). Automatic and control processing and attention. In R. Parasuraman & D. R. Davies (Eds.), *Varieties of attention* (pp. 1–27). Orlando, FL: Academic Press.

Schneider, W., & Fisk, A. D. (1982a). Concurrent automatic and controlled visual search: Can processing occur without resource cost? *Journal of Experimental Psychology: Learning, Memory, and Cognition, 8*, 261–278.

Schneider, W., & Fisk, A. D. (1982b). Degree of consistent training: Improvements in search performance and automatic process development. *Perception & Psychophysics, 31*, 160–168.

Schneider, W., & Fisk, A. D. (1984). Automatic category search and its transfer. *Journal of Experimental Psychology: Learning, Memory, and Cognition, 10*, 1–15.

Schneider, W., & Shiffrin, R. M. (1977). Controlled and automatic human information processing: I. Detection, search, and attention. *Psychological Review, 84*, 1–66.

Shiffrin, R. M., & Schneider, W. (1977). Controlled and automatic human information processing: II. Perceptual learning, automatic attending, and a general theory. *Psychological Review, 84*, 127–190.

Sleeman, D. H., & Brown, J. S. (Eds.). (1982). *Intelligent tutoring systems.* London: Academic Press.

Proceedings of the Research Planning Forum for Intelligent Tutoring Systems (pp. 199–232). San Antonio, TX: Air Force Human Resources Laboratory.

VanLehn, K. (1986). Student modeling in intelligent teaching systems. In *Proceedings of the Research Planning Forum for Intelligent Tutoring Systems* (pp. 49–64). San Antonio, TX: Air Force Human Resources Laboratory.

Wenger, E. (1987). *Artificial intelligence and tutoring systems.* Los Altos, CA: Morgan Kaufman.

Wickens, C. D., Sandry, D., & Vidulich, M. (1983). Compatibility and resource competition between modalities of input, central processing, and output: Testing a model of complex task performance. *Human Factors, 25,* 227–248.

Woolf, B. P. (1987, June). *A survey of intelligent tutoring systems.* Paper presented at the Northeast Artificial Intelligence Consortium, Blue Mountain Lake, NY.

Yazdani, M. (1986). Intelligent tutoring systems survey. *Artificial Intelligence Review, 1,* 43–52.

Technology Assessment: Policy and Methodological Issues for Training

Eva L. Baker
UCLA Center for Technology Assessment
and Advance Design Information

TECHNOLOGY ASSESSMENT

What is technology assessment and what is its purpose? One assesses a situation to make a judgment. That judgment may represent a conclusion (e.g., that was a bad idea), imply a general action (e.g., let's spend more on things like this), or suggest a specific remedy (e.g., whoever thought up that fiasco needs to be punished). Assessment may focus on predictions and may generate estimates of benefit or risk for planning purposes. Assessment looks forward; it answers the question, "where are we now and where shall we go?" *Evaluation,* a term with a dictionary definition similar to assessment, looks back at what has been accomplished. Evaluation asks, "Where have we been and what do we know?" Both functions are decision-oriented. We return to this distinction later.

Many organizations do assessment and evaluation. Let's consider a few major actors on the the national level in order to explore how technology assessment activities have occurred in the past. Perhaps the most visible actor in the area of technology assessment is the Congressional Office of Technology Assessment (OTA). OTA conducts studies requested by members of Congress after review by a bipartisan committee. These studies explore the need for legislative changes, for policymaking rather than for programmatic decisions. OTA conducts its work in the following way: it pools expert knowledge, holds workshops of experts to test ideas and conclusions, conducts field-based observations and interviews, and writes carefully crafted reports.

The OTA does a good job, by all repute, with a task that is at once easy and difficult. An examination of OTA's tasks serves as a reference point for the discussion of training technology assessment. The OTA has it easy because (a) technology assessment is the dedicated purpose of an entire agency principally composed of highly skilled staff; (b) reports are prepared for a single, known audience, but are widely disseminated; (c) OTA receives cooperation because it works for an influential and prestigious group; and (d) staff are disinterested in the outcome of the report. Because the quality of the report, not the content of its conclusions, has personal and organizational consequences, the corruptibility of the process is somewhat reduced. OTA's task is hard because (a) the client is Congress so it needs to be circumspect; (b) it must address technology in all its manifestations, from lie detectors and waste management systems to pacemakers; (c) it has very limited amounts of time to conduct its studies; and (d) the exact uses for studies may not be explicit. OTA helps Congress and the public understand the state of the art of various technologies so that more informed public policy decisions can be made. These decisions are likely to be forward-looking, focusing on whether given regulations are appropriate and whether new technologies look promising for solving national problems. Other agencies perform similar functions. For instance, the National Research Council (NRC), which is outside of government control, conducts studies on a broad array of national issues, including those with implications for education, defense policy, and society as a whole. They also review the utility of particular initiatives, such as military performance testing, or may report on general status, such as the social and economic progress of African-Americans, or make specific recommendations for action, such as how national tests should be revised. The NRC relies on expert judgment to even a greater degree than OTA and therefore takes every precaution to assure objectivity. The findings of both of these agencies are typically widely disseminated and receive strong media attention. Both prepare assessments—that is, they make general estimates of their topic—using a variety of expert sources.

Contrast the work of these two agencies with the responsibilities of the General Accounting Office (GAO), which also reports to Congress. The GAO focuses on what has been accomplished, the adequacy of procedures used, and, as its name implies, the prudence and cost of the endeavor. It also looks at specific programs and organizations rather than general states. They require information from, and make judgments that directly impact on, agencies and their staff. For these reasons, their work comes close to incorporating the concept of evaluation as it is typically used in the social sciences.

In training technology, perhaps because technology products are so concrete, the tradition has been to focus on evaluation—on what has been accomplished. But, for at least four reasons, the concept of technology assessment should be substituted for evaluation in our thinking. First, evaluation, as it is employed in education and training environments, connotes to many a relatively narrow set of methodological choices. Evaluations often are assumed to have certain features. Evaluations appear, for example, to be empirical in nature and as such, are obligated to (a) collect data using designs similar to those employed in experiments (i.e., control groups), (b) use quantitative analysis as the basis for inference, and (c) focus on summarizing and reducing data. Viewing evaluation as bound by constrained methodology is a widespread misperception.

A second hoary belief holds that evaluation should be bisected uniformly into only two pieces. These evaluation components are known widely as summative and formative evaluation. Believers in this analysis categorize studies as either those whose purpose is to make decisions or those whose purpose is to improve programs — as if such functions were mutually exclusive.

A third and seriously limiting conception of evaluation can be traced to the systems approach underlying most evaluation models: the use of limited criteria for judgment. Such models almost always compare the performance of the intervention exclusively against relatively simple requirements (i.e., desired performance objectives) although we know that many more outcomes are usually affected.

Finally, evaluations normally address individual instances or interventions, such as a single algebra tutor. Such instances often are compared rather facilely with an apparently valid alternative (e.g., trainees taught through lecture). Somewhere purveyors of this research lost the idea of sampling, sampling topics, program designers, and instructors. Because of practical constraints, if not methodological impairment, results reported for studies of this type have no generalizability. (See Leifer, 1976, for an excellent analysis.) The lack of generalizability applies to the technology studied (e.g., intelligent tutoring systems, ITS) and for typical comparison conditions (lecturers) in such comparisons.

TRAINING TECHNOLOGIES

What is the range of training technologies to be assessed? We all have different images of existing and ideal training technologies, an assertion that can be verified simply by asking a colleague for a one-sentence definition of the term. One definitional problem is to capture the variability of training technology in a useful way. Table 11.1 lists five dimensions along which training technologies vary.

TABLE 11.1
Dimensions of Training Technology

Equipment intensive <————————> Equipment free	
Mature <————————————> Nascent	
Comprehensive <———————————> Adjunct	
Systems targeted <————————> Multipurpose	
Training specific <————————> Training adapted	

To some, the term *technology* denotes hardware requirements, but this is a good place to remind ourselves that technology is defined in most dictionaries as "systematic treatment" or "applied science." For a process to be labeled a technology, then, it only needs to be replicable, or able to be used in repeatedly with the same consequences. We have come to expect that the consequences of technology use will include both reliable results (e.g., the telephone usually works) and efficiency (e.g., fax is faster and cheaper than overnight mail). To further illustrate this point, we would count as technology certain replicable procedures that exclude hardware trappings. For instance, research-validated procedures used to organize teams of students for learning tasks is a form of technology, even though no hardware would be required for this application. Such procedures are sometimes called *soft technology*. On the other hand, many applications may be equipment-dependent, involving extensive hardware systems, from videodiscs, television, and computers to elaborate simulators designed to model complete environments such as extraterrestrial systems.

The second dimension shown in Table 11.1 relates to technology's level of development, a complex dimension that embraces more factors than those of age. The technology can be classified as nascent or mature. At its outset, new technology has greater risks associated with its exploration and eventual impact; It simply may not pan out. When a technology is mature and a known quantity for certain applications, risk is reduced. However, other liabilities exist. Familiarity may be tinged with contempt and may foster the belief that you only can do what already has been done. This factor may work against the adaptation of a mature technology for new applications. For example, we know well that computer-assisted instruction (CAI) improves efficiency of training (Levin, Leitner, & Meister, 1986). Yet, many potential users may continue to resist their use of CAI because early CAI programs were mundane and demonstrated only limited understanding of learning psychology. Such users cannot imagine how CAI might be changed to become more interesting.

A third dimension of training technology that is relevant to the consideration of technology assessment relates to the centrality of the technology in the overall training or educational plan. We can imagine computer-assisted training where the system bears exclusive responsibility for teaching the trainee. Contrast that situation with one where the bulk of information and practice are accomplished through lecture and workbench activities and where the computer system presents problems for remediation only.

A related issue is whether the training technology is designed exclusively for a particular system or planned to serve many training purposes. Designing a system that trains an individual to interact with a particular system—for instance, to repair a named radar, or to fly a particular airplane—has different conceptual demands and consequences than designing a technology that will be used for a particular first purpose, and simultaneously, maintain a view of a larger set of applications. (O'Neil, and colleagues, discuss an example of this latter sort of technology in chap. 4, this volume.) An extension of this contrast in design foci occurs in the case where the technique or system is developed specifically for training environments as compared with an application adapted from other contexts.

The interrelationships among these dimensions are obvious, and wherever any particular technology falls among them, the juncture has clear implications for technology assessment. Figure 11.1 depicts some of the major sets of training technology elements. The shaded portion displays where intelligent tutoring systems (ITS), the topic of this book, falls within the training technology array.

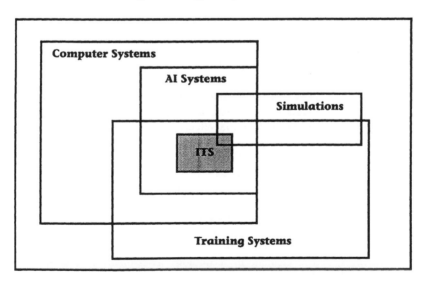

FIGURE 11.1 Schematic of place of ITS in Training Technologies.

Using the dimensions presented earlier in Table 11.1, we would classify ITS as a technology that was hardware-intensive, nascent, conceived typically as a training adjunct, and usually targeted for a particular system. Whether ITS is classified as training-specific or as an adaptation of the other artificial intelligence (AI) technologies depends on one's viewpoint. Probably nothing new for the AI field will come from the development of ITS, so from that perspective ITS is simply an adaptation. If you believe, on the other hand, that tutors require synthesis from a range of disciplines that include psychology, education, and content domains, then ITSs may be viewed as training-specific creatures. Either way, they are comparatively expensive to design and implement on a large-scale basis.

CHARACTERISTICS OF TECHNOLOGY ASSESSMENT

Technology assessment should supplant evaluation if only to avoid the enumerated liabilities of an older term. But exploring the concept of technology assessment is appropriate to our present discussion for a number of important, additional reasons. Consider first that training technology itself — what is being assessed — differs fundamentally from other instructional interventions. Technology is interactive, dynamic, and develops rapidly, often in astounding leaps and surprising directions. Paradoxically, the power of technology continues to expand, as its cost, with relatively small bubbles, continues to drop. Thus, to think of technology as simply another delivery system, comparable to lecture-discussion, is to miss the conceptual boat. Decision makers should not focus only on short-lived races between one instructional delivery system and another. When new technology first gets built and evaluated, it usually fares poorly in comparison to well-established practical alternatives, such as lectures and books. Thus, the initial effects of the technology are almost always underestimated. Studies of technology must be especially sensitive to the notion of technology-push (Glennan, 1967; U.S. Air Force, 1986) — the idea that technology bumps up against the usual requirement-driven programs in odd and unexpected ways — for technology is almost guaranteed to generate, by its very existence, outcomes and applications that were not previously considered by the training system, nor imagined by the technology designer. These new uses may be described mistakenly as side effects, when, in fact, they may be the delayed but central outcomes of the innovation. A critical element in technology assessment, therefore, is identifying when these options represent powerful, useful approaches, goals, or recombination or redefinitions of prior goals.

As a corollary, a new technology, more than other types of innovation, should not be shut off because its superiority on existing goals cannot be demonstrated immediately. For example, one effect of designing tutors may be the development of technology to create new kinds of human performance measures (Baker & Linn, 1985; Collins, 1987; Lesgold, Bonar, & Ivill, 1987) and new ways of conceiving performance tasks (Means & Gott, 1988). It is possible that such practical and conceptual outcomes may be more important than the adaptive wonders of instruction that particular intelligent systems are purported to create. If we are to develop clear traces of the broad utility of technology to meet training needs, studies must involve analyses that range far beyond what the technology designer or any given set of trainees believes or experiences. Policymakers need to be involved early and actively to determine what options should be highlighted, tracked, and ultimately ratified as bonafide new goals and functions.

The detection of the unforeseen has fundamental requirements that policymakers should consider. These requirements involve changing expectations about the purpose of new development. At minimum, policymakers must accept a period of suspended disbelief and a planned commitment to the conduct and the analysis of a network of studies of individual cases of technology. It takes time to execute such studies; thus, these studies cannot be the sole initiative of an individual who is committed for only a limited period of assignment. Some larger, longer-term policy-mechanism must be put in place. To reiterate, the purposes of such investigations focus on not only the differential impact of particular instances — tutor A versus option B — for particular tasks, but the larger and more important task of forecasting the utility of a class of technology. Thus, the explicit goals of technology assessment are twofold: the *case,* usually against a specific training requirement; and the *class,* forecast for known and uncertain future requirements.

Technology Indicators

Both the view of technology assessment and its methodology are more global than that of product evaluation. Although a product evaluation might be interested in relatively well-specified conditions, technology assessment attempts to determine the full range of use. To do so, the model underlying technology assessment should seek to represent thoroughly the conditions that contribute to its impact as well as to take an expansive view of the impact itself.

Two requirements flow from such a model: (a) the system studied must address estimates of input, context, and conditions of implementation as well as the outcomes already specified; and (b) multiple measures of major dimensions must be employed. These requirements result in a *training technology indicator system.*

Educational policymakers at the federal and state levels have adopted the indicators metaphor as a way to assure that they collect data on aspects of policy under their control (e.g., the requirements for teacher training) in addition to those measures they affect only indirectly (e.g., students' standardized test scores). Such an approach is especially suitable when the object of study is technology in light of its potential portability and flexibility. Considered as a system, input (such as requirements and trainee populations) and context and conditions (such as the tasks required, time availability, financing, criticality) and outcomes, (including requirement-driven outcomes and unforeseen effects) present a firmer basis for decision making. Contrast this approach with the more usual evaluation study, which has limited scope. Consider generalizations about the use of instructional tutors based on one carefully done laboratory study with fixed input (the trainees and instructors), limited conditions (a 4-day course on some topic), and one or two outcome measures that can be quantitatively scored. We can trust these findings only when the cost of being wrong is small. As in the field of economics, absolute meaning in assessment does not inhere in any measure, but in the varied behavior of indicators. What becomes important are the interrelationships and the changes in indicator value over time; sophisticated statistical analyses are available to support these causal inferences.

The second component of a technology indicators approach that makes it especially suitable for studying technology is its reliance on multiple measurement of single variables (e.g., achievement). Instead of a single check list, achievement outcomes might be composed of a number of single measures, such as student problem solving, problem identification, efficiency, attitude, and instructor or commander estimate of proficiency. Creating composites of these single measures allows an overall estimate of quality to be determined. Varying the parameters or weightings of individual measures permits a decision maker to examine and make explicit value structures and, at the same time, to study patterns of relationships over time. Such a systematic approach also permits the longitudinal review of policy decisions. Figure 11.2 depicts an indicator model, with boxes identifying elements that would be measured. Notice that multiple measures are depicted only for outcome 1.

The goal of this model is to develop training quality indicators that provide composite estimates of variables and the relationships among them, much as economic indicators provide composite descriptions and forecasts. This indicator assessment perspective, by the way, is apparently useful to state policymakers, legislators, governors, and educational boards

Outcome Model

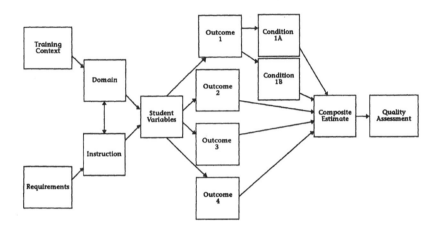

FIGURE 11.2 Model for outcome measurement in Technology Assessment.

and superintendents as they try to determine systematically and longitu-dinally the consequences of policy changes intended to improve the quality of precollegiate educational services (see, for instance, U.S. Department of Education Office of Educational Research and Improvement, 1988). Note that multiple indicator development is a natural opportunity for collabo-ration among branches and services that assess technology. Yet, full-blown quality indicator systems for technology are still a long way off. Many specific problems must be addressed first.

TECHNICAL ISSUES

Although it is easy to describe an ideal technology assessment system, it is unfortunately true that a litany of technical issues must be confronted in order to implement a technology assessment approach to training innova-tions. The assessment design must consider the number of alternative outcome measures for any given set of variables (e.g., instructional context, the timing, valuing and weighting procedures of such variables) as well as the choices among statistical models for analysis. Each of these issues is extraordinarily complex, but in some way, each also presupposes that the outcome measures of interest have been assessed adequately. No one would invest seriously in causal modeling with a fallible criterion. Even the most limited assessment needs high quality outcome data to be credible and to estimate present and predict future impact. One obvious source for identifying outcome measures resides in the goals adopted by the designer during the creation of the new technology. In the case of ITSs, we would look at the assembled empirical base and make a judgment about what should be assessed. Unfortunately, existing ITS literature is a barren source for good examples of outcome measurement. Very few studies address the problem in any systematic or explicit way that exploits the potential power of intelligent systems (see Shute, 1990, for an exception). This criticism holds in part because designers have been so focused on the intricacies of making systems work, or even designing pieces of systems such as an expert problem solver, that whole tutors rarely have been produced, let alone empirically validated. Even when outcomes are measured, the techniques used rarely approach the state of the art in other aspects of achievement measurement. Imagine a not-imaginary example where the designer accommodates outcome assessment by slapping on a standardized measure of learning, or looks at job performance by throwing in a simple check list of correct procedures. Making decisions based on such data is equivalent to listening to a symphony on scratchy LPs when compact discs are available.

How have tutor outcomes been measured in the past? In a series of empirical studies undertaken at UCLA, we (Baker, Aschbacher, Feifer, Bradley, & Herman, 1985) were given the task to evaluate three different tutors that were nominally available or in development at that time. We could find only two such systems that were reasonably amenable to the task: WEST, a program designed to teach number facts in a game strategy (Brown & Burton, 1978) and the program analyzer section of PROUST (Johnson & Soloway, 1987). We hoped to develop a complex set of dependent measures to assess the full range of outcomes for these systems — outcomes that were claimed by the designers and outcomes that could be inferred from system operation. We developed attitude measures and domain-referenced achievement tests based on the designers' articulated goals and, in addition, collected other aptitude measures, such as Scholastic Aptitude Test (SAT) scores or verbal, spatial, and mathematics reasoning scores. We developed measures that we thought captured important goals of each system: in WEST, arithmetic skills and the strategy used to play the game; in PROUST, the quality of the Pascal program generated by students. WEST students did not show much improvement when compared to controls. The particular student computational goals and prerequisites articulated by the designers were sadly mistargeted. That is, students who passed the pretest also passed the posttest without instruction, whereas students who did not possess prerequisites never learned enough to profit from the WEST experience. Strategy, when measured as the solution to particular WEST board problems, was not affected by the WEST practice sessions. In the case of PROUST, the developers ultimately did not permit the use of the program writing measure, preferring an option where students analyzed bugs in Pascal programs (ironically, this was also what the computer did). Our technology assessment experience was not one to lead to great confidence in designer-generated measures. A more positive finding was obtained by O'Neil and Nizamuddin (1989), where they found effects while looking at new outcome measures for treatment variations of Sleeman's Algebra Tutor. (This study was particularly interesting in that, in addition to measures of students academic ability, it systematically assessed students' anxiety reactions.)

So it is very possible to develop outcome measures that are sensitive to technology concerns. Why doesn't this happen more often? One jaded view points out that effects are not measured carefully because it is better not to do so. A second limitation rests in the nature of the interests and expertise of the ITS designer. It is our view that outcome measurement of complex training is so important that it cannot be left to the designer alone to accomplish. Designers may lack the expertise to create good measures. As noted earlier, important training outcomes need multiple measurement across time and conditions to consider effects beyond the short-term achievement of the training goal. These dimensions include retention, robustness of performance across field conditions, transfer, and assessment of underlying constructs to facilitate cross training.

New developments in performance assessment lean heavily on trainee-generated performance, or constructed responses, using constructs from cognitive learning theory to derive scoring attributes (Wittrock & Baker, in press). According to the primary message of this development, measures must map back to characteristics of learning (i.e., elaboration, schema, and problem detection; see Hayes, 1989; Marshall, in press). Such approaches are partially validated by using expert–novice distinctions (Baker & Clayton, 1989; Chi & Glaser, 1980). This concern for the close relationship between learning and measurement conditions contrasts strongly with the majority of current outcome testing practice, in which convenient test formats strongly limit what we are able to say about student performance.

A second direction in performance assessment (Baker, O'Neil, & Linn, in press; Shavelson, Carey, & Webb, in press) involves improved, more sensitive ways to select and train judges of performance. No longer is simple designation as a subject matter expert — or, for that matter, a tutor designer — sufficient to assure reliable and valid rating of performance. Valid judgment must be trained.

There will be some resistance to the dictum of multiple indicators of outcomes, particularly from those stuck in a frozen view of evaluation. Remember that for many the term *evaluation* still calls up the specter of a single, monolithic methodology, largely derived from social science, experimental, and quantitative in nature. That view may have accurately characterized the majority of social science research 20 years ago, but accounts only for a limited proportion of current effort. It also is true that the field of evaluation was fractionated into methodological camps a dozen years ago, with lines drawn between quantitative experimentalists and qualitative interpreters. However, at present, a more balanced blend of methodology is common, and desired. For example, relatively objective forms of performance assessment are often mixed with qualitative analyses of protocols of trainee thinking (Feifer, 1989). Intensive descriptions of processes — for instance, knowledge engineering (Baker, Novak, & Slawson, 1989) — and understanding queries in natural language systems (Baker & Lindheim, 1988) can be combined with surveys and more traditional test forms to provide a more complete explanation for findings.

CRITERIA FOR TECHNOLOGY ASSESSMENT: CHOOSING WHAT GETS ASSESSED

We have discussed methods for collecting information including the use of multiple sources of information. What guidelines can be used for selection and design? Table 11.2 summarizes these criteria for technology assessments.

TABLE 11.2
Criteria for Technology Assessment

Selection Criteria
  I.   Risk-Balanced Portfolio
  II. Potential Benefit to Participants
Design Criteria
  I.   Impact
       • individuals
       • units
       • training systems
  II. Costs

Risk-Balanced Portfolios

Whether empirical or expert-based, a technology assessment effort should include a balanced portfolio of cases. To provide a fair and responsible assessment, these must include efforts representing various levels of risk. Risk can be assessed in terms of the emergent or mature status of the technology, its place in the research and development cycle, its scientific knowledge base, its payoff, the length of its development cycle, the difficulty of the goals undertaken, and its potential for generalizable or targeted use.

Benefits to Participants

Attention should clearly be given to technologies that have higher potential benefit to significant users in any system. How one decides user significance is a matter of prior policy development. Criteria such as the potential number of users, the criticality of their roles, and existing performance deficit, among others, will come into play to make this decision. Important social values should also be considered, including issues of equity and self-worth.

Issues for Review in Technology Assessment

Impact. In addition to the review of benefits to individuals as a selection criterion for the review of technology, gauging its impact should be considered as a main criterion in the design of the assessment. Factors that should be weighed include who will feel the impact, to what degree, and with what anticipated outcome in terms of learning, competency, adaptability, readiness, and so forth. Related to this issue is the impact of the technology on the unit or collectivity to which the individual is assigned. A connected concern is the potential impact on the existing training organization. What changes will need to occur in the training requirements because of technology use? What changes in the training approach or sequence itself are anticipated? How will staffing be affected? Are adjustments anticipated to be major or marginal? How might they be phased?

Costs. Costs of various levels of implementation of the technology need to be projected. This must be computed with normal concerns for life-cycle costs, including start up and maintenance. With technology, cost estimates may be difficult to compute. Consider that the overall cost of computational and visual power will drop over time. But technology creates appetites for better, faster, glitzier implementations that shorten the interval for technology obsolescence and the requirement for reinvestment. The impact of a CAI program developed 10 years ago is surely less than it might be today because of the rapid advances in graphics and distribution of computational support. Thus, the changing context and expectations for technology performance contribute inevitably to shorten the life of any particular implementation. A related concern is how the costs are distributed to agencies, industries, and other funders of technology development work.

Certainly, any assessment will include a set of tradeoffs among criteria such as risk, impact, organizational effects, and costs. The manner in which such tradeoffs are treated probably distinguishes the overall quality of the assessment.

PROCEDURES FOR TECHNOLOGY ASSESSMENT

The goal of technology assessment is to provide a larger view of the utility and potential impact of a class of technology for a set of potential uses. Thus far, we have described how technology assessment is conducted on behalf of the public by national agencies. We have pointed out some shortcomings of the few existing efforts to evaluate objectively in the area of intelligent tutoring and desirable characteristics for future efforts. But the discussion has been abstract. In the operational conduct of technology assessment, what should be achieved? First of all, a given technology should be assessed systematically as a class. Two sorts of analysis are appropriate: empirical analysis and expert analysis (see Table 11.3).

TABLE 11.3
Procedures for Technology Assessment

Empirical Analysis
- Preordinate
- Natural variation
- Post hoc

Expert Analysis
- Panels
- Surveys

Empirical Analyses

An ideal approach to empirical analysis is a design strategy where plans are made to coordinate the investigations of a technology across organizations or agencies. In that way, a range of tasks, contexts, developers, outcomes, and users (or other variables of interest) could be analyzed in parallel natural experiments. This preordinate, empirical approach runs into a variety of difficulties, including funding coordination, competition among agencies, and so on. Certainly it also would be unusual for the full range of variables of interest to be represented in the planned studies. A second alternative is post hoc analyses of the sort conducted by Levin and colleagues (1986), writing on the utility of computer-based instruction. These studies are based on the available literature, usually on existing evaluations of individual systems developed for a unique purpose. Post hoc analyses attempt to generalize to the class of technology. But their utility is also limited. Available studies will differ in quality, in reporting detail, and in nature of comparisons, so inferences drawn from meta-analytical approaches must be interpreted with extreme caution. These studies were not designed with the class of applications of interest to the policymaker in mind, thus significant gaps in knowledge may exist. Yet, some sort of empirical, how-does-it-work evidence is essential to an appropriate assessment.

Expert Analyses

Expert analyses can be conducted through the use of panels of knowledgeable individuals where judgment of utility, future impact, range of applications, limitations, barriers to implementation, and like topics are considered and some kind of consensus is reached. Expert analyses are helpful if the experts have credibility to the policy audiences they are ultimately addressing and if they can be kept to some general set of policy issues and recommendations. Structure for such groups is essential and a policy statement or other product is clearly desirable. Another form of expert analysis can be developed through the use of survey and interview techniques. In these cases, broader samples of experts may be consulted, and the judgment reached will be an aggregation of individual views rather than the group consensus, although this outcome can be altered by use of Delphi approaches to survey consensus. In addition to losing the creative interaction groups can achieve, many times survey or interviews are conducted in a relatively decontextualized way, without sufficient preparation to get the expert up to speed on the particular set of relevant issues. The trade-off is probably breadth versus depth.

It is our recommendation that both empirical and expert approaches should be used in technology assessments. The ideal would be to use preordinate and post hoc empirical studies as well as group and individual expert analyses.

ORGANIZATIONAL ISSUES

Two major types of organizational issues potentially impede the use of more comprehensive approaches to technology assessment. One is the perceived social impediments surrounding assessment. A second is the legitimate organizational boundaries that make such tasks difficult. Consider the social interpretation.

One liability that persists from the era of evaluation is the inferred political impetus of any decision to assess anything. Most efforts at assessment or evaluation provoke some level of resistance, resentment, or defensiveness. No one really believes the slogan "we're here to help," and they are often correct. The evaluatee may believe evaluation is an instrument of aggression (for evaluation only occurs when there is a problem). Program managers, on the other hand, may use evaluation defensively. They may be interested in it primarily as a defense against future assaults, rather than for the information it provides about innovation. Over and above usual paranoia, additional issues deserve comment, because much assessment is a social as well as a technical enterprise. One issue is: Who does the assessment for what ostensible purpose? If the designer of the technology is responsible for assessment, one is not only limited to a particular vision, but also is inevitably confronted with self-interest. Furthermore, designers are more committed to the task of creating systems than to creating systems that result in demonstrable trainee outcomes. Particularly in computer-based technologies, the trick is to make a system run according to prediction. The importance of process is highlighted in an article on AI *Evaluation* by Cohen and Howe (1988). As they describe evaluation, it is limited to an expert review of the quality or process of research efforts. This article was especially heartening for me because it confirmed an earlier conclusion about the distinctions among expectations of high technology researchers, program managers, and evaluation and assessment professionals, and the resulting social complexity of getting the job done.

Societal constraints are a matter of semantics and marketing as well. Researchers may propose to create a training system, program managers may think that is what they bought, and those charged with assessment may assume that training outcomes should be measured. In fact, the likelihood of strong outcome effects increases only with the maturity of the technology. With a new technology, the designers' claims and focus on a training system may simply provide necessary limits for what they perceive as a research problem; the training focus is only a means to conduct research. The researcher may say, and believe, that the chosen task is to develop an intelligent tutor to teach specific outcomes, but the researcher means that *research* will be conducted on an interesting part of the problem of developing a tutor. Researchers are not the same as training system developers, and this fact is demonstrated recurrently by the woeful number of partial systems in the intelligent tutoring community: tutors without student models, tutors with wonderful diagnostic capabilities, tutors without pedagogical modules. Awareness and understanding of the various contexts and subtexts of communication among researchers, managers, and assessors may allow some form of collaborative assessment to work. Program managers can benefit from an understanding of underlying messages, particularly when they may have obtained priority for funding a particular technology program by promising a product for an actual training system.

A more obvious difficulty, especially within newly emerging fields, is the insider–outsider problem. Expertise and expectations differ and suspicions abound, not only between measurement specialists and AI researchers, but among linguists, psychologists, and AIers, and within the AI community, between devotees of one or another approach. We have experienced this phenomenon in our DARPA project on assessing AI systems. We have tried numbers of options to bridge the communication and knowledge gaps, including hiring AI people, providing incentives, using consecutive translation, and throwing ourselves on the mercies of friends. The trade-off is objectivity and detachment for credibility and insight. A solution, of course, is to train people who become proponents and experts in the assessment of technology, but that will happen only when the technology has a surplus of researchers—a self-contradictory state when the focus is new technology. Yet, a few collaborative teams are at work. How they forge successes should be an interesting story that most probably will unfold sometime in the future.

The second organizational issue in technology assessment concerns bureaucratic reality and organizational boundaries. Technology assessment is recommended because it will give program managers a better estimate of where to invest resources. The problems described in this chapter identify requirements for technology assessment: (a) taking a long-range view; (b) focusing on a class of technology rather than single copies; (c) multiple measuring of an integrative set of variables in an indicator system; and (d) infusing assessment expertise into a social situation already made complex by promises and suspicions. These requirements can be met in a situation that assures growth in resources and some spirit of cooperation among decision makers who have agreed to share a vision. The current reality for many technology research and development agencies, private or public, is such that rich resources are a dim memory, fading fast. Bureaucracies also inhibit most forms of cooperation. In the military, the long-standing competition and the vastly different cultural norms among services discourage such interaction. It is possible, however, that cooperation may be the only way to accomplish much at all in a time of declining resources. When risk is shared and relatively low, benefit may be high.

REPORTING

A final area, often overlooked, is concerned with the nature of reporting useful information from assessment for various levels of program and policy decisions. The identification of the full range of audiences is a critical point, as is the understanding that any data or conclusions can be used or misused against you. The challenge is to find ways of communication that will contextualize results appropriately, without endless qualification, reams of tables, or "micromud" descriptions that put off all but the most devoted reader. One area of general interest focuses on identifying the report users' mental models and their options for making effective decisions. If we could apply what we know from cognitive psychology to assist sophisticated decision makers' process and integrate assessment findings, we would develop clues related to what information was most relevant. Furthermore, one might expect that such report readers might themselves need a modicum of training in order to assure that more than one reader would reach one set of conclusions given similar findings.

RESEARCH AND DEVELOPMENT IMPLICATIONS

Short-Term Research and Development

The issue enumeration given earlier leads directly to some recommendations for research and development activities to advance the field. First, in the general area of technology assessment of ITSs, it will be important to categorize systematically the existing and developing Defense-supported tutors by attribute, technical approach, and training task. UCLA has undertaken this task for DARPA in the area of natural language (NL) understanding systems and has created a sourcebook of the problem types that natural language systems address. A second short-term project involves the creation of advisory or assessment authoring systems particularly suited to technology assessment problems. A prototype system has been developed at UCLA on the narrow problem of reliability for criterion referenced tests, and costs for a library of such aids are relatively small. A third activity might be a case study analysis of an attempt at class-oriented technology assessment of ITSs, using naturally occurring and planned assessments. Fourth, research on decision maker's mental models could be conducted to provide a better understanding of assessment and reporting requirements.

Long-Term Studies

The design of seriously planned embedded assessment systems that includes the full range of input, process, and outcome data, such as individual differences, process, trainee performance, retention, and transfer data could be undertaken in a long-term study.

ACKNOWLEDGMENTS

This research reported herein was conducted with partial support from the Office of Naval Research, pursuant to Grant No. N00014-86-0395; and Advanced Design Information. However, the opinions expressed do not necessarily reflect the position or policy of these agencies and no official endorsement by these agencies should be inferred.

The author also wishes to thank Rebecca Frazier for her insightful suggestions.

REFERENCES

Baker, E. L., & Clayton, S. (1989, June). *The relationship of text anxiety and measures of deep comprehension in history*. Paper presented at the Conference of the Society for Test Anxiety Research, Amsterdam, The Netherlands.
Baker, E. L., Aschbacher, P., Feifer, R. G., Bradley, C., & Herman, J. (1985). *Intelligent*

computer-assisted instruction study (JPL Contract No. 956881). Los Angeles: UCLA Center for the Study of Evaluation.

Baker, E. L., & Lindheim, E. L. (1988). *A contrast between computer and human language understanding.* Los Angeles: UCLA Center for the Study of Evaluation.

Baker, E. L., & Linn, R. (1985). *Institutional assessing and improving educational quality* (Proposal to the National Institute of Education for the Center on Student Testing, Evaluation and Standards). Los Angeles: UCLA Center for the Study of Evaluation.

Baker, E. L., Novak, J., & Slawson, D. (1989). *Feasibility study of an AI testing advisor* (Report to the Office of Educational Research and Improvement). Los Angeles: UCLA Center for the Study of Evaluation.

Baker, E. L., O'Neil, H. F., Jr., & Linn, R. L. (in press). Performance assessment framework. In S. J. Andriole (Ed.), *Advanced technologies for command and control systems engineering.* Fairfax, VA: AFCEA International Press.

Brown, J. S., & Burton, R. R. (1978). Diagnostic models for procedural bugs in basic mathematical skills. *Cognitive Science, 2,* 155–192.

Chi, M. T. H., & Glaser, R. (1980). The measurement of expertise: Analysis of the development of knowledge and skill as a basis for assessing achievement. In E. L. Baker & E. S. Quellmalz (Eds.), *Educational testing and evaluation: Design, analysis, and policy* (pp. 37–47). Beverly Hills: Sage Publications.

Cohen, P., & Howe, A. (1988). How evaluation guides AI research. *AI Magazine, 9*(4), 35–43.

Collins, A. (1987). *Reformulating testing to measure thinking and learning* (Report No. 6869). Cambridge, MA: BBN Systems and Technologies Corporation.

Feifer, R. G. (1989). *An intelligent tutoring system for graphic mapping strategies* (Tech. Rep. No. UCLA-AI-89-04). Los Angeles: UCLA Computer Science Department.

Glennan, T. K., Jr. (1967). Issues in the choice of development policies. In T. Manschak, T. K. Glennan, Jr., & R. Summers (Eds.), *Strategies for research and development.* New York: Springer-Velag.

Hayes, J. R. (1989). *The complete problem solver* (2nd ed.). Hillsdale, NJ: Lawrence Erlbaum Associates.

Johnson. W. L., & Soloway, E. (1987). PROUST: An automatic debugger for Pascal programs. In G. P. Kearsely (Ed.), *Artificial intelligence and instruction: Applications and methods.* Redding, MA: Addison-Wesley.

Leifer, A. (1976). Teaching with television and film. In N. L. Gage (Ed.), *The psychology of teaching methods* (pp. 302–334). Chicago, IL: The National Society for the Study of Education.

Lesgold, A., Bonar, J., & Ivill, J. (1987). *Toward intelligent systems for testing* (LRDC Tech. Rep. No. ONR/LSP-1). Pittsburgh: University of Pittsburgh Learning Research and Development Center.

Levin, H., Leitner, D., & Meister, G. (1986). *Cost effectiveness of alternative approaches to computer assisted instruction* (Rep. No. 87-CERAS-1). Stanford, CA: Stanford University, Center for Education Research at Stanford.

Marshall, S. P. (in press). Mathematics: What cognitive skills do parents offer children? In T. Sticht (Ed.), *The intergenerational transfer of cognitive skills.* Norwood, NJ: Ablex.

Means, B., & Gott, S. P. (1988). Cognitive task analysis as a basis for tutor development: Articulating abstract knowledge representations. In J. Psotka, L. D. Massey, & S. A. Mutter (Eds.), *Intelligent tutoring systems: Lessons learned* (pp. 35–57). Hillsdale, NJ: Lawrence Erlbaum Associates.

National Science Board. (1987). *Science and engineering indicators* (Rep. No. NSB-87-1). Washington, DC: U.S. Government Printing Office.

O'Neil, H. F., Jr., & Nizamuddin, K. G. (1989, July). *Effect of anxiety in intelligent computer-assisted instruction.* Paper presented at the 10th International Conference of the Society for Test Anxiety Research, Amsterdam, The Netherlands.

Shavelson, R. J., Casey, N. B., & Webb, N. M. (1990). Indicators of science achievement. Options for a powerful policy instrument. *Phi Delta Kappan, 71,* 692–697.

Shute, V. J. (1990, June). Rose garden promises of intelligent tutoring systems: Blossom or thorn? In *Proceedings from the Space Operations, Applications, and Research Symposium* (SOAR '90).

U.S. Department of Education Office of Educational Research and Improvement. (1988). *Creating responsible and responsive accountability systems: Report of the OERI State Accountability Study Group.* Washington, DC. Author.

U.S. Air Force (1986). *Project Forecast II: Executive summary.* Washington, DC. Author.

Wittrock, M. C., & Baker, E. L. (Eds.). (in press). *Testing and cognition.* Englewood Cliffs, NJ: Prentice-Hall.

The Future of Intelligent Tutoring Systems

Carol Luckhardt Redfield
Southwest Research Institute

Kurt Steuck
Air Force Human Resources Laboratory

Imagine a first-grade classroom in a private school with about 10 children. In this classroom, the teaching–learning activities are almost completely individualized. There are 1 to 3 children in each reading and math group. The curriculum covers a wide set of topics including social interaction skills. In short, the teacher can plan and deliver instruction that is appropriate for each of the children's needs — almost. During a math lesson the teacher gives a child a multiple-choice worksheet that has 75 questions with three options (a, b, c) for each question. The teacher, seeing that the student has answered the first three questions correctly, moves on to another pupil. The first student then proceeds to answer the remaining 72 questions by marking option "a" (only about a third were correct). What happened here? Was it a failure by the teacher to monitor each student continuously? Was the student distracted by other students or activities? Did the student not understand the instructions? (Actually, the student thought that if you had three "a"s in a row all of the rest had to be "a.")

This private school story shows that human-to-human teaching is very difficult. Teachers cannot achieve totally individualized or effective instruction. Only in true one-on-one situations can a teacher monitor a student's behavior and progress. In addition, competing goals could hinder the educational process. For instance, in the classroom described, it may have been more important for the student to learn responsibility for completing an assignment or to develop self-control to ignore distractions. Furthermore, Bunderson and Inouye (1987) cited research pointing out that true one-to-one, face-to-face, teacher–student interaction in the typical elementary classroom occurs as little as 2 minutes per day. This shocking piece of data more strongly emphasizes the potential impact intelligent tutoring systems (ITSs) can have on education by adapting instruction to the individual student. In short, human-to-human teaching is very difficult, so we have even a greater task in making computerized training effective.

During the forum on ITSs that led to this book, Frank Hughes of National Aeronautics and Space Administration's (NASA) Johnson Space Center described a scenario in which training occurred on a manned space station. In his remarks, he challenged the ITS community to develop portable or embedded tutors so we can "take the tutor with us." With future developments in space exploration, NASA will not be able to train individuals on all aspects of a mission before a launch. Instead, they will have to train crew members while they are orbiting Earth (NASA, 1987), on the way to the Moon or Mars, or on a Moon base. For example, NASA may teach the explorers about a particular astronomical observatory while on the ground, but wait to teach them how to use that system until they are in space. This implies that in the future ITSs must be transportable to a variety of locations and educational settings. It also challenges us to build ITSs so that they can be used in a diverse set of domains.

The aforementioned two examples have several implications for the intelligent tutoring field. They deal not only with how researchers develop ITSs, but also how they use ITSs in training settings. Tutors must represent domain expertise, deliver effective instruction, and respond to changing student needs.

Future ITSs need to know "what to teach." This domain knowledge includes declarative knowledge, procedural skills, and higher order thinking skills, such as metacognitive knowledge, reasoning abilities, and problem-solving skills. The ITS also needs to be able to explain itself. That is, it needs to be able to articulate when and why it is necessary to do a particular domain activity.

Future ITSs need to know "how to teach." They will need to embody a subset of the human instructional repertoire. We use *subset* to indicate that computer-based training systems will never truly take on all characteristics and abilities of human teachers. However, ITSs will aid humans and have capabilities to deliver instruction in qualitatively different ways than their human counterparts. To do so, ITSs will need a variety of teaching skills to present information, monitor student performance, diagnose student weaknesses, and manage instruction. This latter point — the ability to manage or control the teaching–learning process — may be the most challenging of problems for ITS researchers.

Future ITSs need to know "who" they are teaching. Educational systems for kindergartners or seniors in high school will differ in many ways from those preparing bioengineers for living in space. In other words,

ITSs will need to consider the nature of the learner as each enters the learning situation. Just as important, however, an ITS will need to change dynamically as a student traverses the curricular path. The tutor will need to adapt to each student's progress and individual characteristics. These individual differences may include differing rates of progress, prior training and background, specialty areas, and curriculum mastery to name a few.

Although future ITSs will need to know "what," "how," and "whom" to teach, the diversity of educational settings and uses will require ITSs of the future to take on a variety of extra characteristics. Our future training systems will need to be:

- applicable to individual or team training;
- flexible for diverse sets of domains and varying student schedules;
- flexible for job-aiding or job-training;
- transportable/distributable to a variety of educational settings;
- available to all levels of education and computer sophistication;
- easy to modify and upgrade; and
- reliable across time and conditions.

Our challenge, then, is to make the training system capable of delivering effective one-to-one training while meeting these demands.

The remaining portions of this chapter highlight several areas of ongoing research and application. It then embarks on the risky business of forecasting characteristics of the next generation of ITSs and those beyond the next generation. Although we acknowledge that infinite possibilities could arise, we want to give the reader an idea of the direction the field may be taking in the next several years. The chapter ends with a description of a few emerging trends in the evolution of ITSs.

TODAY

So where are we today? What issues are today's researchers addressing? What technologies are being researched and developed? Certainly many answers to these questions are found in this book and other current research literature. We have extracted several characteristics of ITSs that are more refined than the traditional taxonomy of interface, expert, student, and instructional modules. This set of characteristics is not exhaustive, but rather is representative of the areas of interest in recent research studies. It also includes topics that concern future training. These represent the aspects of ITSs that we are discussed in the remainder of this chapter. Table 12.1 contains the ITS characteristics and a brief description of each.

Review of Our Authors

The interface is an important feature of an ITS because it is the window through which the student interacts with the domain and instructor (Bonar, chap. 3). Today's input or *sensing* devices include mice, keyboards, joysticks, trackballs, digital pads, touchpads, light pens, voice recognition systems, touch-screens, and graphics tablets (Bunderson & Inouye, 1987). Output or *acting* devices include low- and high-resolution graphics monitors, interactive videodisc, digitized and synthesized audio systems, and printers. Digital video interactive (DVI) has recently begun to work its way into research and application areas.

Although in the past interactive styles were limited to graphics and

TABLE 12.1
Characteristics and Supporting Technologies

Category	Characteristics Discussed in Text
Interface	devices, operations, interactive styles
Instructional design	model-based vs. theory-based; curriculum issues
Authoring	computer-aided design systems, intelligent guidance modifiable
Strategies	variety, interaction with domains; individual vs. team training
Executive control	adaptive in strategies and to student; responsive to student and setting; flexible, self-improving
Domain	multiple-database domains; flexible design use; increasing number of domains; integrated, networked databases; granularity of knowledge; design structure of database/ domain; techniques for filling in structure
Evaluation	effectiveness, affordability, transportability, accessibility
Hardware	nature of memory, processing, input/output devices, speed
Availability	more domains, military and industry, general public
Purpose/goal of ITS	use of knowledge; proficiency, mastery, familiarity
Environmental setting	team teaching, embedded training, job-aiding vs. training

text, Swigger (chap. 2) points out that menus, icons, and windows have become standards for ITSs. Advances in clicking and dragging technology now allow us to pull down and push up menus, select, highlight, move, and throw away icons, and open, close, frame, cycle, and bury windows.

Swigger also points out that the issues facing developers today involve how to communicate knowledge to the student and how to manage human–computer interactions. In chapter 3, Bonar discusses the importance of the communication issue, positing that domain knowledge as well as an ITS's teaching and diagnostic knowledge are embedded in a tutor's interface. If we adopt this viewpoint, the importance of the interface during the design and development phases of a tutor increases. As a result, Bonar proposes the development of an authoring methodology that creates direct manipulation interfaces that represent expertise, accomplish specific tasks, are easy to use by novices, and help a novice's progression to expert levels of performance.

Authoring systems for more traditional computer-based training applications have been available in the marketplace for several years now. These authoring systems typically have graphics and text editors, branching options, and auxiliary video capabilities, such as interactive videodisc. The end product is a training system with limited knowledge of student performance, restricted tutoring flexibility, and static domain knowledge. Tutorials that come with commercialized word processors and spreadsheet programs are examples of what have been built with traditional authoring systems. In chapter 5, Pirolli concludes that many previous authoring systems are not sufficient for producing effective computer-assisted instruction due to a lack of instructional design guidance. Whereas traditional ID theory-building has taken years, recent advances in cognitive psychology and ITS research have expanded the instructional design domain. Specifically, work in the areas of expert and student modeling, interface design, tutoring strategies, and knowledge engineering has implications for instructional design practices.

Three systems now in development shed more light on the state of the art. These systems, Instructional System Design Expert (ISD Expert), Expert Computer Managed Learning (Expert CML), and Instructional Design Environment (IDE) differ along several research issues or dimensions. For example, systems differ in the instructional design expertise required of their intended users or audience. ISD Expert is designed for novice instructional designers; IDE for sophisticated designers. In contrast, Expert CML has greater flexibility because it is designed for individuals with varying degrees of instructional design expertise.

ITSs by default adopt at least one instantiation of instructional design principles in teaching their students. These instantiations, however, may not be based on sound theoretical principles, instead using instructional techniques that have not been verified, given the instructional context. Tennyson and Park (1987) called such cases *model-based* training systems and described today's ITSs as being model-based. That is, current ITSs use particular instructional design techniques or approaches, but without having verification of those techniques. In the future, they claim, ITSs will be theory-based in that the instructional approach will have been verified for that educational context.

While authoring systems have focused on generating text and graphics, Woolf (chap. 6) researches authoring systems that capture the underlying knowledge about delivery and management of instruction. She designed and developed several tools to aid in acquiring, representing, and reasoning about basic elements of tutoring. Examples include tutorial topics and prerequisites, specific tutoring activities, and common misconceptions. Note that these tools not only elicit and represent the experts' domain knowledge, but also their knowledge about how and when to perform the instructional activities.

For an ITS to be truly individualized and responsive to the particular student's needs, the system needs to be able to make "management" decisions about the current instructional context. Again, Woolf developed a tool for acquiring, representing, and using this kind of control knowledge. Whereas these tools require a relatively sophisticated user today, they point out the direction and issues involved in providing ITS authoring tools for nonprogramming individuals.

In addition, ITSs vary in the instructional strategies used to convey the domain knowledge to the learners. Kearsley (1987) categorized computer-based systems as coaches, diagnostic tutors, microworlds, mixed initiative tutors, and articulate expert systems. Kyllonen and Shute (1988) presented a list of learning strategies that includes (but is not limited to) learning by analogy, learning from examples, and learning from observation and discovery.

Moreover, ITSs need to have a large repertoire of instructional strategies available for handling the multitude of instructional needs that might arise. In chapter 4, O'Neil, Slawson, and Baker approach this problem by developing a framework for domain-independent instructional strategies and domain-dependent instantiations of those strategies. They have synthesized from existing instructional theory formal rules that are written in explicit if-then format for applications across different domains. These domain-independent rules are then "grounded" in domain-specific instantiations. There is a key advantage with this effort because ITS developers can embed the rule sets within a tutor to enhance its instructional strategy repertoire.

There are many aspects of domain knowledge to consider when

discussing the present and future of ITSs. Some concern the way knowledge is represented and used; others concern the nature of the databases that store that knowledge. In the former case, a single, well-designed domain representation may allow an ITS to teach several types of knowledge, such as declarative knowledge and procedural skills. Furthermore, how an ITS reasons about, expands, and uses the domain knowledge depends on the design of the database and inferencing algorithms available when the ITS is developed. Thus a significant design issue is the granularity of the knowledge stored within the database, which must be appropriate to the instructional purposes. This granularity must be considered when constructing the database itself. Knowledge engineering techniques directly affect veracity and completeness of the domain information available to the ITS.

In chapter 7, Acker, Porter, and their colleagues point out that current ITSs are limited in their ability to use and present domain knowledge. Typically, researchers build a tutor with stores of text prepared for simple reproduction when needed. As they point out, this requires the developer to anticipate every use of the knowledge and implement means for those uses. The combinatorial explosion of concepts and potential uses rapidly makes this an unwieldy approach. As a result, ITSs have been traditionally limited in breadth and depth where the use of domain knowledge is concerned.

Porter's team at the University of Texas is exploring alternative methods for extending the representations and uses of domain knowledge. They have designed a multifunctional botany database so an ITS can use it to generate coherent explanations for different types of questions. The tutor can teach highly complex, integrated, basic knowledge while employing only one multifunctional database. Though this effort is now in a research environment, it has the potential to be applied in university or public education settings.

In chapter 8, Reisbeck and Schank study an alternative to the dominant rule-based reasoning approach for representing and using domain knowledge. Traditionally, frames, propositions, or semantic nets represent domain facts and if-then rules represent domain procedures. The alternative — case-based reasoning — represents domain knowledge in cases or examples that are learned and then applied to new situations (i.e., problems). Reisbeck and Schank believe that this is a more accurate model of human cognition and a better approach for developing ITSs. One significant implication of this research is that training systems may be able to avoid some of the problems encountered in developing and maintaining large rule-based systems.

Many training systems focus on knowledge-rich domains. In these domains, performance of a task is heavily dependent on large and elaborate stores of knowledge. In knowledge-rich domains, accuracy in performing the task is important, but speed may not be. In contrast, high performance domains require people to be accurate and fast. For example, Federal Aviation Agency (FAA) air traffic controllers and console operators at NASA launch facilities must react quickly and precisely to rapidly changing environments. Individuals working in high performance domains must learn how to carry out the procedures in an *automatic* fashion. Fink (chap. 9) and Regian (chap. 10) describe issues and approaches to training in which the knowledge required has become automatic. An everyday example of this kind of task is driving a car. Initially, new drivers focus most of their attention on depressing the gas pedal, using the brake, turning the steering wheel, and so on. After a few weeks of experience, drivers are able to traverse corners and familiar routes while paying more attention to other aspects of driving, such as the strategy of defensive driving.

In chapter 11, Baker reminds us that typical evaluations of ITSs have taken a limited, traditional approach in assessing a system's instructional effectiveness. Adopting a mutually exclusive distinction between formative and summative evaluations, using restricted methodologies, making judgments based on a narrow range of criteria, and evaluating a single instantiation of a tutor limits this approach. Along these lines, Steuck and Fleming (1989) proposed a three-dimensional taxonomy for planning and conducting evaluations. The dimensions cover the point in the development cycle in which the evaluation is being conducted, substantive research issues, and methodological issues. By crossing the three dimensions, researchers can develop systematic evaluation plans that not only include, but go beyond the traditional assessments of cost and training effectiveness.

Baker argues that a focus on technology assessment should replace our current evaluation methodologies. This requires that studies focus on the environmental or instructional context of the ITS, the nature of the trainees and training requirements, and the conditions of implementation, to name a few, in addition to training outcomes. This forces researchers to employ multiple measures in their assessments of ITSs.

The focus of a technology assessment, however, is much broader than an evaluation of a single instantiation of that technology. A technology assessment focuses on the field under study instead of one or two examples of that technology. The goal of this approach is to avoid some of the limitations of focusing short-term goals and benefits. We do not want to miss opportunities to promote the technology under development even though a particular evaluation was less than favorable.

Other Issues and Concerns

Although this book does not directly address computer hardware as a major topic, hardware has profound implications for nature of current and future generations of ITSs. Processing speed and capacity limit computerized systems in their ability to emulate human cognitive characteristics. Input and output devices constrain training opportunities due to limitations in the way humans can interact with computers. Data storage and communication devices directly affect the types and amount of knowledge that can be conveyed to the learner. They also indirectly affect the nature in which that knowledge can be conveyed.

Many research labs have relied on AI workstations containing specialized processing boards (e.g., LISP boards), up to 8MB RAM, one or more harddiscs, a mouse, network in local area network, and so on. Rarely are these expensive systems found in large quantities in training facilities. On the other hand, recent advances in general purpose platforms have helped the use of lower-end systems, such as MacIntosh IIs and PCs. In the research labs these systems commonly have 3-8MB RAM, large harddiscs, and a mouse. Labs are also upgrading to platforms with 32 bit microprocessors and data paths. These systems have also begun to work their way into larger scale training facilities.

Hardware in the home and public school settings is very different from the labs. Apple IICs, IIGSs, Commodores, small PCs, and MacIntoshes are the mainstay computing systems. Typically, RAM ranges from 64K to 1024K with 512K being very common. Keyboards, color monitors, and printers are the main input/output devices. It is quick to see that full-blown ITSs will cause a fairly dramatic change in hardware in general education settings in order for widespread implementation to occur.

There is a wide gap between training systems available to the public and those under development in today's research labs. Whereas a fair number of traditional computer-based training systems are in use, instructional developers have applied ITS technology to fairly few domains, largely because the field is extremely young and has room for growth. Today ITSs tend toward training students in areas that require higher order cognitive processes, such as diagnosing diseases, troubleshooting malfunctions, operating and maintaining complex equipment, and understanding and applying scientific principles. These domains include, but are not limited to, mathematics, algebra, physics, weather, medicine, writing, computer programming, electricity, electronics, console operations, and complex physical devices, such as nuclear power plants and jet engines. However, ITSs remain in research labs and university settings and have not yet made their way into the public educational systems.

Increasingly adults are becoming exposed to tutorial systems through the proliferation of word processing and spreadsheet programs. Usually these tutorials are electronic page turners with minimal interactions between the computer and the user. If the learner is required to make any response at all, the program is capable of only minimal response checking. That is, it checks to see if students typed what they were instructed to type.

Tutoring systems in the school setting are not as sophisticated as those in research labs. Understandably, this is due in part to limitations in hardware and resources available for computer classes. Whereas researchers enjoy the use of sophisticated workstations, educators in the classroom must make do with a motley assortment of generally low-end personal computers. There is also a lack of effective courseware readily available for use. Finally, teachers lack knowledge of or familiarity with computers. In some cases, teachers either do not have the initiative or are not reinforced for showing initiative to use computers in their classrooms.

NEXT GENERATION

What will users be requesting and demanding of ITSs in the next generation? The world in which ITSs are used will probably be paced even faster than it is today. Information, of course, will be a dominant industry and technology. By the year 2000, 95% of all jobs will involve some time in handling highly computerized information (Cetron, 1988). As a result, workers will need to meet basic skills in information processing. Furthermore, many people will have multiple careers throughout their lifetimes. Trends show that on average the next generation of workers will change jobs more than five times (Cetron, 1988). Quicker, more effective training and retraining will be in demand.

There will be many applications of ITSs in industry, the military, and more importantly, in homes and public and private schools and universities. Industry needs to reduce the cost and time required for on-the-job training and avoid costly mistakes. The military needs training for large groups of people. By the year 2000, the space station *Freedom* should be orbiting with a permanent crew. We may see an experimental lunar base in 2005 with a crew of about eight (NASA, 1989). In the Lunar Evolution Case Study, there is a requirement that autonomous, on-site, crew training be available for all safety critical systems operated by the crew. Long-range space voyages will need to take many kinds of expertise along so the crew can have access as needed. Practical issues such as cost-effectiveness, real-time response, integration capability with other systems, and system integrity will be important factors in developing the next generation of ITSs.

Research in the next few years will continue to address current basic problems with ITSs. Rosenberg (1987) noted that two basic flaws in current ITS theory are the lack of a substantiated model of learning and the inadequate testing of systems—issues addressed elsewhere in this volume. The successes and failures of working systems will drive the need for and development of models of learning that can be applied to ITSs. After bringing intelligent tutors to the public, there will be many places to collect data and perform studies to get complete and conclusive information. The existence of training environments in which to observe and experiment is probably the most important aspect of the next generation.

Some specific predictions have been made for the next few years. Future ITSs will facilitate discovery and experimentation by allowing the user to try many solutions to see what happens (Harmon, 1987). Littman (1987) noted that by 1992, a complete curriculum tutor for introductory programming, including handling simple bugs and programs up to about 150 lines, could exist. Duncan (1989) foresaw that in 1995, at the very least, an ITS would have:

- a large 19-inch display,
- an optical disc for interactive video,
- high quality voice output,
- an authoring system for creation, and
- user networking capability.

Otherwise, tutoring systems will continue to be defined for a specific domain and constructed with production rules. Duncan also wrote that ITSs will host many ill-defined domains, be student-oriented, and able to do simulations, so an ITS could serve as a laboratory where investigations can occur. To be student-oriented, the system would keep track of and consider the student's history with the system, learning style, purpose in being tutored, and attention state. The ITS's response would be partially based on these items. Dede (1988) had the most extensive and detailed description of a system for the year 2005, mostly centered on the interface and hardware and software environment of the ITS. Dede predicted that the ITS of 2005 will have:

- a large panel display with three dimensional (3D) graphics, thousands of colors and millions of pixels resolution, a dual erasable optical disc storage system with a few gigabytes, and very powerful hardware (distributed parallel processors, 100 logical inferences per second per million instructions per second, object knowledge base of 1,010 objects, and 80 megahertz clock speed);

- limited voice recognition, varied interface functionalities, and on-screen teleconferencing availability;
- embedded coaches and tutors for both novice and experienced users, with collaboration emphasized through group decision support tools;
- a user credit card or "megacard" with a few megabytes of memory; and
- hypermedia and associated networks, satellite links, and connectivity with many systems so an emulation of any other system can run programs.

The megacard capability would impact modeling the student. It could store the student model and other background information about the user very easily. The student model will be constantly changing and growing with the student's knowledge of the domain and problem-solving process. Greater use of hypermedia and emulation would impact the expert module, because new representations and accesses would be available for the expert's use. The instruction module would also benefit by the availability of simulations from other systems. System tools are becoming easier to use and have greater capabilities, consequently there will be advancements in the expert model. For example, representations will be flexible, adaptable and able to handle more complicated domains. As hardware capabilities increase, interfaces for ITSs will be positively impacted with more available options. In general, improvements and extensions over the next 5 to 15 years will probably be made within each of the major components of ITSs. Radical changes in the overall ITS paradigm will probably not occur during this time. Nonetheless, ITSs will be applicable to more instructional environments and will appear more in everyone's daily activities.

What the next generation will then provide for the future is a new set of problems, as well as, some much needed evaluations and data. Results from tutoring that are not effective will help determine areas that need to be reevaluated and improved. For example, in the next generation, studies should show whether graphics or text is more valuable for increasing educational effectiveness, and under what conditions. Any interface problems will become apparent with extensive research. The lack of a model for instructional design will become a major issue for standarization of ITSs. During this next generation, experimentation should determine the effective use of an ITS during training. That is, for some domains, we will know under what conditions it is better to use an ITS, a three dimensional simulator, or an actual apparatus.

In the next generation, ITS researchers will be delving deeply into the student modeling issues. They will attempt to take into account different learning types of students and the students' assumed or background knowledge. ITSs will need to be written so that they address the student's requirements, expectations, needs, and background information.

How the student regards the ITS is very important in determining the effectiveness of the ITS. A student's behavior with an ITS is partly determined by the background knowledge of the student, what the student anticipates the ITS can do or accomplish, and what the student's purpose is in interacting with the ITS. A student's purpose could range from just getting off the system as soon as possible to mastering a certain skill. How the ITS determines and alters a student's actions and purpose is an issue that researchers will need to address.

Challenges for the domain expert module will most likely be in training ill-defined types of knowledge such as nonalgorithmic skills. For example, training management skills with an ITS is not feasible now. If management involves aligning on a purpose, defining and delegating tasks, giving clear instructions, making requests, following up tactfully, and completing the project, how is this trained? Still, the domain of management is not clearly defined so that it can be trained by an ITS. Social skills are also too nebulous for training by an ITS. Harmon (1987) noticed that about half of the human problems occurring in industry have to do with noninstructional domains such as motivation, attitude, and incentive.

In the next generation, evaluations of ITSs will become more systematic and sophisticated. Researchers will adopt methods used in other areas of social science to enhance their evaluations. For example, we will become more aware of the need for greater control and more elaborate reporting required by meta-analyses. In turn, meta-analyses of intelligent instructional techniques will begin to appear. As researchers develop better evaluation methods, we must take care that we are not getting inflated effectiveness results due to the novelty of having a new way to learn or the attention a student gets with working on something "new and improved." As we begin to report success stories, the robustness and generalizability of our findings will come under scrutiny by educational decision makers. Evaluators will need to provide them with information that will allow the development of this technology to continue in the next generation and propel us on into the one after that.

BEYOND THE NEXT GENERATION

What society will need from training systems 20 to 30 years from now is even harder to predict than in the period 10 to 20 years from today. Paradoxically, it is easier to predict what ITSs will look like. With advances in AI and other technologies, ITSs will emulate humanlike capabilities more and more. Thus, because we know something about human training now, we can describe future computerized training systems.

What will our children and grandchildren be doing on a daily basis? If your children are in a home or office environment, they may call for their all-purpose holographic monitor where many media forms have merged, including newspapers, television, magazines, and telephone. They could then request tutoring on how to design and fly those old-fashioned ultra-lights, including instruction on the aerodynamics of the aircraft. The monitor will be a doorway to a multipurpose communication system, worldwide information network, and development environment on a grand scale and encompassing many technologies. In short, there will be a less clear distinction between training and the other functions that computerized systems will have.

The ITS will be able to explain itself and its strategies in ways that are trackable by the student. The student will be able to ask why the ITS did a particular action and the ITS will be able to answer in a way that the student can understand. The ITS may even have insights into the student's learning patterns. Natural language interfaces may begin to be feasible, although they probably will be user-specific. Human instructors will be able to modify and upgrade the tutors directly. More importantly, there will be various teaching strategies available to the ITS from which to select, based on directions from the instructor, the learner type (such as verbally or spatially oriented), domain type, and target tasks. There should be a multidimensional theory of instructional design that the ITS can use to choose and change teaching strategies based on the student's responses and the performance criteria.

The kind of expertise available through ITSs will expand to include areas such as innovation, creativity, and intuition. The definitions of creativity, intuition, and intelligence may alter because of what researchers discover in these training settings. We can see evidence that this is already beginning today in the area of higher-order cognitive skills. Gott (1988) pointed to evidence that such higher-order skills, such as expert problem solving, can be trained. Another domain that will be very important for this time frame is organizational meta-skills to manage information and skills. It will be critical to develop this meta-skill of determining what skills are useful and needed. There will be so much information available, a new management scheme for handling information will need to be developed and made trainable simply because it will be in demand.

If indeed one of the more significant results of the next generation is the application of ITSs in major training arenas, the most significant accomplishment following that might be in the maturation of assessment methodologies. Although there will be advances in evaluation techniques in previous generations, the field will not mature until ITSs have been widely implemented. A continuing issue will be to identify the components of an ITS which need further examination when an ITS is not effective. Within 20 years, we should begin to see some form of embedded assessment that will dynamically alter and adapt an ITS as it is being used.

EVOLUTION

Obviously, we can envision many changes as a result of ITS research. They will positively impact our research and theories on the teaching-learning process. In addition, they will cause changes in the way we view and design ITSs themselves. These two changes will in turn force changes in the way evaluations or assessments of ITS are conducted. Finally, the relationship between intelligent training systems and the sociology or context in which ITSs are used will mature with time.

Learning Theory

We believe that continued investigations of ITSs will have a profound impact on learning theory as we know it today. Currently, research on teaching and learning theory focuses on instructional strategies and individual differences. In the educational research literature, these are called *treatments* and *aptitudes,* respectively, and an approach that blends these two foci is called Aptitude $_3$ Treatment Interaction (ATI) research (Cronbach & Snow, 1977). However, obtaining meaningful ATIs has been extremely difficult and thus this approach has not taken a predominant role in the field as it was expected to do.

It is expected that ITSs will greatly influence the nature of research on teaching and learning. ITSs can collect data on student performance unobtrusively throughout the entire course of learning. This will allow researchers to explore the direct relationships between aptitudes, instructional strategies, and student outcomes. If researchers exploit this ability, they may be able to find more robust, meaningful ATIs.

ITS researchers can add to the ATI "equation" two more dimensions described by Kyllonen and Shute (1988). As we learn more about knowledge types (K) being trained and the domains (D) in which the instruction is occurring, we can explore more complex relationships. For instance, aptitude by treatment by domain interactions (ATDIs) may be more meaningful for both theory and practice than the simpler ATIs found previously. Or, we may find that relationships are generalizable across domains and that aptitude by treatment by knowledge type interactions (ATKIs) are more educationally meaningful.

In short, we envision an evolution from research efforts focusing on single dimensions, such as the effects of aptitudes or treatments on student outcomes, to more complex forms of relationships. We see a growing number of ATIs being discovered and more research investigating ATDIs and ATKIs. Eventually, beyond the next generation, the field may evolve to exploring relationships between all four dimensions: aptitude, treatment, domain, and knowledge type.

ITS Paradigm

Concurrent with changes in teaching and learning theory, we may see changes in ITSs themselves. Up to this point, we have not seen many variations in the way ITSs have been described. Table 12.2 shows the components of four different implementations or theories of ITSs over the years 1973–1989. The components fill the roles of interface, teacher model, student model, domain knowledge, or control in the ITS. After 1973, the control of the ITS has mostly been incorporated into the other modules.

This is not to say, though, that the field has been stagnant. What we have seen is a refinement of the components into subcomponents. For instance, we can divide the teacher module into a variety of submodules

TABLE 12.2
ITS Components

Roles	1973	1982	1984	1989
Interface		user interface		intelligent interface
Teacher	teaching operations	tutoring knowledge	teaching generator teaching administrator	instructional expert
Student	student history	bug catalogue	student model student history	student model
Domain	domain knowledge	domain expert		domain expert
Control	guidance rules			

that have different responsibilities in instructing a student. For example, a student diagnostic submodule compares student performance to a representation of an expert's performance. After determining the student's strengths and weaknesses, another subcomponent may specify what instructional objectives have not yet been met. The system then passes these results to an instructional planner that sequences the instructional activities required to met each of those objectives. Another module, the interface or communication module, then enacts the instructional activities scheduled by the instructional planner. All this means that whereas the overall structure of an ITS or paradigm has not changed much over the past 20 years, significant advancements have been made in the field.

Although there may be a period in which refinements are still made to today's paradigm, we envision that an evolution will begin. The four components of an ITS, the interface, instructional model, student model, and expert model may begin to shift greatly in their definition and functionality. The instructor and expert modules may merge as one unit. The interface may be absorbed into the instructor, or vice versa, because the distinction between the two is not always clear and may not be useful.

Perhaps the interface, teaching, student, and expert modules are not as separable as we have been assumed. In dealing with these four distinct areas, researchers will see how to combine some of these areas and develop a different set of distinctions that may be more effective for ITS productivity.

Evaluation Paradigm

In order for dramatic advances to occur in ITS paradigms and learning theory, evaluation methodology must also advance. Researchers need to extend traditional methodologies beyond the focus on short-term goals.

A step toward adopting a technology assessment approach as advocated by Baker (chap. 11, this volume) might be to borrow evaluation techniques used in more advanced areas of social science research. For instance, the teacher behavior and instructional strategy research areas have well-established paradigms. In this area, researchers go to great lengths to control extraneous variables, measure an extensive set of preinstructional variables, and use multiple outcome measurements. For example, Anderson, Evertson, and Brophy (1978) derived over 500 variables from data they collected in a large-scale study on effective teaching in reading groups. From this, they determined that 55 variables were important for future consideration. ITS research would benefit by adopting evaluation methodologies from established research areas such as those mentioned here.

More creative or innovative approaches will develop over the years. Initially we will see meta-analyses of ITS evaluations appear in the review literature. Later we may see systems that have on-line, embedded evaluation capabilities that record both a student's behavior and the instructional activities undertaken by the ITS. This possibility would give us more precise information about the relationship between instructional activities and learning outcomes.

Meta ITS-Training Theory

In addition to altering the framework of ITSs, an evolutionary step could be developing, implementing, and training a meta-theory of knowledge. Also, intelligent tutors could become self-generating, that is, we might imagine an ITS that produces ITSs. ITSs could become teachers of certain skills and could own certain knowledge along with teaching other qualities of a person who has that skill or knowledge. An evolutionary step in assessment could be to evaluate not only mastery of skills or knowledge, but also to determine higher-order skill attainment, as suggested in Dede (1988).

Sociology

Over the next few generations we will see dramatic changes in the sociology of computerized training systems. Today there is resistance to using computers in many educational settings. Instructors and administrators have little experience with computer applications in education and have little evidence to persuade them to implement systems on a large scale. Many adults are not familiar with computers, few schools have more than a hand full of small microcomputers, and those that are in schools are not well used (Ridgway, 1988).

This is a problem in this generation, but it will not be so in future generations. Children, adolescents, and young adults view computers as an essential and commonplace aspect of their daily lives. As these individuals assume leadership positions, their favorable attitudes toward computers will influence decisions about implementing computer-based training.

In addition, in future generations a migration of computer-based training (CBT) systems will occur. As computers become more pervasive in our daily lives, we will see CBT systems initially spread from traditional instructional settings such as training centers and schoolrooms to the various job sites. The evidence of this comes from the nature of the systems being developed in research labs. Many tutors are focused on complex, technical domains such as those being developed within military and industry settings. The impetus for the change will be both advances in technology and a growing need for onsite training.

Later, the migration will take systems into the home. As hardware advances, the ability to deliver robust instruction effectively and cheaply will in turn advance. As a result, parents devoted to providing the best education possible for their children will become early adopters of the new technology.

CONCLUSION

What we have done in this chapter is to suggest some possible directions ITS research and applications may take. We have assumed that the overall goal of ITSs is to deliver effective individualized instruction. For instance, we believe that eventually ITSs will help that first-grade teacher mentioned at the beginning of this chapter catch her pupil before the student makes too many mistakes. We foresee that computerized systems will be embedded in daily workplaces, whether on Earth or in space, serving as both a job-aid and a job-trainer. With scientific advances in computer science, psychology, and education, computers will become more humanlike in their teaching abilities. The ITS community has already taken major steps toward developing effective and efficient ITSs. Although the future looks promising, significant issues and problems still remain. Many questions need to be answered, and we encourage you, the reader, to address the challenges presented in this book.

REFERENCES

Anderson, L. M., Evertson, C. M., & Bropy, J. E. (1978). *An experimental study of effective teaching in first-grade reading groups* (Report No. 4072). Austin, TX: The Research and Development Center for Teacher Education.

Bunderson, C. V., & Inouye, D. K. (1987). The evolution of computer-aided educational delivery systems. In R. M. Gagne (Ed.), *Instructional technology: Foundations* (pp. 283–318). Hillsdale, NJ: Lawrence Erlbaum Associates.

Cetron, M. J. (1988). Class of 2000: The good news and the bad news. *The Futurist, 21*(6), 9–15.

Cronbach, L. J., & Snow, R. E. (1977). *Aptitudes and instructional methods: A handbook for research on interactions.* New York: Wiley.

Dede, C. (1988). Probable evolution of artificial intelligence-based educational devices. *Technological Forecasting and Social Change, 34,* 115–133.

Duncan, P. C. (1989, October 4–6). Aerospace technical training: The state of the art and forecasting for the future. *Proceedings of AIAA Computers in Aerospace VII Conference* (pp. 420–428), Monterey, CA.

Gott, S. P. (1988, November). Technical intuition in system diagnosis, or accessing the libraries of the mind. *Aviation, Space, and Environmental Medicine, 59,* A59–A64.

Harmon, P. (1987) Intelligent job aids: How AI will change training in the next five years. In G. Kearsley (Ed.), *Artificial intelligence and instruction: Applications and methods* (pp. 165–190). Reading, MA: Addison-Wesley.

Kearsley, G. (1987). Overview. In G. Kearsley (Ed.), *Artificial intelligence and instruction: Applications and methods* (pp. 3–10). Reading, MA: Addison-Wesley.

Kyllonen, P. C., & Shute, V. J. (1988). *Taxonomy of learning skills* (AFHRL-TP-87-39). Brooks AFB, TX: Manpower and Personnel Division, Air Force Human Resources Laboratory.

Littman, D. C. (1987, April). Intelligent tutoring systems: Today and tomorrow. *Conference Record of Electro/87 and Mini/Micro Northeast: Focusing on the OEM.* Electronic Conventions Management, New York, NY.

National Aeronautics and Space Administration. (1987, January). *Space station program definition and requirements: Space station system requirements* (JSC 30000). Houston, TX: NASA Lyndon B. Johnson Space Center.

National Aeronautics and Space Administration. (1989). *Office of Exploration Study Requirements Document FY 1989 Studies.* Houston, TX: NASA Lyndon B. Johnson Space Center.

Ridgway, J. (1988). Of course ICAI is impossible . . . worse though, it might be seditious. In J. Self (Ed.), *Artificial intelligence and human learning: Intelligent computer-aided instruction* (pp. 28–48). London: Chapman & Hall.

Rosenberg, R. (1987, November). A critical analysis of research on intelligent tutoring systems. *Educational Technology, 27*(11), 7–13.

Steuck, K. W., & Fleming, J. L. (1989). *Issues in the evaluation of intelligent tutoring systems.* Paper presented at the annual meeting of the American Educational Research Association, San Francisco, CA.

Tennyson, R. D., & Park, O. C. (1987). Artificial intelligence and computer-based learning. In R. M. Gagne (Ed.), *Instructional technology: Foundations* (pp. 319–342). Hillsdale, NJ: Lawrence Erlbaum Associates.

Wenger, E. (1987). *Artificial intelligence and tutoring systems.* Los Altos, CA: Morgan Kaufmann.

Author Index

Subject Index